Disney Trivia

from the

Vault

Secrets Revealed and Questions Answered

Disney Trivia from the Vault

Secrets Revealed and Questions Answered

By Dave Smith

Chief Archivist Emeritus of The Walt Disney Archives

EDITIONS

NEW YORK

The Official Community for Disney Fans

Disney.com/D23

Table of Contents

ASK  DAVE

Beginning with the July 1983 issue of *Disney Channel Magazine*, I began answering Disney trivia questions from Disney Channel viewers. My column, called "Exploring the Archives" and later simply "Archives," continued until January 1994. When *Disney Magazine* began, the column moved to that publication with the new title of "Ask Dave." After *Disney Magazine* ended, the column moved to the online "Disney Insider" and, most recently, the D23 (Disney's community for Disney fans) Web site. So for almost thirty years, I have been answering Disney trivia questions in print from Disney enthusiasts the world over. Throughout this period, many readers have told me that the "Ask Dave" column was the first thing they turned to.

After over 1,100 "Ask Dave" questions—many bringing up interesting information that had not been published elsewhere—I felt that it would be a fun idea to compile some of the questions in a book, divided by topic. Readers can open to any page and find some interesting facts relating to Disney history. Some of the answers have been edited and enhanced to bring them up to date. I hope you find as much joy in perusing this book as I did in digging up answers to the questions in the first place.

Dave Smith
**Chief Archivist Emeritus
Walt Disney Archives**

ACKNOWLEDGEMENTS

Many people deserve thanks for helping me with this book, especially Walt Disney Archives staff members Becky Cline, Robert Tieman, Alesha Reyes, Mike Buckhoff, Edward Ovalle, Rob Klein, Shelly Graham, and Yvette Khalafian. Special thanks go to my good friend and colleague Steven Vagnini, whose layout talents and advice helped me get the book started, and who then provided continuing advice along the way. Nate Tarampi and Max Lark provided digital files of the "Ask Dave" questions from "Disney Insider" and D23, and John Johnson and Alex Williams helped me compile the *Disney Channel Magazine* questions. Additional thanks go to friends and colleagues, including Bruce Aguilar, Tony Anselmo, Justin Arthur, Keith Burrell, Steven Clark, Rob and Zinnia Cress, Tyson Ervin, Ruston Harker, Lenny Larsen, Ryan Letts, Paula Sigman Lowery, Julian Lowy, Michael Maney, Brainard Miller, Martin Munoz, Trevor Nelson, Matt Pilla, Russell Schroeder, Clay Shoemaker, Moises Torres, Michael Vagnini, and James Wilson. Family members Jean Marana, Kathy Eastman, and Gil and Val Eastman provided welcome support. I also extend my gratitude to Wendy Lefkon at Disney Editions. And above all, thank you to the Disney fans who took the time to write in their questions.

Dave "Ask Dave" Smith
Burbank, CA

ANIMATED
FEATURES

Q In the movie *WALL·E*, the directive not to return to Earth was called A113. In *Toy Story 3*, the license plate on a van is shown as A113. What is the significance of this number? John, Windsor, CT

A —The number, which can be found in many Pixar films, is the room number of the animation classroom at CalArts (California Institute of the Arts) where some Pixar students studied.

Q In the early fifties, I owned a record (a 45 rpm on colored vinyl if I remember correctly) of a song called "Never Smile at a Crocodile" by comedian Jerry Lewis. Having discovered *Peter Pan* at about the same time, I always associated the record with "Tick Tock" from the animated film. Do you know if there was any connection, or was it just coincidence and early marketing strategy? Marcus, Corona Del Mar, CA

A —The 45 rpm record of "Never Smile at a Crocodile," as sung by Jerry Lewis, was released by Capitol Records in 1953. "Following the Leader" was on the flip side. While "Never Smile at a Crocodile" was written for *Peter Pan*, it is not sung in the film—there are only portions of the tune used in the background score. After the film was released, the song was recorded by several different singers, including the Paulette Sisters and Sterling Holloway. It was also released on sheet music.

Q Was *Fantasia* the first movie to have stereophonic sound? Justin, Appling, GA

A —While there were stereophonic sound recordings in the 1930s, *Fantasia* was the first commercial motion picture to be exhibited in stereo, in 1940. Leopold Stokowski, who did the stereo recording for *Fantasia*, had in 1937 recorded *One Hundred Men and a Girl* in stereo for Universal, but the nine tracks were mixed down to one for that film's release.

Q I have two questions. First, who voices the sportscaster in the Goofy cartoons on football and basketball? I believe he also does the same thing in the shorts called *Football Now and Then* and *Moochie of Pop Warner Football*. Second, in what venues was *Fantasia* first shown in its first-run, road-show phase with Fantasound? I saw on the old *Fantasia* DVD that there weren't more than a dozen venues ever equipped for Fantasound. I know it was shown at the Broadway Theater in New York City, the Carthay Circle Theatre in Los Angeles, the Geary Theater in San Francisco, and the Majestic Theater in Boston. I was told it was also shown in this way in Cleveland, Chicago, and Detroit. But do you know what the rest of the cities are? Michael, Granite Bay, CA

A —The narrator of the Goofy "how to" cartoons was John McLeish, who was an animator and story man at Disney in the 1940s. Besides the four theaters you mentioned, *Fantasia* also was shown originally at the Aldine Theater in Philadelphia, the Hannah in Cleveland, the Apollo in Chicago, the National in Washington, D.C., the Ford in Baltimore, the Erlanger in Buffalo, the Fulton in Pittsburgh, the Wilson in Detroit, the Minnesota in Minneapolis, and the Royal Alexandria in Toronto.

Q When making the older animated films, how long did it take to record the voices? Did all the actors needed for a scene stand in one room to record, as shown in the *Disneyland* episode *A Story of Dogs*, or did they do it separately, as is common practice today? Spencer, Camarillo, CA

A —For the early animated films, the actors generally did their voice recording separately. This is still true for more recent films. If there is interplay in a scene, then the producers might decide to have two or more actors record together. The actors would be called in a number of times over the three or more years that the film was in production as new dialogue was added or changes were made. This caused a problem, especially for adolescents, whose voices might change during production.

Q **I have enjoyed listening to the songs "Jiminy Cricket," "Three Cheers for Anything," "Honest John," and "Turn on the Old Music Box," which were all deleted from the film *Pinocchio*. However, there are two more songs that were deleted from that film: "As I Was Saying to the Duchess" and "Monstro the Whale." Has Disney ever released these songs to the public, or if not, are there plans to release them in the future? I would really love to listen to them. Jeremiah, Fairfax, VA**

A —The sheet music for "Monstro the Whale" and "As I Was Saying to the Duchess" is published in Russell Schroeder's book, *Disney's Lost Chords, Volume 2* (2008). I am not aware of any recordings of the two songs.

Q **In *Lilo & Stitch*, Lilo's bedroom door has a sign with the word *kapu* written on it. What is the meaning of this word? Blake, Winslow, IL**

A —*Kapu* means "keep out" or "off limits" in Hawaiian.

Q **Is it true that the Disney animators are no longer drawing the characters? I heard that Disney did away with them in 2004 and went to doing everything on computers. This is a great loss of talent if this is true. Thanks for your time. Terry, Pensacola, FL**

A —There are still animators. Some have adapted to drawing on the computer rather than on paper, but occasional films still are made with drawings done on paper. *Winnie the Pooh* was the most recent.

Q I recently watched the first *Toy Story* and noticed that the gas station Woody and Buzz are left at is Dinoco. The same Dinoco symbol is in *Cars* on the King. I'm guessing it is the same one. Is that true? Are there any other common items represented throughout the Disney•Pixar movies? I know that the *Toy Story* characters are in *Finding Nemo* in the dentist's waiting room. Melanie, Ohio

A —Dinoco (as seen in *Cars*) is an in-joke reference to the original *Toy Story*. As for other common items, the most popular one is the Pizza Planet truck, which is hidden in all Pixar films except for *The Incredibles*, and the A113 letter-number sequence, which is a reference to an animation classroom at CalArts; it appears somewhere in almost every Pixar film.

Q Who came up with the look of the Dwarfs' cottage in *Snow White and the Seven Dwarfs*? Was it Walt Disney himself? Julie, Maryville, TN

A —The design, created by Disney layout artists, was loosely based on Bavarian forest cottages (but not on any one specific building). Artist Ken Anderson built a full-sized model of the cottage that the staff could use to help stage the action and determine camera angles.

Q Wart's voice is much deeper at the end of the movie than it is at the beginning; you can also hear this deeper voice scattered throughout the film. Did more than one actor provide Wart's voice? Erin, Nutley, NJ

A —Ricky Sorenson was fourteen years old when he first voice-tested for the role. By the time the movie was released, Sorenson was seventeen years old, and his voice had changed. To try to match his younger voice during retakes, Robert and

Richard Reitherman, sons of *The Sword in the Stone*'s director, Wolfgang Reitherman, filled in.

Q

In *Alice in Wonderland*, the riddle, "Why is a raven like a writing desk?" is never answered. What is the correct answer? Cristina, Tucson, AZ

A

—That riddle appears in Lewis Carroll's book *Alice's Adventures in Wonderland*. Carroll received constant inquiries about the riddle. He claimed that there was no answer; he had made up the riddle without thinking of one.

Q

When did Verna Felton die? J.K., Akron, OH

A

—The great character actress, who supplied voices for many well-known Disney animated characters such as the Fairy Godmother in *Cinderella* and Flora in *Sleeping Beauty*, died at the age of seventy-six in 1966.

Q

I have been told that *Beauty and the Beast* was not the first Disney film to have a stage version performed in New York. If it indeed wasn't, which film was? George, Concord, MA

A

—The answer is *Snow White and the Seven Dwarfs*. There had been earlier stage versions of Disney's *Snow White and the Seven Dwarfs*, but the first major production was mounted in 1969 in St. Louis. Although the production was successful, it was a decade before the show moved to New York City. It opened on October 18, 1979, at Radio City Music Hall, where it ran for thirty-two performances.

Q

As a little girl in the sixties, I saw *Snow White and the Seven Dwarfs*. I could swear that there was a scene showing the Dwarfs making Snow White's coffin. When the video was released, I bought a copy, but there was no such scene included. Am I imagining that scene? Lois, Boca Raton, FL

A —There has never been such a scene in the film. There is some footage of the Dwarfs making a bed for Snow White, which you might have seen. That scene, which was also included in books, and another scene of the Dwarfs eating soup, were never finished and never made it into the film.

Q In *Pinocchio*, the scene in which Lampwick changes into a donkey is so effective and frightening. And the scene in *Snow White and the Seven Dwarfs* in which the huntsman tried to kill Snow White is also scary. Were there other scenes cut from the final versions of these films because they were considered too terrifying? John, Bethpage, NY

A – One scene of the witch at her cauldron from *Snow White and the Seven Dwarfs* never made it into the original film, but it was included in bonus material on a DVD release. Other very frightening scenes were probably dispensed with during story-meeting discussions.

Q Who did the voice of the Horned King in *The Black Cauldron*? Katy, Iowa City, IA

A —British actor John Hurt provided the Horned King's voice. He also appeared in Disney's *Night Crossing*. Later, he narrated *The Tigger Movie*.

Q I have two drawings that were done by the Disney artist Harry Holt on September 19, 1987. What movies did Harry Holt draw for? Joan, Northbrook, IL

A —Harry Holt joined the Disney staff in 1936, with his first animation work on a Silly Symphony called *Woodland Café*. He worked on such features as *Snow White and the Seven Dwarfs* and *Pinocchio*, though as an assistant animator, he received no film credit. He later worked as a sculptor for Walt Disney

Imagineering and Walt Disney World; after he retired, he returned to staff an animator's desk at the Magic Kingdom's Preview Center, where he continued to delight Guests with his drawings.

Q **Disney's _Bambi_ is based on the work of a German-speaking author, Siegmund Salzmann, who went by the pen name Felix Salten. Was Walt Disney familiar with German literature? Was Salten's work available in English back then? Scott, Bridgewater, MA**

A —Felix Salten's _Bambi, ein Leben im Walde_ (_Bambi, a Life in the Woods_) was first published in English in 1928. MGM Studios producer Sidney Franklin purchased the movie rights to the book in 1933. After he determined that it would be hard to make the movie in live action, he brought the story to Walt Disney and suggested an animated film. Walt acquired the rights in 1937, and Franklin was engaged to collaborate on the film.

Q **Did the animators of _Fantasia/2000_ include the then-unbuilt Walt Disney Concert Hall in the film? In the live-host sequences, the background looks similar to the shapes of the concert hall. Larry, La Jolla, CA**

A —I checked with Don Hahn, who directed those parts of the film. He says that the shapes were meant to look like abstract sails on a sailing ship and were not consciously made to look similar to the Walt Disney Concert Hall, designed by Frank Gehry.

Q **Who was the model for Walt Disney's first feature character, Snow White? H.I., Portland, ME**

A —The live model for the character of Snow White was Marge Belcher. After the production of the film, she married Disney animator Art Babbitt and later dancer Gower Champion, becoming Marge Champion of the well-known Marge and

Gower Champion dance team. The model for Snow White's prince was Harry Stockwell, the father of actors Guy and Dean Stockwell.

Alice in Wonderland's Mad Hatter wears a "10/6" on his top hat. Can you explain what the 10/6 means? Sophia, Alameda, CA

—It looks like a fraction, but it is not. The 10/6 is the price of the hat, ten shillings sixpence, in the former currency of Britain. There were twelve pence in a shilling and twenty shillings in a pound. In 1971, this complicated money system was changed to a decimal-based one, doing away with the shilling.

Who does the singing voice of the Golden Harp in the "Mickey and the Beanstalk" segment of _Fun and Fancy Free_? Marsha, Los Altos, CA

—The singer was Anita Gordon. She was a movie and TV actress/ singer who passed away in 2006 at the age of ninety-two. She was the uncredited singing voice for Pamela Tiffin in _State Fair_ (1962) and for Jean Seberg in _Paint Your Wagon_.

Is Harryhausen's, the restaurant in _Monsters, Inc._, named after the animator who did the stop-motion animated monsters in the old live-action Sinbad movies? Cathy, Glenvil, NE

—Yes, Harryhausen's is a tribute to special-effects wizard Ray Harryhausen, who worked on _Jason and the Argonauts_, the Sinbad films, and many other movies.

I have the movie poster from Disney's fiftieth anniversary release of _Snow White and the Seven Dwarfs_. I've noticed that Sleepy's left hand has five fingers, but his right hand has only four. All the other Dwarfs have only four fingers.

Was this an error? Was it ever corrected? Robert, Chatham, Ontario, Canada

A —You definitely found a mistake on that poster; I never noticed it before. As far as I know, the error was never corrected.

Q **Many Disney movies include cameos by other Disney characters. Belle appears in *The Hunchback of Notre Dame*; Pinocchio, Sebastian, and Beast all show up in *Aladdin*. Does Tinker Bell appear in any other Disney movie? Bobby, Whittier, CA**

A —Other than the appearance of the *Lady and the Tramp* dogs in *One Hundred and One Dalmatians*, such Disney character cameos are pretty much from the last three decades. Tinker Bell makes appearances in *Who Framed Roger Rabbit* and *The Black Cauldron*.

Q **Once when I was very young, I saw a Disney cartoon whose name I can't remember. However, to this day I sing one of the songs over and over. The lyrics go, "Johnnie Fedora met Alice Bluebonnet in the window of a department store. 'Twas love at first sight and they promised one night they'd be sweethearts forevermore." Can you tell me the name of this cartoon? Joan, Lapeer, MI**

A —The song "Johnnie Fedora and Alice Bluebonnet" is one of the ten segments from the 1946 feature *Make Mine Music*, Disney's first postwar "package" picture. *Make Mine Music* has been released on video and DVD.

Q **My favorite Disney movie is *Sleeping Beauty*. I've studied its history so much that I feel I know everything about it, except one thing: who provided the voice for Aurora's mother, the Queen? I have not been able to find the answer anywhere. Though she has only two lines in the film, I can't help but feel**

that somewhere this must be documented. Please solve this great *Sleeping Beauty* mystery! Byron, Richmond, KY

A —You have been unable to find this credit published anywhere because we have never been able to find it. Unfortunately, although we have lists of many of the people who came in to record for the film, the lists do not mention which roles they performed. It has been suggested that it could have been Verna Felton, who provided the voice of the fairy Flora. At least she was around if they needed someone to speak the two lines.

Q I've heard of storyboards used for Disney animation. On those boards, is every line and scene displayed? Brittany, Marstons Mills, MA

A —Storyboards normally depict, in sketches, each scene of an animated film; any dialogue is on a slip of paper pinned below the corresponding sketch. But whether every line and scene is displayed is questionable; as with a script of a live-action film, changes can be made during production. The animators and directors might make minor changes after the storyboards are completed, the actors doing the voices might suggest slight changes in the dialogue, or there could be changes made during the editing of the film. The concept of the storyboard originated at the Disney Studios in the 1930s, but it is now used throughout Hollywood for all types of movies. The word "storyboard" is often erroneously used today to refer to a story sketch, but the storyboards are four-by-eight-foot boards on which story sketches are pinned.

Q In *The Little Mermaid*, who does the voices of Ariel's sisters? One of them sounds like Susan Ruttan, from *L.A. Law*. Also, I read on the Internet that Richard Chamberlain voiced someone in the movie. Did he? Vicki, Pittsburgh, PA

A —Only two of Ariel's six sisters have credited voices—Susan Ruttan, as you suspected, did Andrina, and Debbie Shapiro did Aquata. Richard Chamberlain is not listed as part of the cast of the Disney film, though he did narrate a 1974 animated film of *The Little Mermaid*, produced by *Reader's Digest*.

Q In *Sleeping Beauty*, when the three fairies slip into Maleficent's castle, they almost fly into a sleeping guard. I think the guard's face looks like a young Marc Davis. Did Disney animators ever put self-portraits in their films? Ralph, Modesto, CA

A —I don't know if this particular guard is a caricature of animator Marc Davis, but caricatures of animators certainly appear in many of our films. Ward Kimball and Fred Moore can be seen in *The Nifty Nineties*, Walt Disney and a few animators turn up in *Ferdinand the Bull*, and several artists are in crowd scenes in *Aladdin*.

Q My sister recently received a video of *The Jungle Book*. Who voiced the vulture barbershop quartet? Also, how many of *The Jungle Book* voice actors are still living? Amanda, North Charleston, SC

A —The vulture voices were Lord Tim Hudson (Dizzy), J. Pat O'Malley (Buzzie), Chad Stuart (Flaps), and Digby Wolfe (Ziggy). We don't keep track of actors after they have appeared in our productions, so it is not easy to answer your question about who is still around. The film came out over four decades ago, and most of the cast members, such as Louis Prima, Phil Harris, Sebastian Cabot, Verna Felton, Sterling Holloway, and George Sanders, are no longer living.

Q My brothers and sister and I were playing the Disney Charades Game, and we came across a card of a cat called Rufus. We believe he is from *The Rescuers*, but the card says he is from *The Great Mouse Detective*. Who is right? Stephanie, Ottawa, IL

A —You are correct; Rufus is the elderly cat who befriends Penny in *The Rescuers*. Felicia is the overweight cat who acts as executioner for Ratigan in *The Great Mouse Detective*.

Q One of our most prized possessions is an original lobby card from *Snow White and the Seven Dwarfs* that shows a Christmas scene in which Dopey is nailing stockings to the fireplace mantel. Was a Christmas sequence planned for the film and then cut after the lobby cards were made? Franc and Alan, New York, NY

A —No, there was no Christmas scene planned. Often when a film is released around Christmastime, special promotional art is produced to tie the film in with the holidays. *Snow White*'s original release date was four days before Christmas in 1937.

Q Please help me settle a discussion with my brother. Does the song "Heigh-Ho" in *Snow White and the Seven Dwarfs* go by another name? Daria, Philadelphia, PA

A —It is titled on the original sheet music "(The Dwarfs' Marching Song) Heigh-Ho." The first part is omitted in recent Disney songbooks and has almost never been used.

Q Are *Pocahontas*, *Oliver & Company*, and *The Rescuers* the only Disney animated features that take place in the United States? Anais, New Windsor, NY

A —No, you left out *Dumbo*, *Lady and the Tramp*, and *The Fox and the Hound*. There are also segments of the package films of the 1940s that were set in the United States. The locale of *Bambi*

is not stated in the movie and could have been America, though Felix Salten, the author of the book on which the film was based, was raised in Vienna. [Since this 2000 question, one can add a slew of films: *Chicken Little, Lilo & Stitch, Brother Bear, Home on the Range, Meet the Robinsons, Bolt*, and *The Princess and the Frog*, not to mention almost all of the Pixar films.]

Q I already have your book *Disney A to Z*, but I want to ask you for more about Tommy Luske, the boy behind the voice of Michael in *Peter Pan*. Joanna, Piraeus, Greece

A —Thomas Charles Luske was the son of Disney animation director Hamilton Luske, and he was five years old when *Peter Pan* was released. When he grew up, he married and lived in Baywood, California, where he worked as a cabinetmaker. He was killed by a drunk driver in 1990, at the age of forty-two. He had two daughters.

Q Who is the man behind the voice of Shere Khan, the tiger in *The Jungle Book*? Is he still alive, and has he played in other movies? Catherine, Antwerp, Belgium

A —George Sanders did the voice of Shere Khan. Following a distinguished thirty-six-year career as an actor (he played Thomas Ayerton in Disney's *In Search of the Castaways*), he passed away in 1972, five years after the release of *The Jungle Book*.

Q I purchased four different covers of *A Bug's Life* when it appeared on videocassette. I was surprised when I came across a fifth cover (featuring Hopper) not previously announced in any advertisements or *Disney Magazine*. Was this meant to be a surprise for fans? Greg, Milan, IL

A —Yes, the Hopper cover was added at the last minute to be a bonus for Disney fans.

Q In *The Rescuers Down Under*, the initials "R. Z." are on Percival McLeach's garage. Do they stand for anything? Tasha, St. Paul, MN

A —Not as far as I know. There is no one on the film's list of credits with those initials.

Q In *Lady and the Tramp*, who is the gentleman who provides the voice for Tramp? Also, what was the title of the book that inspired the movie? Deana, Reading, PA

A —Tramp's voice was provided by Larry Roberts; according to the Internet Movie Database (imdb.com), this was his only acting credit. The idea for the book actually came from a short magazine story by Ward Greene titled "Happy Dan, the Whistling Dog," but at the time of the film's release, he revised and enlarged his story into a *Lady and the Tramp* book.

Q In the *Ultimate Disney Trivia Book* that you wrote, there are some questions about a film I've never heard of called *The Black Cauldron*. I was wondering why this film doesn't seem as popular or well known as the rest of Disney's animated films. Also, in *Alice in Wonderland*, the voice of the White Rabbit sounds a lot like Mr. Smee in *Peter Pan*. Is it the same voice? Stefanie, Elk Grove Village, IL

A —*The Black Cauldron* was the first Disney animated feature to receive a PG rating, because of the scariness of its villain, the Horned King, and his horde of sinister warriors. It got a mixed reception at the time of its release in 1985, but still has many fans. It was released on videocassette in 1998 and on DVD in 2000 and 2010 (the twenty-fifth anniversary release).

You have a good ear for voices—both the White Rabbit and Mr. Smee were voiced by Bill Thompson. He also did many other Disney characters, including Jock in *Lady and the*

Tramp, King Hubert in *Sleeping Beauty*, and Uncle Waldo in
The Aristocats.

Q I noticed in the introduction to the written version of A. A. Milne's classic that Pooh's original name was "Edward Bear." In the video of *The Many Adventures of Winnie the Pooh*, however, the narrator in the introduction says Pooh's original name was "Edwin Bear." Which is correct? Jodie, Superior, CO

A —You have caught a mistake on the video. Edward Bear is correct.

Q How did Disney come up with the name Megara for the heroine in *Hercules*? It's my last name. Terry, Erial, NJ

A —According to Greek mythology, Hercules married Princess Megara of Thebes. Although devoted to her and their children, in a fit of madness inflicted on him by Hera, Hercules slaughtered his family. Obviously, Disney did not want to stick too closely to the original story.

Q My dad and I were watching *Snow White and the Seven Dwarfs*. At the end, we noticed that Snow White kisses only six Dwarfs good-bye. Was there a reason for this, or was it a mistake? Andria, Dayton, OH

A —At the close of the film, Snow White is seen kissing only six of the Dwarfs good-bye. Sleepy is the one not shown. Veteran animator Frank Thomas explained that this was one of the final scenes done prior to the release of the film, and the timing of the scene, plus the fixed length of the Prince's arms (he could scoop up only three at a time), prevented all seven Dwarfs from appearing. According to Frank, he was rushed at the end of production of the film and didn't pay attention, so that in the planning of the scene one of the Dwarfs was left out. In retrospect, he would have changed the staging to include them all.

Q In *Cinderella* there are two girl mice named Suzy and Perla. I've been told that Suzy is the mouse wearing a green dress and Perla is the mouse wearing a pink dress. However, there are many different mice wearing pink and green dresses in the film, and their identities remain a mystery to me. Exactly which two mice are Suzy and Perla? Also, which mice are named Mert, Bert, Luke, and Blossom? Daniel, Issaquah, WA

A —The mice are named in studio production records. We can identify Mert, Bert, and Luke (though not individually) as being the three male mice with Jaq at the beginning of the first mice sequence. In the dressmaking sequence, Suzy is the lead girl mouse in yellow sitting on a spool, studying the illustration of the dress in the fashion book. Perla and Blossom were not individually identified in the production notes, which often just stated "Girl Mouse" instead of an actual name.

Q I discovered after purchasing my video of *Sleeping Beauty* that it was the first animated film to be released in the 70 mm Technirama format. Were there any other early wide-screen animated Disney films? William, El Cajon, CA

A —Disney only used 70 mm Technirama for *Sleeping Beauty* and *The Black Cauldron*. But earlier, Disney had pioneered the use of a different wide-screen process (CinemaScope) in an animated feature with *Lady and the Tramp* (1955) and even earlier in the short *Toot, Whistle, Plunk and Boom* (1953).

Q I was looking at my *Hunchback of Notre Dame* sound track when I noticed that on the song "A Guy Like You," it had listed Mary Wickes/Mary Stout as the voice of Laverne. Does this mean that two people provided her voice? I never heard anything about it before. Cheri, Longview, WA

A —Mary Wickes died during the production of *The Hunchback of Notre Dame*, so additional lines of dialogue in the movie were supplied by Jane Withers. Mary Stout was used to finish the songs.

Q **In your book *Disney A to Z*, in the entry for *One Hundred and One Dalmatians*, you have Lisa Davis listed as the voice of Anita and Cate Bauer as the voice of Perdita. But the entry for Perdita says she was voiced by Lisa Daniels. Was this a mistake? Susan, Edison, NJ**

A —I can see your confusion. According to studio records, Perdita was voiced by both Cate Bauer and Lisa Daniels. Daniels is listed much later in the credits, so we assume she did only a small part of the character's dialogue. Since voice recording for an animated film often takes place over several years, occasionally a voice actor is unavailable for retakes, and another actor has to be called in. You may recall on *The Hunchback of Notre Dame*, Mary Wickes passed away during the production of the film, and some lines for Laverne had to be supplied by Jane Withers. Anita was voiced by Lisa Davis. The presence of the two Lisas (both with last names beginning with D) in the film's credits has confused many people.

Q **In the movie *Hercules*, when Herc and Pegasus are putting their hand- and hoofprints in the cement, it says "To Sid" on other cement squares around them. What is the reason for this? Matthew, Chula Vista, CA**

A —The original owner of the fabled Chinese Theatre in Hollywood was Sid Grauman, and he is the one who began the tradition of having stars put their hand- and footprints in cement in front of his theater. Besides the reference to him in *Hercules*, he is caricatured in the early Mickey Mouse cartoon *Mickey's Gala Premiere*.

Q **I would like to know who sang "Colors of the Wind" in *Pocahontas*. I know Vanessa Williams sang the popular version of that**

wonderful song, but I like the movie version better. Roxanne, Huntington Beach, CA

A —Musical-theater actress Judy Kuhn sang "Colors of the Wind" in the movie. Kuhn is featured on the cast recordings of *Sunset Boulevard*, *Les Miserables* (as Cosette), and *Chess*. She also has a solo album of show tunes called *Just in Time: Judy Kuhn Sings the Music of Jule Styne*.

Q *The Lion King* **is often called the first Disney animated feature created from an original story (not from a fairy tale, children's book, etc.). Doesn't that distinction belong to** *The Aristocats***? Linda, Yatesville, PA**

A —*The Lion King* was the first original story developed by the Disney Feature Animation department. *The Aristocats* was originally created by staff writers Tom McGowan and Tom Rowe and producer Harry Tytle as a live-action television show, with Disney executives later deciding to do it in animation instead.

Q **I recently saw a showing of rare Disney footage and was especially impressed with "Clair de Lune," which was cut from** *Fantasia***. Why was that cut? Rachel, Webster, NY**

A —"Clair de Lune" would have made *Fantasia* too long, so it was cut from the film. The animation was saved and used with the song "Blue Bayou" in *Make Mine Music* instead. The "Blue Bayou" animation with the "Clair de Lune" music was released in the 1970s as part of an educational film called *Creative Film Adventures, # 2*.

Q **Was Figaro in** *Pinocchio* **the first cat in a major role in a Disney film? R.M., Sun Valley, CA**

A —There were two earlier cats who had fairly major roles. In Walt Disney's early silent Alice Comedies, the costar was an animated cat named Julius. The other cat was the villain Peg Leg Pete. Pete, a nemesis of Mickey Mouse, actually debuted before Mickey, also in the Alice Comedies.

Q **Was the Walt Disney animated version of *Alice in Wonderland* the first one on film? C.B., Yonkers, NY**

A —No. There were several silent versions and three in the sound era, two with actors (1931 and 1933) and one with puppets (1950). Walt Disney had an early silent series, the Alice Comedies, about an Alice character who visited Cartoonland.

Q **During the Korean War, my father met a Disney animator named Joe Rinaldi, who was covering the war for one of the wire services. He created a pencil Mickey Mouse sketch for me. What can you tell me about Mr. Rinaldi? Does the print have any value as a collectible? J.P. Jr., Charlotte, NC**

A —Joe Rinaldi was a story man for Disney from 1937 to 1964; two of the films he worked on were *Dumbo* and *Cinderella*. He died in 1974. Artwork of individual Disney animators rarely has great collectible value. It is unusual to find a piece signed by an artist, because they were encouraged not to sign artwork outside the Studio, and pieces from the Studio were never signed.

Q **I know that Disney animators are famous for slipping little surprises into their feature films. So I'd like to know if my eyes deceived me when I saw *The Hunchback of Notre Dame*. When Quasimodo is singing "Out There" early in the film, his view from the top of the cathedral overlooks the streets of Paris. Might I have seen *Beauty and the Beast*'s Belle walking down the street in her blue dress and apron, face buried in**

a book? I loved the film—and would love to know the answer. Tony, West Hollywood, CA

A —Yes. According to the two directors, Kirk Wise and Gary Trousdale, not only is Belle in a cameo in *Hunchback*, but Pumbaa from *The Lion King* is in there too, being carried suspended from two poles. And the Magic Carpet from *Aladdin* can also be seen, being held up by a salesman.

Q My wife says that when she was young she saw *Snow White and the Seven Dwarfs*, and at the end Dopey spoke, saying good-bye to Snow White. Is this true, or is my wife dreaming? D.H., Gouldsboro, PA

A —She may have been; Dopey never spoke in *Snow White*.

Q When my husband viewed the video of *Bambi*, I think he caught a mistake at the end of the forest fire sequence, where a baby animal suddenly disappears. Was he seeing things? G.G., Salinas, CA

A —We congratulate your husband on his eagle eye in catching a mistake most people fail to notice. At the time Walt Disney made *Bambi*, money was very tight, and he could not afford to redo many scenes. So when the camera department, while photographing the cels on the background, inadvertently shifted the cel of the "missing" baby to the right, the error was deemed too minor to go to the expense of reshooting. Because this happened when they were making the original master negative, the mistake appears in all prints of *Bambi*, including the one prepared for videos and DVDs.

Q Can you tell me what was used to create the sound of the dragon's teeth snapping in *Sleeping Beauty*? J.W., Lakewood, CA

A —To answer your question, we went right to the "dragon" himself—sound-effects man Jimmy Macdonald. Macdonald said he used ebony castanets, the kind that are on a handle rather than the kind you hold in your hand. This way he had complete control and could match whatever tempo the action required. You might also like to know that the sound of the dragon's flame breath was created with a government-issue flamethrower!

Q **I've always been a great fan of the Disney creation Jiminy Cricket, voiced by Cliff Edwards. My mom says she remembers a time when Sterling Holloway lent his voice to Jiminy—but I've never found substantiation for her recollection. Nathan, Canterbury, CT**

A —As far as I have been able to find out, Sterling Holloway never did the voice of Jiminy Cricket.

Q **I've seen *Sleeping Beauty* quite a few times. Her dress is blue throughout most of the film, but much of the recent merchandise has her wearing a pink dress. Do you know why? Emily, Santa Clara, CA**

A —Merchandisers usually make a color decision based on what they feel will sell best. During the duel between Flora and Merryweather at the end of the movie, we see the color of the dress changing back and forth from pink to blue. Thus, merchandisers have two colors from which to choose.

Q **Is it true that *Bambi* held its world premiere outside the United States? Was it the first Disney movie to do this? Where was the premiere? Gregg, Juneau, AK**

A —*Bambi* had its world premiere in London on August 8, 1942, five days before its release in the U.S. It was the first Disney film to premiere abroad. Other animated features that premiered outside the U.S. have included *Saludos Amigos*, *The Three Caballeros*, *Alice in Wonderland*, and *Treasure Planet*.

Q **I have heard that the Academy gave out special Oscars for *Snow White*—a big one and seven small ones. Is this true? Are they all the same figure, or were the small ones in the shape of each Dwarf? Where are they located now? Ellen, Montebello, CA**

A —It was one special award: a full-size Oscar and seven Dwarf-size Oscars arranged in a stair-step arrangement on a wooden stand. The award, like all of the awards presented to Walt Disney personally, is the property of the Walt Disney family. It was on display for a while in The Walt Disney Story attraction and as part of the One Man's Dream exhibit at Walt Disney World, but it can now be seen in The Walt Disney Family Museum in San Francisco.

Q **I find the original *Pinocchio* book somewhat dark and not like the animated classic at all. Was it Walt's idea to make the book into a movie, and where did he get the inspiration? Susan, Long Beach, CA**

A —Walt, along with some of his animators, saw a stage production of *Pinocchio* in Los Angeles, and it inspired him to make his own animated version.

Q **My parents were visiting Walt Disney World, and their bus driver would ask them trivia questions. They couldn't answer this one: "What is Cinderella's last name?" Would it be Charming? Melinda, Chubbuck, ID**

A —Her stepmother is Lady Tremaine, so Tremaine would likely be Cinderella's last name.

Q **Where does the story of *Cinderella* take place? Carrie, Poland, NY**

A —We can assume France, since it is from a French fairy tale, but we never mention a location in our film.

Q **In the movie *Peter Pan*, what's the name of the alligator that wants to eat Captain Hook's hand? I've heard him referred to as Tick-Tock, but I am not sure if that is his name. Julie, Anaheim, CA**

A —It is a crocodile, not an alligator. He is unnamed in the *Peter Pan* film, but in later comic book stories he was called Tick-Tock.

Q **I was wondering if you could tell me what the Ferrari said in Italian to Guido at the end of *Cars*? Julie, Long Beach, CA**

A —When Luigi faints, the Ferrari says, "*Spero che il tuo amico si riprenda. Mi dicono che si eta fantastici.*" Perhaps you know an Italian who can translate that for you.

Q **I have heard rumors about lyrics to "The Second Star to the Right" that were not used. I also heard they had something to do with *Alice in Wonderland*. Could you tell me about them? Gabrielle, Houston, TX**

A —Composer Sammy Fain, with lyricist Bob Hilliard, wrote some of the songs for *Alice in Wonderland*, including one called "Beyond the Laughing Sky." It was not used in *Alice*, but since Sammy Fain was also the primary composer on *Peter Pan*, and presumably everyone liked the melody he had written earlier, new lyrics were written by Sammy Cahn, and it became "The Second Star to the Right."

Q **In the animated *Alice in Wonderland*, when the walrus is under the sea talking to the oysters, why does the letter R in "March" glow bright red when the mother is looking at the calendar? Kimberly, Duncan, OK**

A —The R flashes due to the old proverb that one should only eat oysters in months that have an "R" in their name. Until the advent of modern harvesting methods, it was common for oysters taken in the summer months to be of poor quality. The flashing R was a warning to the baby oysters.

Q **What is the significance, if any, of the name "Mater" as the name of the tow truck in *Cars*? Is it a reference to the country term for tomato? Jim, Myersville, MD**

A —The name Mater was actually taken from the nickname of Douglas "Mater" Keever, a devoted fan at Lowe's Motor Speedway, near Charlotte, North Carolina. *Cars* director John Lasseter met Mater and was impressed by him on a research trip for the film in 2001. Keever had received the nickname as a kid working with "tuh-maters" on his parents' farm.

Q **I've been researching this question for years, but have never found an answer. In *Lady and the Tramp*, whose initials are in the heart? Brian, Bayport, NY**

A —We have never been able to determine who the initials that are carved on the tree belong to. Even the animators who worked on the film did not know. It was suggested that someone who worked on the film put his initials with his girlfriend's inside the heart, but there is no one credited on the film who has those initials.

Q **Where did the story of Dumbo come from? Duane, Golden, CO**

A —*Dumbo* was based on a story by Helen Aberson and Harold Pearl that was first published in a scroll-like item called a Roll-A-Book. None of these Dumbo Roll-A-Books have ever surfaced. After the intense work on the major productions of *Snow White and the Seven Dwarfs*, *Pinocchio*, and *Fantasia*, Walt Disney and his artists were looking for a simple little story that they could turn into the next animated feature. *Dumbo* fit the bill.

Q **Could you tell me if *The Rescuers* was released for showing in UK cinemas, and if so, when? I did not see any mention of a UK release date, although it shows 1977 as the release date in the United States. Lynda, London, UK**

A —*The Rescuers* was also released in the UK in 1977, beginning in limited release that October in the West End. It played with the featurette *Arizona Sheepdog*. The general release was in December 1977.

Q **No one has been able to give me the answer to this question, so please help! In Disney's *Aladdin*, Aladdin says that something is written on the Genie's lamp before he rubs it. What does it say on the Genie's lamp? Angela, Mountain View, CA**

A —In the film, we never know. Aladdin, in examining the lamp, says, "I think there is something written here, but it's hard to make out." When he rubs the lamp to try to read the inscription, the Genie pops out, and we never learn what it was that was written on the lamp.

Q **Although *Cinderella* is my very favorite Disney film, *Snow White and the Seven Dwarfs* has a special place in my heart, as I believe it is the first film I ever saw as a child. Could you please tell me if *Snow White* was rereleased for the first time in the summer of 1942? Louise, Sherman Oaks, CA**

A —The first official reissue of *Snow White and the Seven Dwarfs* was in February 1944, though the film remained in release in selected cities for a number of years after its 1937 premiere, and it is very possible that you did indeed see it in 1942.

Q **I was lucky to win lot No. 32, the *Fantasia* 1940 and 1977 programs, at the D23 Expo Live Auction. I was surprised at the great condition these programs are in and the wonderful detail of the color plates. I was wondering if you could tell me more about them and where they came from. Gerard, Sydney, Australia**

A —First, congratulations! The programs were extra copies that had been saved at the Disney Studios. The 1940 program was the only place where one could get the filmmakers' credits when one went to see the motion picture because there were no credits on the screen. The 1977 program was created for *Fantasia's* fifth reissue to make it appear as much of a special event as it was when it was first released.

Q **I've read that *The Aristocats* was based on a story by Tom McGowan and Tom Rowe. Were they storywriters for the Disney Studios who came up with the idea, or were they authors whose book *The Aristocats* is based on? If so, what is the name of that book? I collect the books that all Disney features are based on, and I've never been able to find one for *The Aristocats*. Holly, Burke, VA**

A —*The Aristocats* did not come from a book, so you can call off your search; Walt Disney simply bought the story idea from the two authors (who were not Disney employees) in 1963. It was seven years until the film was released, four years after Walt died.

Q Could you tell me a bit about Marc Davis's proposed animated feature *Chanticleer*? I know Mel Leven wrote a few songs for the picture and actress Robie Lester was signed on to voice one of the principal characters. Any other names who worked on the picture during its long and ultimately tragic preproduction? David, Birmingham, AL

A —According to Charles Solomon's book *The Disney That Never Was*, *Chanticleer* was first discussed at the Disney Studios as a possible animated film in 1937. Preliminary story work continued on and off for three decades, with Ken Anderson and Marc Davis working on it in the 1960s. The concept was finally dropped for budgetary and other considerations, such as the complaint, "You can't make a personality out of a chicken!" Mel Shaw was unsuccessful in trying to resurrect the idea in 1981. Much of Marc Davis's artwork for the proposed film ended up in a 1991 book from Disney Press entitled *Chanticleer and the Fox*.

Q In the original *Fantasia*, Deems Taylor comments that *The Nutcracker Suite* isn't played much anymore and most people don't know it. I have a hard time believing that's the case. Is it true (at least for 1940), or was Mr. Taylor just poking fun at the popularity of the ballet? Did *Fantasia* bring *The Nutcracker Suite* to popularity, or is there more to the story? Matthew, Gilbert, AZ

A —Actually, in *Fantasia*, famed music critic Deems Taylor's exact words are, "You know, it's funny how wrong an artist can be about his own work. Now, the one composition of Tchaikovsky's that he really detested was his *Nutcracker Suite*, which is probably the most popular thing he ever wrote." *The Nutcracker Ballet*, from which the suite was drawn, did not have the same popularity, and it was not until the mid-1950s that it gained the fame that it has today.

Q I couldn't help but notice that the villain in the film *Up* is named Charles Muntz. I was wondering if this was a conscious connection to Charles Mintz. Was this thought of, or am I reading too much into things? Charelle, Elizabethtown, PA

A —The artists made no connection to Charles Mintz, who distributed some of Walt Disney's earliest cartoons. In *The Art of Up*, the artists did say, "If you were to blend Errol Flynn, Clark Gable, Howard Hughes, and Walt Disney into one heroic 1930s man, that would be Muntz."

Q Why did Disney choose to make so many fairy tales? Did Walt love them, or did they lend themselves well to animation? Robert, Brooklyn, NY

A —When you select a well-known fairy tale to adapt, you already have a built-in audience for your film. People who know the story are often eager to see how Disney would present it.

Q Is there any chance Disney will make the sound tracks from *Melody Time, Make Mine Music,* or *The Adventures of Ichabod and Mr. Toad* available on CD or on iTunes? I have always wanted to have recordings of the music from these films, but cannot find them anywhere. Reed, location not given

A —Randy Thornton of Walt Disney Records has been leading an effort to digitally release original Disney albums (previously available through the decades on vinyl) on iTunes. As of now, sound tracks to the animated features in question have not been released. However, versions of songs from these films have been made available: a rendition of "The Headless Horseman" (*Ichabod*) on iTunes's *Walt Disney Records Archive Collection, Volume 1* and "Blame it on the Samba" (*Melody Time*) on *Saludos Amigos (Music from the Motion Picture)*.

Q **Was a man named Dick Ruhl doing work for Walt in the 1960s? Ernest, Sapulpa, OK**

A —Dick Ruhl worked as an in-betweener (animator) at the Disney Studios for less than a year in 1944. He died in 1991.

Q **Is it really true that *Sleeping Beauty* saved The Walt Disney Company from going bankrupt? Doug, Sylmar, CA**

A —No. The profits from *Snow White and the Seven Dwarfs*, and later from *Cinderella*, helped get the Company in a profitable mode, but *Sleeping Beauty* was not quite in the same category. *Sleeping Beauty* was a very expensive film for its time (more than $6 million), and it did not prove to be a tremendous box office success in its initial release. Two years ago, with its fiftieth anniversary, critics and fans took a second look at *Sleeping Beauty* and reaffirmed its place as one of the most strikingly designed animated features.

Q **I am a huge Tink fan! When was Tinker Bell "born," and when was the Mary Martin version of *Peter Pan* created? Jan, Gilbert, AZ**

A —Tinker Bell was actually "born" in the play *Peter Pan*, which J. M. Barrie wrote in 1904. The Disney film was made in 1953, and for the first time the fairy was something other than a flitting glimmer of light. Mary Martin and Cyril Ritchard starred in a new musical version of *Peter Pan* on Broadway in 1954; that version was aired as a TV special by NBC for a number of years beginning in 1955.

Q **On a recent reissue of *The Jungle Book*, it's mentioned that the film is the last personally overseen by Walt. Wasn't it also the last to use hand-inked cels (prior to the switch to the Xerographic process)? Dave, Lakewood, CO**

A —No. *The Jungle Book* also used the Xerographic process for the cels. The process was first used in a feature for a few scenes in *Sleeping Beauty* and then for the entire film in *One Hundred and One Dalmatians*.

Q I've heard that the Disney animators had live fawns at the Studio to act as models for *Bambi*. How did they do the elephants for *Dumbo*? Did they visit the zoo a lot, or were they less worried about making them seem "elephant-like"? Jorge, Tempe, AZ

A —The Disney artists regularly visited the Los Angeles Zoo because it was just a few miles from the Disney Studios. But at least once they had an elephant at the Studio; the artists are shown drawing it in *The Reluctant Dragon* feature.

Q I've heard that Walt Kelly, who drew the *Pogo* comic strip, worked for Disney for a while. What projects did he do? Richard, Baltimore, MD

A —Kelly worked at the Disney Studios from 1936 to 1941, starting as a story man and later doing some animation of Mickey Mouse in *The Little Whirlwind* and *The Nifty Nineties*. He also aided Ward Kimball in a little animation in the "Pastoral Symphony" sequence of *Fantasia*.

Q I've heard that Walt Disney invented the multiplane camera. How does it work? Ruben, Tampa, FL

A —Well, it wasn't actually Walt himself but staffer Bill Garity who perfected the camera. To get a feeling of depth and dimension in an animated production, the camera filmed downward through as many as six layers of background elements painted on glass. If there were characters in the scenes, they would be painted on celluloid. One of the Disney multiplane cameras is currently on display at The Walt Disney Family Museum in San Francisco.

Q **Did any of the Disney animated films use rotoscope techniques? Can you explain exactly what rotoscoping is? Greg, Ventura, CA**

A —Animators were able to take live-action film footage of actors, print the frames, and use the images to help them with their animation. The original rotoscopes actually projected the images onto glass. While some rotoscope users would simply trace the action, Disney animators usually used the printed images only as a guide.

Q **Why doesn't Cinderella's prince have a name? Shari, Ithaca, NY**

A —It is actually Snow White's prince that is just known as the Prince, just as that film has the Queen and the Witch. These characters may have been named in published versions of the story, but were not for the Disney film. The prince in *Cinderella* is Prince Charming.

Q **Is it possible to buy maquettes from the making of Disney's animated movies? James, Madison, WI**

A —The early plaster models, now called maquettes, that were made for the use of Disney animators were never sold to the public, though some that were given to animators after a film's completion have occasionally turned up at auction. A few maquettes have been reproduced for sale in art galleries and at the Parks in more recent years.

Q **In Walt's day, how long did it take to make most of the classic animated features? Anastasia, Astoria, NY**

A —It usually took about three years to make an animated feature, with perhaps a couple years in story work and preparation and a year in actual animation.

Q **How did the animators come up with the look of Jiminy Cricket? An insect seems like a hard choice to make into a sympathetic character! Carla, Pittsburgh, PA**

A — There was a cricket in Collodi's original Pinocchio story, but he had only a minor role. Walt felt Pinocchio needed a conscience and had Ward Kimball work on the character. Ward recalled that Jiminy "started out as a pretty ugly-looking insect from which all the somewhat grotesque insect appendages and characteristics ultimately had to be eliminated."

Q **At the end of each Pixar movie there's a credit listing Pixar babies. Are those the babies born during the making of that film? Jennifer, Burns Harbor, IN**

A —I checked with Christine Freeman, the archivist at Pixar, and here is her answer: "The babies listed in the credits were born to Pixar employees during the making of the current film and after the issuing of the credits for the previous film. A baby born after the credits deadline can be eligible for the credits for the next film."

Q **I understand that the voice of Jiminy Cricket was an entertainer named Ukulele Ike. Can you tell us anything about the man and his relationship with Disney? Walt, Alexandria, VA**

A —Cliff Edwards, the performer who also appeared onstage as Ukulele Ike, was the original voice of Jiminy Cricket in *Pinocchio* in 1940. He later voiced the character in *Fun and Fancy Free*, in later television cartoons, and on phonograph record albums. Edwards passed away in 1971.

Q Was the same actress the voice of both Cinderella's evil stepmother and Maleficent? Also, is she the voice in the crystal ball in Disneyland's Haunted Mansion? Diana, Upland, CA

A —Eleanor Audley provided the voices of Lady Tremaine and Maleficent, as well as Madame Leota, the head in the crystal ball in Haunted Mansion. It's little-known, but she also played a cook on an episode of *The Swamp Fox* on TV in 1960.

Q I have a two-year-old son who loves to listen to Disney songs. Right now he loves the Seven Dwarfs. When we listen to the song "Heigh-Ho," I could swear I hear Burl Ives's voice as one of the singers. Is this true, or am I just hearing things? Casey, Independence, MO

A —Burl Ives did not sing on the sound track of *Snow White and the Seven Dwarfs*—he did not begin working in the industry until almost a decade after it was released. Ives's primary work for Disney was in *So Dear to My Heart* and *Summer Magic*, and he also did the voice for Eagle Sam, the host of America Sings at Disneyland.

Q I'm trying to find a DVD of Donald Duck videos from the 1940s to early 1950s. I've purchased DVDs with some cartoons from those years, but want the specific Donald Duck short in which Pluto swallows a magnet and Donald gets involved. It's hilarious. We originally had it on 8 mm film, but it's long since deteriorated. Also, it was obviously a silent movie. Can you tell me about this particular cartoon and if sound was added? Woody, Davenport, FL

A —The Pluto-and-the-magnet cartoon was actually the first Donald Duck–starring cartoon, titled *Donald and Pluto* (1936). That cartoon was originally made with sound, though a silent 8 mm version was sold for home use. It appeared most recently on the *Walt Disney Treasures: The Chronological Donald, Volume One* DVD.

Q **What is the name of the queen in *Sleeping Beauty*? She is just referred to as "Queen." Angela, Saylorville, IA**

A —She was never given a name in the Disney film.

Q **I was wondering what they did with the live-action storybooks that were shown at the beginning of *Snow White*, *Cinderella*, and *Sleeping Beauty*. Are they kept in the Archives? Rachel, Salina, KS**

A —Yes, we have all three of those books in the Archives. The *Sleeping Beauty* book is especially handsome, with its bejeweled cover.

Q **I've heard that the sorcerer's name in *Fantasia* is Yensid, "Disney" spelled backward. I can't find any verification beyond word of mouth. Is this true, or is it a Disney myth? If true, is there a story behind it? Randy, Victoria, MN**

A —It's true. "Yensid" appeared in *Fantasia* books from 1940, the year the movie was released, but is nowhere in the film. Walt later used the credit "Retlaw Yensid," which is his whole name spelled backward, for a story credit on the 1966 feature *Lt. Robin Crusoe, U.S.N.*

Q **Which film featured the circus bear that fell off a train, ended up in the wild, and fell in love? Also, was that the bear's only film? Bill, Cazenovia, NY**

A —Bongo the circus bear was featured in the 1947 film *Fun and Fancy Free*. Bongo, who originated in a story based on a

Sinclair Lewis article, later appeared in Disney books as well as comic books, but no other films.

Q **I have a big question about Timothy, the mouse from *Dumbo*. His full name is Timothy Q. Mouse. What does the "Q" stand for? Justin, Appling, GA**

A —We are never told.

Q **I am looking for some information about singer Dora Luz (date of birth and death, career, collaboration with Disney Studios, etc.) from *The Three Caballeros*. If you have some anecdotes about the movie, do not hesitate! Karl, France**

A —Surprisingly, the press material for *The Three Caballeros* has very little information on Dora Luz. It simply mentions that she was a Mexican radio songstress and recording star making her film debut. She sang "You Belong to My Heart (Solamente una vez)" in the film and also recorded the song "Destino" for the aborted 1946 film project with Salvador Dali.

Q **Was there ever an animator with Disney Productions with the initials E. M. L.? Brenda, Spokane, WA**

A —I do not know about the middle initial, but with the initials E. L. there were Eric Larson (one of Walt's Nine Old Men), Edward Lovitt (a background artist on *Fantasia* and *Bambi*), and Edward Love (an animator on *Fantasia*).

Q **Why was Captain Hook shown in *Disney Channel Magazine* in two pictures, each with his hook replacing a different hand? Which is correct? I know James Barrie used the right hand in his book. R.N., Livermore, CA**

A —I figured that the best way to get an answer to your interesting question was to go to the source, Frank Thomas, who animated the character. Frank explained that there were many meetings of the animation staff during which they tried to decide how to handle the hook. While they realized that Barrie had the hook on the right, they saw problems with that in animation. They wanted Hook to be able to make gestures, to write, and to perform other actions that are simpler to do with the right hand. So they made the decision to place the hook on the left. This made their animation of the character a lot easier. Regarding the inconsistency in the published photos, sometimes in page layout a photo is "flopped" for aesthetic reasons. In this case, that led to an inadvertent error, putting Hook's hook on his right arm— which was wrong.

Q **Why was the name of famed illustrator Kay Nielsen listed in the credits for *The Little Mermaid*, since he has been dead for many years? T.R., Lake Park, GA**

A —After the success of *Snow White and the Seven Dwarfs*, Walt Disney began dozens of projects. One of them was *The Little Mermaid*, and Walt asked Kay Nielsen to prepare some story sketches. With the coming of World War II, *The Little Mermaid* was shelved and the project was not revived until the 1980s. At that time, the Disney artists decided to give him screen credit because his early sketches helped inspire them. Nielsen is better known at Disney for his concept sketches for the "Night on Bald Mountain" segment in *Fantasia*. One of his most famous credits elsewhere is illustrating the fairy-tale book *East of the Sun, West of the Moon*.

Q **Is the "Ben Wright" in the credits for *The Jungle Book* the same Ben Wright who did the voice of Grimsby in *The Little Mermaid*? M.S., Los Angeles, CA**

A —Yes; the same actor provided the voice for Rama the Wolf in *The Jungle Book*. Even earlier, he had voiced Roger Radcliff in *One Hundred and One Dalmatians*. Mr. Wright passed away in July 1989.

Q **I have a photo of a Disney "Danny the Lamb" character. Could you explain who this lamb is? S.W., Londonderry, NH**

A —Danny the Little Black Lamb was featured in the Disney film *So Dear to My Heart*, which was released in 1949. The film starred Bobby Driscoll as a boy trying to raise a black lamb that was constantly getting into mischief. Danny inspired a number of merchandising items—a watch, a book, and a plush figure—which are quite popular with collectors today.

Q **How did the producers of *The Little Mermaid* come up with the name of Ariel for the title character, since the mermaid is not named in Hans Christian Andersen's story? Did they name her after the servant spirit in Shakespeare's *The Tempest*? S.F., Fremont, CA**

A —To get an answer to your question, I called producer Ron Clements, who had the original idea for *The Little Mermaid* as an animated film. Ron tells me that while he had known of the character in *The Tempest*, he did not consciously think of that play when he came up with the character's name. The name Ariel just sounded right to him at the time.

Q **Do the boxes for the videocassettes of the Disney animated classics utilize artwork from the original theater lobby cards? D.D., Pinole, CA**

A —In all cases, the video boxes for the Disney animated classics feature new artwork. In fact, new poster art was usually prepared each time the films were rereleased. Poster styles and tastes have changed over the years; what may have been eye-catching in 1940 is not necessarily so now.

Q **The narrator's voice for *Peter and the Wolf* sounded so familiar; who was it? B.M., San Luis Obispo, CA**

A —The narrator was Sterling Holloway. He did the voices for many Disney characters (among them the Cheshire Cat and Winnie the Pooh), so it is no wonder you recognized the voice.

Q **Can you tell me about Felix Salten, who wrote *Bambi*? S.L., Provo, UT**

A —Salten was born in Budapest in 1869, but was educated in Vienna. He wrote several adult novels and plays, but is best known for *Bambi*, first published in English in 1928.

Q **Where did José Carioca, the charming parrot in *Saludos Amigos*, get his name? D.S., Los Angeles, CA**

A —A native of Rio de Janeiro, Brazil, is often called a "carioca" in Portuguese (Brazil's national language). Since José was a Brazilian parrot, what name could have been more appropriate?

Q **Didn't Walt Disney's critics have a nickname for *Snow White and the Seven Dwarfs* during its production? R.H., Newark Valley, NY**

A —*Snow White* was referred to as "Disney's Folly." They changed their tune, of course, after it became a huge success. Walt Disney often had prophets of doom who scoffed whenever he attempted something that had never been done before.

Q I was surprised to hear Bette Midler singing "Baby Mine" in *Beaches*. Wasn't that song from an earlier Disney film? P.O., Prattville, AL

A —"Baby Mine," with lyrics by Ned Washington and music by Frank Churchill, was originally written for and used in *Dumbo* (1941).

Q I remember the names of Donald Duck and José Carioca, but who was the third caballero in *The Three Caballeros*? He was a rooster. T.L., San Juan, Puerto Rico

A —The rooster was named Panchito, and his voice was provided by Joaquin Garay II. One interesting fact: thirty-five years later, a pint-size pickpocket in *Herbie Goes Bananas* was portrayed by Joaquin Garay III, following a family tradition, as he was the son of the actor who had provided Panchito's voice.

Q Who provided the voice for the female church mouse in *Robin Hood*? The voice sounds so familiar. S.K., Huntington Beach, CA

A —That was Barbara Luddy. Ms. Luddy also did the voices of Merryweather in *Sleeping Beauty* and Lady in *Lady and the Tramp*, so that is why her voice is so familiar.

Q Why did Walt Disney pick *Snow White and the Seven Dwarfs* as the story for his first animated feature? L.K., Bowie, MD

A —When Walt was a newspaper boy in Kansas City, he saw a major presentation of a silent film version of the story starring Marguerite Clark. The screening was held at the city's Convention Hall in February 1917, and the film was projected onto a four-sided screen using four separate projectors. This movie made a tremendous impression on its fifteen-year-old viewer because he was sitting where he could see two sides of the screen at once.

Q Was *The Sword in the Stone* based on a book? L.R., Compton, CA

A —While Walt Disney dug deeply into folklore for many of his animated classics, for *The Sword in the Stone* he turned to a contemporary novel by the well-known English author T. H. White. *The Sword in the Stone* was published in 1938 and immediately became popular. The author later revised and rewrote the novel, along with two other books in his Arthurian cycle, and combined them with a new concluding section into a saga called *The Once and Future King.*

Q In *Alice in Wonderland,* there seems to be a moment during the mad tea party when the film briefly switches to black and white as the White Rabbit's watch is smashed. Was this intentional? D.C., Beavercreek, OH

A —That brief black-and-white segment in *Alice in Wonderland* was probably created to show the life passing out of the White Rabbit's watch. The same effect was used in "The Sorcerer's Apprentice" in *Fantasia,* when Mickey Mouse chops the broom into pieces.

Q Is it possible that Tramp in *Lady and the Tramp* and the adult Bambi were voiced by the same person? The voices sound the same. A.K., Colorado Springs, CO

A —No, there were two different actors. Larry Roberts was the voice of Tramp; the voice of the adult Bambi was provided by John Sutherland. Neither of these actors was used in any other Disney animated feature.

Q Did the Disney Studios reedit *Cinderella?* When I saw it at our local theater, the words for "The Work Song" were not the words I remembered. D.A., Carson, CA

A —There was no new editing done on *Cinderella*. Often the song in a film is quite different (and usually shorter) than the version found on records or published as sheet music. Perhaps your recollection of "The Work Song" is from a record version.

Q **Who provided the original voices for Mickey and Minnie Mouse?**
C.F., Racine, WI

A —Walt Disney was the voice of Mickey Mouse from Mickey's beginnings until the late 1940s, when Walt became too busy to fulfill the task. The original voice of Minnie was Marcellite Garner, who worked in the Ink and Paint Department at the Disney Studios.

Q **Whatever happened to Peter Behn, the boy who did the cute voice of Thumper in *Bambi*? T.L., Wheeling, WV**

A —We wondered ourselves, so some years ago we put an article in newspapers nationwide. One reader in Florida was a friend of Peter Behn's and gave him a call. Peter then called the Studio. He had been working in the real estate business in Vermont.

Q **I recall Roy Rogers singing in a Disney film, but I don't remember which one. Can you help? J.C., Albuquerque, NM**

A —In *Melody Time* (1948), Roy Rogers and the Sons of the Pioneers sing one of my favorite songs from a Disney film, the hauntingly beautiful "Blue Shadows on the Trail." In the film, Rogers and his group are sitting around a campfire with child stars Bobby Driscoll and Luana Patten, and they use the song to introduce the story of Pecos Bill.

Q **In the early 1920s Walt Disney made a few cartoons starring the character Alice, who was played by Virginia Davis (and later on by Margie Gay). Are these cartoons still around? N.R., York, ME**

A —From 1923 to 1927, Walt Disney made fifty-seven of the Alice Comedies as silent films, so it was quite an extensive series. Today, however, many of the films seem to be lost. Through diligent searching, we have been able to find prints of about thirty of them, which we have in our collection. Several of them had been retained by Virginia Davis herself, and she presented us with original nitrate prints. Alice of the comedies is named after Lewis Carroll's Alice, but her escapades bear little resemblance to Carroll's *Alice's Adventures in Wonderland*. Walt Disney's *Alice in Wonderland*, based on the Lewis Carroll novel and its equally famed sequel, *Through the Looking Glass*, was released in 1951.

Q **Is it true that Tinker Bell was modeled after Marilyn Monroe? B.B., Hayward, CA**

A —While Marilyn Monroe was at the peak of her popularity in 1953, the year *Peter Pan* was released, the animators who worked on the film assured me that Monroe was not the model for Tinker Bell. The actual model for the fairy was actress Margaret Kerry.

Q **Why are different boys' voices used as the voice of Christopher Robin in *The Many Adventures of Winnie the Pooh*? D.P., Key West, FL**

A —The initial Disney Winnie the Pooh films were made over a period of several years, from 1966 to 1974. Boys' voices change, so it was not possible to continue using the same voice for each film. The three Pooh featurettes in the film were not originally meant to be seen at the same time.

Q **Who were Walt Disney's "Nine Old Men"? M.L., Derby, KS**

A —After Franklin D. Roosevelt spoke of his "Nine Old Men" on the Supreme Court, Walt remarked that he had his own "Nine Old Men," referring to his key animators at the time. They were Les Clark, Marc Davis, Ollie Johnston, Milt Kahl, Ward Kimball, Eric Larson, John Lounsbery, Woolie Reitherman, and Frank Thomas.

Q **Why did the Disney Studios never make a sequel to *Fantasia* during Walt Disney's lifetime? H.C., South Orange, NJ**

A —*Fantasia* was considered to be ahead of its time and took years to break even at the box office. However, Disney used the same format as *Fantasia* for *Make Mine Music* and *Melody Time*, but with popular instead of classical music. Did you know there was a segment prepared for *Fantasia* that never made it into the final film? The segment was produced to go with Debussy's "Clair de Lune." Disney finally decided the piece did not fit, so the animation was shelved. But when *Make Mine Music* was in production a few years later, the animation was brought out again and used with the song "Blue Bayou" instead of "Clair de Lune." In 2000, the Disney Studios finally made a sequel, *Fantasia/2000*.

Q **Sterling Holloway was a familiar voice in many Disney films. What happened to him? S.S.O. and F.O., Dearborn Heights, MI**

A —Holloway retired in the 1970s and lived in Laguna Beach, California, until his death in 1992. The previous year he had been honored as a Disney Legend. His distinct and recognizable voice was first used by Walt Disney as the stork in *Dumbo* way back in 1941. The quality of the voice was such that Disney animators loved working with it. So Holloway gave further performances during the next four decades, including Flower the skunk in *Bambi*, the Cheshire Cat in *Alice in Wonderland*, Kaa the snake in *The Jungle Book*, Amos the mouse who befriended Ben Franklin in *Ben and Me*, Roquefort the mouse in *The Aristocats*, and Pooh in *Winnie the Pooh*.

Q **I heard that during the film's production Tramp from *Lady and the Tramp* had other names. Is that true? C.E., Trona, CA**

A —In early script versions, Tramp was first called Homer, then Rags, then Bozo. A 1940 script introduced the twin Siamese cats. Eventually known as Si and Am, they were then named Nip and Tuck.

ANIMATED SHORTS

Q I know that Mickey has two nephews: Morty and Ferdie; Donald has three nephews: Huey, Dewey, and Louie; and Goofy has a son, Max; yet I don't ever recall hearing about Mickey or Donald's siblings or Max's mother. Can you tell me more about this younger generation of Disney characters and how they came to be? Rachael, Littleton, CO

A —Disney artists only created characters when they were needed for a story; in the theatrical cartoons no sibling was ever created for Mickey Mouse, and only in some early cartoons did Goofy have a wife. We are told in *Donald's Nephews* that Donald's sister was named Dumbella, but she never appeared in a cartoon. A multitude of relatives for the characters were created for comic books and comic strips.

Q Was *Steamboat Willie* the first Mickey Mouse cartoon? I heard that there were two silent cartoons before *Steamboat Willie*. Is that true? Hakop, Van Nuys, CA

A —*Steamboat Willie* was the first Mickey Mouse cartoon released, and as such its release date is regarded as Mickey's "birth." Two silent cartoons, *Plane Crazy* and *The Gallopin' Gaucho*, were made earlier the same year (1928), but they were not released until after *Steamboat Willie*, when sound could be added to them.

Q On the Walt Disney Treasures set *The War Years*, it is stated that some of the films hadn't been seen since World War II. However, I seem to recall both *Chicken Little* and an edited *Reason and Emotion* shown on *The Wonderful World of Disney*. (Both had Ludwig Von Drake in the narrator's role.) Am I imagining things? Orville, Greenville, SC

A —You are correct. *Chicken Little* appeared in *Jiminy Cricket Presents Bongo*, airing on September 28, 1955, and both that cartoon and *Reason and Emotion* appeared in *Man Is His Own Worst Enemy*, airing on October 21, 1962.

Q   **Who sang the original song "A Cowboy Needs a Horse," and is it available as an MP3? Judy, Oceanside, CA**

A   —"A Cowboy Needs a Horse" was sung in the film by Jeanne Bruns, Gil Mershon, Bob Wacker, Gene Lanhan, and Dick Byron. I have seen several MP3 listings on the Internet.

Q   **We were always under the impression that *Steamboat Willie* was the third Mickey Mouse cartoon to be produced but the first one released, on November 18, 1928. However, a few Web sites note *Plane Crazy* as being released on May 15, 1928, six months before *Steamboat Willie*. Was this a true release date or, perhaps, just a private viewing for distributors? Joseph and Chrissy, Modesto, CA**

A   —The May 15 date was a preview of the silent version of *Plane Crazy* at a single theater in Los Angeles; the film did not have its official release until after sound was added. It opened at the Mark Strand Theatre in New York on March 17, 1929, four months after *Steamboat Willie* premiered.

Q   **I've been trying to remember the name of that old Silly Symphony cartoon about the Easter bunny. I think it was from the 1930s. Renee, New York, NY**

A   —That cartoon, Disney's only Easter-themed film, was *Funny Little Bunnies* from 1934. It was the first cartoon that Wolfgang Reitherman, who later became a director, helped animate.

Q   **I own a Disney story record for *Winnie the Pooh and the Honey Tree* that includes a Sherman Brothers song. The song, "Mind**

Over Matter (Will Make a Pooh Unfatter)," is sung as a lullaby by Kanga to comfort Pooh while he's stuck in Rabbit's hole. On the video and DVD releases of *The Many Adventures of Winnie the Pooh,* you can hear a brief march-tempo version of the song as Christopher Robin and the gang head to Rabbit's house to pull Pooh free from his predicament. Was this scene with Kanga's lullaby cut out of the original animated feature, or did the record add extra scenes and music? Bob, Whippany, NJ

A —Nothing has been cut from the film; extra material has often been added to recordings.

Q I have a 16 mm black-and-white cartoon, about four minutes long, called *Mickey's Repair Shop* (copyright 1935, Walt Disney Productions), starring Mickey Mouse and Peg Leg Pete. One odd thing was that at the beginning of the cartoon, Pete's left leg is a peg leg, but later on, it is his right. Was this just a mistake? Anthony, New Fairfield, CT

A —This shortened cartoon was actually part of *Mickey's Service Station*. The Disney animators often had problems remembering which of Pete's legs was supposed to be the peg leg. This cartoon is a good example of how the peg leg could switch sides.

Q I've been looking for a certain Disney cartoon for years. I don't remember the title, but it was about Lambert, a very sheepish lion. Where can I find this short? Monica, Napa, CA

A —*Lambert, the Sheepish Lion,* directed by Jack Hannah, was released in 1952 and nominated for an Academy Award. A stork mistakenly delivers Lambert, a lion cub, to a flock of sheep. At first Lambert's pals make fun of him for being different, but later Lambert's leonine ways save the flock from a wolf. *Lambert* was released on the *Melody Time* DVD as a bonus feature.

Q I grew up in Moscow in the former Soviet Union, and I have always thought that Goofy is a wolf. That's because in Russian cartoons, wolves look like Goofy! I've searched the Internet for an answer as to what Goofy is, and most of his fans define him as "an anthropomorphic dog." Is he a wolf, an anthropomorphic dog, or something else altogether? Andre, Forest Hills, NY

A —This is an interesting interpretation of Goofy; we have never heard him described as a wolf before. Goofy has doglike features, and indeed his original name was Dippy Dawg, but essentially he was created as a human character: talking, walking upright, wearing clothes, etc.

Q I remember an old Disney cartoon from the 1930s or 1940s about Mother Goose characters, but I've completely forgotten the title. Can you help? Jae, Chicago, IL

A —You're thinking of *Old King Cole*, a color Silly Symphony cartoon. It was made in 1933. In the film, characters from Mother Goose rhymes come out of a book and attend a lively ball at King Cole's castle; later, the king has trouble getting them to go home. There was also a 1938 cartoon, *Mother Goose Goes Hollywood*, in which Hollywood stars of the period portray nursery rhyme characters.

Q What is the name of the cartoon in which Mickey, Minnie, and Pluto are walking along a frozen river when Pluto jumps in the water and pulls out a sack of kittens, which Mickey and Minnie then take home? Steve, Largo, FL

A —That cartoon is *Mickey's Pal Pluto*, released on February 18, 1933, and directed by Burt Gillett. When Pluto rescues some kittens, Minnie and Mickey take them home, making Pluto jealous. In 1941 the cartoon was remade in color and released as *Lend a Paw*, which won an Academy Award for Best Cartoon.

Q **Where can I find the lyrics to the original song that Chip and Dale sang? Carol, Malvern, PA**

A —Here they are:
> I'm Chip . . .
> I'm Dale . . .
> We're just a couple of crazy rascals
> Out to have some fun.
> When Chip and Dale
> Start cooking up some trouble
> You can bet it gets well done.
> Folks all say
> We are the cutest two . . .
> To tell the truth
> I think so too!
> I'm Chip
> No, I'm Chip!
> A great sensational corporation
> We are Chip and Dale!

Q **I saw a Disney cartoon years ago about shipping guinea pigs through the mail. Can you tell me about this cartoon? Kathy, Pierrepont Manor, NY**

A —*Pigs Is Pigs* was released on May 21, 1954, and was nominated for an Academy Award. It was taken from a famous story written by Ellis Parker Butler. A character named McMorehouse is collecting his two guinea pigs from the post office. He argues that the animals are pets and not pigs, so the shipping charges should be cheaper.

Q **I once saw a Disney animated film in which Donald Duck gets lessons on the mathematics of shooting billiards. When was this cartoon made? Scott, Marysville, WA**

A —The film to which you refer is *Donald in Mathmagic Land*. It was made in 1959 for theatrical release, and it was also shown in 1961 on the very first *Walt Disney's Wonderful World of Color* program. It has been a very popular educational film in schools.

Q While staying at the Polynesian Resort at Walt Disney World, my husband and I discovered an animation cel in the lobby that featured Mickey and Minnie in tropical attire. The plaque beneath said it was from *Hawaiian Holiday.* Can you tell me any more about this cartoon? Maureen, Barling, AR

A —*Hawaiian Holiday* was released in 1937; it featured the Disney gang enjoying themselves on the tropical isles. The cartoon was released in 2001 on the *Walt Disney Treasures: Mickey Mouse in Living Color* DVD.

Q Some of my coworkers told me that Chip and Dale were in Looney Tunes cartoons before they were featured in Disney cartoons. Are they correct? Elyce, Oceanside, CA

A —No, they were never Looney Tunes characters. They made their debut in the Disney cartoon *Private Pluto* in 1943.

Q Who originally was the voice of Minnie Mouse? Did the actress ever do other Disney things? Who else has voiced Minnie through the years? Jerry, Tucson, AZ

A —Since Minnie Mouse did not have many lines in the early cartoons, an actress was not hired at first to do the work. Instead, Walt used a woman from the Ink and Paint Department, Marcellite Garner. Succeeding her were Leone Ledoux, Thelma Boardman, Ruth Peterson, and Ruth Clifford. Besides voicing Minnie, Garner did the meows for kittens in several cartoons. Russi Taylor has provided the voice of Minnie Mouse since 1986.

Q I remember a Ranger Brownstone cartoon where the ranger tried to get the bears to clean up the national park by singing about using sticks to pick up paper and then put the paper into bags. Is this cartoon available on video? Matthew, Placentia, CA

A —The ranger's name is J. Audubon Woodlore, of Brownstone National Park, and the cartoon you recall is called *In the Bag*. That cartoon was released on DVD in 2005 on *Walt Disney Treasures: Disney Rarities*.

Q I am a Cast Member at one of the Disney Stores here in England. A Guest asked us a question she had heard in a quiz on a BBC radio show to which we have been unable to find an answer: What is the name of Donald Duck's boat? Liz, Quarry Bank, West Midlands, England

A —It is possible that there are several boats with different names owned by Donald Duck, given the huge number of cartoons, comic book stories, and comic strips he appears in. For example, in the classic 1942 *Donald Duck Finds Pirate Gold* comic book, Donald has a small boat named the *Daisy II*. In Mickey's Toontown at Disneyland, Donald's boat, which is also his house, is the *Miss Daisy*.

Q In a book I have about Disney, there is a story by Dick Kelsey based on *The Song of Hiawatha*. Has Disney ever thought of animating *Hiawatha*? Ivan, Clare, Australia

A —Walt Disney made a Silly Symphony cartoon called *Little Hiawatha* in 1937. His artists worked on story sketches for a feature-length picture, but it was never made. There was a *Little Hiawatha* comic story in Sunday papers from 1940 to 1942 as well as a Little Golden Book and several comic books.

Q I saw a short film on Disney Channel's *Vault Disney* featuring a girl being chased by lions. The girl was real, but everything else was a cartoon. I thought that *Mary Poppins* was the first movie to mix live people and cartoons in the same scene. Can you tell me what I saw? Katie, Garden City, NY

A —The cartoon you saw was *Alice's Wonderland* (1923), the pilot film of the Alice Comedy series and the only one produced by Walt Disney in Kansas City. Virginia Davis was the girl who played Alice. These cartoons were the first to immerse a human figure in a cartoon environment, though cartoon figures had interacted in human spaces before. Walt Disney continued trying different techniques in such films as *The Three Caballeros*, *Song of the South*, and *Melody Time*. *Mary Poppins* was the culmination of everything he had learned from these earlier attempts.

Q I recall reading in a Disney magazine that besides Mrs. Lillian Disney, Mickey Rooney was somewhat influential in Mr. Disney's changing Mortimer Mouse's name to Mickey Mouse. Is this correct? Rosalie, East Chicago, IN

A —Mickey Rooney was only seven years old when Mickey Mouse was created and named. While he had made some short film comedies as Mickey McGuire at that time (his real name was Joe Yale), he was not yet well known, so the story is doubtful. There is no evidence that Walt Disney knew Mickey Rooney, and even if he did, would he have asked for advice from a seven-year-old boy? Walt Disney always told the story that it was his wife who had come up with the name of Mickey Mouse.

Q Sound technology was available in 1928 when Walt Disney made *Steamboat Willie*. Why did he wait until 1929 and *The Karnival Kid* to have the mouse utter his first words? Avani, Ann Arbor, MI

A —My guess is that many of the first cartoons were made without dialogue so that they would have greater success when shown in foreign countries, since the studio wouldn't have to worry about translations and dubbing. Also, the plots of the earliest cartoons didn't require Mickey to speak.

Q **Who does the voice of Goofy? Christie, Rochester, NY**

A —The current voice of Goofy is Bill Farmer. Originally, Goofy's voice was created and supplied by Pinto Colvig, who once was a circus clown.

Q **What was the title of the last black-and-white Silly Symphony? Scott, Stevensville, MI**

A —The last black-and-white Silly Symphony was *Just Dogs*, released the same day (July 30, 1932) as *Flowers and Trees*, the first color one. The last film of the Silly Symphonies series was the 1939 remake of *The Ugly Duckling*, which won a Best Cartoon Academy Award. The last black-and-white Disney cartoon was a Mickey Mouse one—*Mickey's Kangaroo*, in 1935.

Q **When is Pluto's actual birthday? I know he was around back in 1930 in *The Chain Gang*. Barbara, Discovery Bay, CA**

A —*The Chain Gang* was Pluto's first film. We have come up with actual "birthdays" for only three of our characters—Mickey Mouse, Minnie Mouse, and Donald Duck. The birthdays are based on the dates when their first cartoons were released in theaters, so they are actually anniversaries of films instead of birthdays of characters. Since actual release dates of cartoons in the early 1930s are difficult to establish, we just go by the year for Pluto (1930) and Goofy (1932). For the feature films, it would be presumptuous for us to assign a birthday to, say, Snow

White, when the character was established in folktales long before we ever made our movie. The same would be true even with characters from our short cartoons, such as the Three Little Pigs, who had their birth in folklore.

Q **I have a copy of a song by former Monkee Davy Jones called "Happy Birthday Mickey Mouse." It's from 1978, and I assume it was made to commemorate Mickey's fiftieth birthday. Was this song authorized by the Disney company? Was Davy Jones involved in any other Disney project besides this one and a 1977 appearance in *The Bluegrass Special* on *The Wonderful World of Disney*? Alison, Buffalo Grove, IL**

A —The song "Hey Ra Ra Ra—Happy Birthday Mickey Mouse" was actually written by Al Kasha and Joel Hirschhorn, but was sung first by Davy Jones "and a Million Kids" on a Warner Bros. record in England in 1978. The song was copyrighted by Disney. Jones appeared only in *The Bluegrass Special* for Disney.

Q **My uncle had an interview with Walt Disney for an animator's job. Although he was not hired, Mr. Disney was kind enough to give him a tour of the Studio. My uncle watched one animator who would draw, then go to a large mirror and start laughing, then go back and continue drawing. Sometime later, my uncle saw a cartoon that had as one of its main characters a horse who had a laugh just like the animator he had seen. Any idea which cartoon it might have been? Ron, Elko, NV**

A —A gag with a horse laughing was a common one in Disney cartoons of the 1930s, 1940s, and 1950s, usually when something funny happened to its rider, so without further information it would be impossible to determine which one you are referring to. A couple of cartoons with laughing horses are *The Cactus Kid* and *How to Ride a Horse*.

Q **Who was the first animated Disney dog after Pluto and Goofy? Was it Nana in *Peter Pan*? Sarah, Milwaukee, WI**

A —According to John Grant's *Encyclopedia of Walt Disney's Animated Characters*, the first named dog after Pluto and Goofy (though Goofy was technically portrayed as a human character) was Fifi, who appeared initially in *Puppy Love* in 1933. The first major dog in the animated features was Bruno, in *Cinderella* (1950).

Q **I hear that Mickey Mouse had a few cameos in live-action films in the 1930s. Is *Hollywood Party* considered the first feature film appearance of Mickey Mouse? Jake, Springfield, VT**

A —Actually, *Hollywood Party* is not the first. It was released in 1934, but in 1933 part of the Mickey Mouse cartoon *Ye Olden Days* appeared in the Fox film *My Lips Betray*. *Hollywood Party*, from MGM, was the first feature film for which new animation of Mickey Mouse was prepared.

Q **Many moons ago, my husband and I viewed a Donald Duck cartoon video. During one of the segments, Donald's head transformed into what appeared to be an old radio. The transformation was similar to that of a character turning into a lollipop to indicate being a sucker. We did not understand the implication, so we viewed the video several times. The radio was labeled "Wingfoot." Can you help us figure out what we saw? Susan, San Dimas, CA**

A —That wasn't a radio you saw, but the heel of a shoe—Donald was meant to feel like a "heel." "Wingfoot" was either the brand name of a type of shoe heel or a made-up name that people would associate with shoes (as a play on the words "wing tip").

Q While vacationing in Italy, I saw a Mickey Mouse cartoon starring "Topolino." How come? R.T., Kent, CT

A —Mickey's name differs from country to country. In Italy he's Topolino, in Greece Miki Maous, in Hungary Miki Eger, in Sweden Musse Pigg, in Finland Mikki Hiiri, and in Norway it's Mikke Mus.

Q Are Mickey and Minnie, or Donald and Daisy, married? J.N., Springfield, VA

A —Neither Mickey and Minnie, nor Donald and Daisy, have been married in any of our cartoons or comic stories.

Q Were Mickey Mouse's two nephews, Morty and Ferdie, ever in a cartoon? I know they were in the comic strips. Joseph, Spring Hill, FL

A —Mickey has two unnamed nephews in *Mickey's Steam Roller* (1934). That may be their only screen appearance, though some have said that Tiny Tim in *Mickey's Christmas Carol* was Morty.

Q My granddaughter Claudia would like to know when Mickey Mouse lost his tail. Her Mickey and Minnie dolls have no tails, yet her uncle's old Mickey doll does have a tail. Lee, Saugus, MA

A —Tails have been used on Mickey Mouse dolls, cartoons, and comic books off and on since the beginning. My answer is that if the tail is not showing, it is inside his pants.

Q Is there a reason why Mickey has only four fingers (and no thumb)? Lorie, Sherman Oaks, CA

A —The reason is actually very simple—it makes the hand easier to draw.

Q Many years ago, I saw a short featuring Mickey and Goofy having breakfast in a runaway trailer. I'd love to find this cartoon again; can you tell me the title? Marimelle, Pasay City, Philippines

A —The cartoon you recall is *Mickey's Trailer* (1938). In the U.S., it is on the Disney Treasures DVD *Mickey Mouse in Living Color*, which was released in 2001, and also on a videocassette entitled *The Spirit of Mickey*.

Q It's well known that Mickey Mouse was created soon after Oswald the Lucky Rabbit was licensed away from Walt. What ever happened to Oswald? Patrick, Paducah, KY

A —Animation pioneer Walter Lantz, at Universal, continued making Oswald cartoons and comic books for many years. Lantz is better known for Woody Woodpecker. In recent years, Disney was able to reacquire the rights to Oswald from Universal. Oswald cartoons were released on DVD; he can also be found on current Disney T-shirts and other merchandise, and he is in the 2010 *Epic Mickey* video game.

Q My favorite character is Donald Duck. Did Walt create Donald and Goofy as well? Lauren, Wheaton, IL

A —Walt did not personally create any of the characters; it was a joint effort with staff artists, since Walt himself wasn't an accomplished artist.

Q The Walt Disney Studios produced quite a few movies for the United States government during World War II. Plus, I remember seeing a series of Disney educational films when I was in school. Could you tell us a little about the history of these two projects and whether we'll ever get to see these forgotten treasures again? Greg, Tulsa, OK

A —Disney did dozens and dozens of training and propaganda films using animation for the government during World War II, and when the war was over, we used the techniques we had learned to produce educational films for other companies and for schools. The wartime films have no relevance today, but later educational films, such as *Donald in Mathmagic Land*, are still used in schools today.

Q **I remember while growing up watching several "I'm No Fool"-themed short movies in school featuring Jiminy Cricket. How many of these movies were produced, and what were their titles/themes? Thanks. Ken, Frisco, Texas**

A —There was *I'm No Fool as a Pedestrian*, *I'm No Fool Having Fun*, *I'm No Fool in a Car*, *I'm No Fool in an Emergency*, *I'm No Fool in Unsafe Places*, *I'm No Fool in Water*, *I'm No Fool on Wheels*, *I'm No Fool with a Bicycle*, *I'm No Fool with Electricity*, *I'm No Fool with Fire*, and *I'm No Fool with Safety at School*. Some of these titles were originally shown on the *Mickey Mouse Club*; others were made years later as educational films.

Q **I remember Little Toot, a little tugboat trying to prove himself to the other boats. There was another cartoon about a sports car and one about a house. I liked how they showed the life of a "lifeless" object. Unfortunately, I don't know where to find them or, for that matter, even their names. Do you, by any chance? Dezyrie, Lodi, CA**

A —You are thinking of *Susie, the Little Blue Coupe* and *The Little House* (both special cartoons from 1952). Another classic of the animated inanimate is *Johnnie Fedora and Alice Bluebonnet* from *Make Mine Music* (1946). *Little Toot* was originally in *Melody Time* (1948). Over the years, these all have been released on DVD.

Q My husband and I have always wanted to know what kind of dog Pluto is. My husband says he is a poodle, but I say some kind of retriever. We recently visited Walt Disney World in Florida and asked the person who works with the characters at Chef Mickey's in the Contemporary Resort and he didn't know. We asked several Cast Members around the Magic Kingdom and they didn't know either. Can you help? Michelle, Hialeah, FL

A —Pluto was never meant to be any particular breed—in other words, he is a lovable mutt. In his first appearance in the 1930 cartoon *The Chain Gang*, he was a bloodhound.

Q I recently watched one of Walt Disney's cartoons called *Pluto's Sweater*. Minnie had a cat in the cartoon, but I didn't listen carefully enough to hear the name. What is it? Did this cat appear in other cartoons? Andrew, Seattle, WA

A —The cat is Figaro, and he first appeared in *Pinocchio* in 1940. Figaro appeared in several short cartoons after that, including *Figaro and Cleo* and *Figaro and Frankie*.

Q Why is Goofy the only Disney dog that can talk? Alicia, Stockton, CA

A —Goofy was actually created as a human character with doglike characteristics, so, yes, he wears clothes and talks. But there are other Disney dogs that talk—witness the casts of *Lady and the Tramp*, *Oliver & Company*, *The Fox and the Hound*, etc.

Q Have all the Oswald the Lucky Rabbit cartoons been found? Ryan, Huntingtown, MD

A —There are still a number of Oswald cartoons (and earlier Alice Comedies) that have not surfaced. It is possible that no prints of them exist anywhere. Not only was early film stock nitrate-based and combustible, but it was often destroyed for its silver content.

Q I've seen Internet sources say Pixar's earliest short, *The Adventures of André and Wally B.*, from 1984, came on before *Toy Story* during its original theatrical release, in 1995. Honestly, I don't remember seeing this short at all before the movie started. Is this an Internet hoax, or is it the truth? Bryan, Asheville, NC

A —Kind of a long answer here, Bryan. *The Adventures of André and Wally B.* was not Pixar's earliest short; it was made by John Lasseter and Lucasfilm for a SIGGRAPH computer conference two years before Pixar was founded. Thus, *Luxo Jr.* (1986) is considered Pixar's first short. There was no Pixar short included with the theatrical release of *Toy Story* in 1995, but later laser disc and DVD releases included *Tin Toy* because of the feature film's roots in that short. The tradition of including a short with a Pixar feature in theaters began with *Geri's Game*, which was released with *a bug's life* in 1998. Disney Home Entertainment put out a videocassette anthology called *Tiny Toy Stories* in 1996 which may have added to the confusion about *The Adventures of André and Wally B.* because it included that Lucasfilm short along with four Pixar shorts. *André* is often bundled in with the others because it is a CGI landmark and a major step in the creation of Pixar as we know the company today.

Q Why does Mickey wear gloves? Brandon, SD

A —Mickey Mouse didn't have gloves in his earliest cartoons, but they were added when he played the piano in *The Opry House* (1929), the fifth Mickey Mouse cartoon, and from then on he wore them. The animators figured it was easier to draw Mickey's hands if they were in gloves, with white outlined in black having more readability than black on black.

Q — **Are Chip and Dale brothers, or really good friends? Renee, Santa Ana, CA**

A —Even though Bill Justice, who first drew Chip and Dale, mentioned in his autobiography, written fifty years after the characters were created, that he thought of the two as "simply little brothers," the company has never officially acknowledged that. In the cartoons they were always depicted as friends.

Q — **I remember a cartoon when I was a child where the capitalist system and profit were explained (I believe to Donald Duck). Is that cartoon available anywhere? Gordon, Rosamond, CA**

A —The film you recall is *Scrooge McDuck and Money* (1967). While it was available for many years to schools and libraries, it has not been released on videocassette or DVD for public sale.

Q — **Is it true that Mickey Mouse once appeared in a non-Disney movie with the Disney Studios' permission? If so, how did that come about? Tom, Seattle, WA**

A —Mickey Mouse animation was done by Disney, under contract, for the 1934 MGM film titled *Hollywood Party*. Mickey appears with Jimmy Durante in a scene introducing a quasi–Silly Symphony cartoon called *The Hot Choc-late Soldiers*. Other films have had scenes with Mickey cartoons showing in a movie theater, though this did not constitute new animation, and all were used by permission from Disney.

Q — **Did Walt Disney have a favorite Mickey Mouse short? Sam, location not given**

A —I don't believe he ever said anything about a favorite, but he did keep the original script for *Steamboat Willie* in his desk drawer, which is an indication that he had a fondness for that film.

Q **Is Mickey's rival, Pete, a cat? In the older black-and-white cartoons with Alice and Oswald, he sometimes looks like a bear. Kyle, Imperial Beach, CA**

A —Pete is indeed meant to be a cat, at least a humanized cat. Sometimes he was drawn with a peg leg and was known as Peg Leg Pete; other times he was known as Black Pete. He was actually one of the earliest of the named Disney characters, debuting in the silent Alice Comedies several years before Oswald and Mickey.

Q **Was Walt Disney there at the premiere of the first Mickey Mouse cartoon? Kat, Salt Lake City, UT**

A —We do not know for sure, but he was in New York on November 18, 1928, when *Steamboat Willie* premiered at the Colony Theater, so it is likely that he was there. I certainly would have been there if it was my film. We have here in the Archives the actual program for the Colony Theater for that day. *Steamboat Willie* was the first film on the program, which started at noon. Walt may have been our source of that program, having brought it or sent it back to the Studio.

Q **Before the feature presentation of *Swiss Family Robinson* and other classic Disney movies is a short cartoon (*Swiss* had a short in which Donald Duck and a cricket were shipwrecked). When these movies first played in theaters, did they play a Disney short? Jessica, Mission Viejo, CA**

A —Until the mid-1950s, movie theaters would normally show a double feature, including a cartoon and a newsreel, on a continuous basis throughout the day. You could enter the theater at any time you wished, and if you got in during the middle of a film, you could just remain until that film started again. Things changed as multiplexes were built and theaters began showing only individual features at selected times during the day, no longer renting cartoons or newsreels to go with them.

Q **I am looking for a cartoon that was in movie theaters in the fifties. It was about a car that got stolen by gangsters and went through horrific adventures, ended up in the junkyard, and then was salvaged by a teenager, who turned it into a street rod. I believe the cartoon was the name of the car, but I can't remember. Pam, New Orleans, LA**

A —You are remembering *Susie, the Little Blue Coupe* from 1952. It was released on DVD in 2006 in *Walt Disney's It's a Small World of Fun! Volume 2.*

Q **On the Disney *Sing Along Songs* videos on VHS, there was an owl as the teacher in a classroom with some singing birds. I remember when I was a kid seeing that cartoon, but I don't remember its name. Is that opening taken from another older cartoon? David, Long Beach, CA**

A —Professor Owl in his classroom was actually used in two Disney cartoons: *Adventures in Music: Melody* and *Toot, Whistle, Plunk and Boom* (both 1953). The former was the first Disney cartoon in 3-D; the latter was the first in CinemaScope.

Q **Who are Huey, Dewey, and Louie's parents? Do they appear in any of the cartoons? Sarina, Montreal, Quebec, Canada**

A —According to the cartoon *Donald's Nephews*, Donald receives a postcard from his sister, Dumbella, saying she is sending the three for a visit. That is the only time we ever hear of Dumbella, and a father's name is never mentioned.

Q **I heard that Walt Disney never actually drew Mickey for any theatrical cartoons. Is that true? Did he design Mickey, or was that someone else as well? Linda, Vancouver, BC, Canada**

A —Walt relied on his chief animator, Ub Iwerks, to help design Mickey Mouse for him. By that time, 1928, Walt was no longer animating, but had instead moved into story work and direction. The only Mickeys he drew were occasionally at the request of autograph seekers.

Q **Who did the "ya-ha-hooey" sound that Goofy always makes? John, Madison, WI**

A —Pinto Colvig, who was the original voice of Goofy, originated that famous yell, used primarily when Goofy was falling a great distance. Others copied it in later years, and it remains a distinctive trademark of the Disney cartoons.

Q **In *How to Dance*, Goofy cuts the rug in front of a bandstand with the Firehouse Five. Was the music really performed by the Firehouse Five, or was that just an in-joke? Did they perform in any other Disney cartoons? Sheila, Cleveland, OH**

A —The Firehouse Five Plus Two, the Dixieland jazz group of Disney artists led by Ward Kimball, did indeed perform for the sound track of *How to Dance*. They later appeared as guests on several of the Disney evening television shows and on the *Mickey Mouse Club*.

Q **I have an original cel from the fifties (complete with separate background) and wondered what movie it is from. It is a smiling Donald Duck with a cute bee standing next to him offering**

what looks like half of a coconut. He has the other half in his other hand. Jean, Sarasota, FL

A —Without actually seeing the cel, I would say that it is probably not a bee, but Bootle Beetle, who appeared with Donald and the coconut halves in the cartoon *Sea Salts* (1949).

Q **Humphrey the Bear appeared in one or two Disney cartoons. I think one featured Donald Duck; the other just had Humphrey and the park ranger. I'd love to find these on DVD but have had no luck with title searches. Any ideas? Lisa, Colorado Springs, CO**

A —The bumbling grizzly bear Humphrey appeared in seven cartoons, beginning with *Hold That Pose* in 1950. In five of those cartoons, he starred with Ranger J. Audubon Woodlore. Not all the cartoons have been released on DVD.

Q **One of *The Wonderful World of Disney* episodes featured a demonstration on pin-striping a car, but I don't recall if this was a show segment or the entire show. The artist received a call just after he started painting two dots/stripes. While on the phone, the dots raced all around the car. After hanging up, he saw what they had done. What was this from? David, San Jose, CA**

A —The film—*Dad, Can I Borrow the Car?*—was originally released in theaters in 1970 and aired on television in 1972.

Q **Mickey looked a lot different in the beginning. Why did the makers change his look? Sam, Santa Monica, CA**

A —Over the years, art styles have changed, and different artists have drawn Mickey Mouse. The main change came in the late

1930s when animator Fred Moore convinced Walt Disney that puffing out Mickey's cheeks and changing his eyes would make him cuter. His costume has also been made more contemporary as the years have passed.

Q **I remember a World War II–era animated short where Donald Duck received war bonds in his mailbox, but I can't remember the name of the film. Also, was it in the United States or Canada? Russ, Ocala, FL**

A —Wow, that is an obscure film. *Donald's Decision*, made in 1942, was one of four shorts made for the National Film Board of Canada to show the advisability and necessity of buying Canadian war bonds. It reused animation from previous Donald Duck cartoons.

Q **I once had the pleasure of meeting Roy Disney at the Newport Beach Film Festival, in California. He was showing some shorts that hadn't been seen in a long time or had never been seen. There was one about a little girl selling matches, I think. It was very sad. Can you tell me the name of that short, and is it available to purchase? Jill, Garden Grove, CA**

A —*The Little Matchgirl* is a short cartoon about a poor, young girl who finds visions of happiness in the flames of the matches that she lights to keep warm. It is set to the music of Alexander Borodin's String Quartet no. 2, third movement. The cartoon was nominated for an Academy Award and released on *The Little Mermaid* DVD in 2006.

Q **While Disney publications give June 9 as Donald Duck's birthday, both *The Three Caballeros* and *Donald's Happy Birthday* show Friday, June 13 as his birthday. Which date is correct? K.N., Rockledge, PA**

A —Since several dates had been used for Donald Duck's birthday in the past, we decided to make Donald consistent with Mickey Mouse. For Mickey's birthday, we use the date of his first cartoon, *Steamboat Willie*, so for Donald's birthday we now use June 9, the release date of *The Wise Little Hen*, in which Donald made his first appearance.

Q Was there ever a short film with Mickey Mouse as a train engineer? I believe it was a silent film in black-and-white about the little train that could. Linda, Apollo, PA

A —There was an early Mickey Mouse black-and-white cartoon from 1929 called *Mickey's Choo-Choo*, where Mickey is a train engineer and he and Minnie have some harrowing adventures when one of the cars breaks away from the train with Mickey and Minnie on top. This was a sound film, but shortened silent versions were released for use with home projectors. In 1941's *The Reluctant Dragon*, the little Casey Jr. train, which would later appear in *Dumbo*, made its debut. There was also a color cartoon, *The Brave Engineer* (1950), which featured Casey Jones trying to get his train to the station on time. You may also be thinking of *The Little Engine That Could*, a non-Disney book by Watty Piper with illustrations by Lois Lenski, published by Platt & Munk in 1930.

Q Could you tell me something about Horace Horsecollar? When is his birthday? Why isn't he used in more Disney cartoons? P.K., New Fairfield, CT

A —Horace Horsecollar made his debut in the Mickey Mouse cartoon *The Plowboy* (1929) and was usually paired with Clarabelle Cow. We do not have an exact release date for that cartoon, so we have been unable to assign Horace a birthday. Horace was always an awkward character. (After all, real horses stand on four legs and have hooves.) Perhaps that is one of the reasons why he has not been used more.

Q **Could you please explain how the voices of Chip and Dale are done? I've always assumed the tape recordings are sped up. E.H., La Habra, CA**

A —The voices of the chipmunks are recorded at a slow speed, about a third slower than normal, then played back at regular speed.

Q **What was Walt Disney's first animated cartoon? J.R., Lexington, KY**

A —When Walt Disney was a young man living in Kansas City, Missouri, in 1920, he made his very first cartoons, called Newman Laugh-O-grams, for the Newman Theater. They made fun of current events in the city.

Q **Is Mickey Mouse right-handed or left-handed? J.O., Alameda, CA**

A —Mickey Mouse is usually drawn right-handed, but sometimes there are situations where he works better left-handed. It is easy to take such liberties with an animated character.

Q **Why did Walt Disney stop making short cartoons in the 1950s? R.G., Kansas City, MO**

A —Disney produced about 450 short cartoons during the thirty-year period that shorts were popular in movie theaters. By the mid- to late 1950s, cartoons got too expensive to produce, and the theaters, which had switched to double features, were no longer buying cartoons or other short subjects such as newsreels and travelogues. Today, with many theaters back to showing single features, there could be a place for cartoons again. Disney's first experiment, *Tummy Trouble*, released with *Honey, I Shrunk the Kids*, was a big success. There have been short cartoons released with many of the Disney•Pixar animated features.

Q **What can you tell me about *Donald in Mathmagic Land*? I teach architecture and find it very useful with my classes. T.L., Hingham, MA**

A —*Donald in Mathmagic Land* was originally released in theaters in 1959 on a bill with *Darby O'Gill and the Little People*. Two years later it had the honor of being introduced by Ludwig Von Drake and shown on the first program of *Walt Disney's Wonderful World of Color*, when the TV series moved to NBC. The film was made available to schools and has become one of the most popular educational films ever made by Disney. As Walt Disney explained, "The cartoon is a good medium to stimulate interest. We have recently explained mathematics in a film and, in a way, excited public interest in this very important subject."

Q **While I have heard that Disney's *Flowers and Trees* was the first color cartoon, didn't Ub Iwerks produce *Fiddlesticks* in color a year earlier? T.S., Clifton, NJ**

A —*Flowers and Trees* (1932) was the first *full*-color cartoon. It was the first to use Technicolor's new three-color process, which made possible a complete palette of colors. Earlier color processes, such as that used in *Fiddlesticks*, were two-color processes, and were limited in their ability to portray realistic colors. Walt Disney had the foresight to sign an exclusive two-year agreement with Technicolor for the use of their new process in cartoons, giving him a great head start over the other cartoon producers.

Q Walt Disney's early character Oswald the Lucky Rabbit looks very much like Mickey Mouse. Were parts of Oswald used in designing Mickey? G.G., Chelmsford, MA

A —You are very observant. Walt Disney never said that he used elements of Oswald in designing Mickey Mouse, but it seems obvious from looking at the two characters that he did. Furthermore, both characters were drawn by the same man, Ub Iwerks, within a year of each other.

Q Is T. Hee a real person? I have seen his name on the credits for Disney cartoons and have wondered if it was a joke. S.K., Montpelier, VT

A —Yes, T. Hee is a real person. It's a great name for an animation story man, isn't it? T. (Thornton) Hee worked at the Disney Studios on and off for three decades as director, stylist, and story man. He also served as an animation instructor and was renowned as a caricaturist.

Q Did the changes in Mickey Mouse's appearance, such as the perspective ears that were used for a short time, lead to a loss in popularity? J.M., Thunderbolt, GA

A —*The Pointer*, in 1939, was the first cartoon that featured a drastically new look for Mickey. His body became more pear-shaped than round, and pupils were added to his eyes, making them more expressive. In the early forties, animators gave him perspective ears—shadowing them to give a three-dimensional effect—but this change was short-lived. I'm not sure why the animators stopped using the perspective ears; they probably found it was a lot of extra work and wasn't noticed by many people. Later changes consisted mainly of new costumes, taking him out of shorts, for instance, and putting him in more contemporary clothes. Most changes in Mickey Mouse have come about gradually, so there has been no noted public response.

Of course, Disney stopped making Mickey Mouse cartoons in 1953 (except for *Mickey's Christmas Carol* in 1983), but discontinuance was not because the cartoons were unpopular. There were two problems with Mickey Mouse cartoons. One—a problem with all cartoons—was that in the fifties, movie theaters began showing double bills, and thus cut out cartoons and shorts. The second problem was that as Mickey Mouse became a symbol, cartoon writers found it increasingly difficult to write stories for him. It was easier to write stories for Donald Duck or Goofy, for example—characters who weren't so perfect.

Q **Even though *Steamboat Willie* was the first "talkie" cartoon, Mickey Mouse doesn't actually say any words in the film, does he? B.M., Cincinnati, OH**

A —That's right. While Mickey made some squeaks in *Steamboat Willie*, his first actual words did not come until *The Karnival Kid* (1929). This was Mickey's ninth cartoon.

Q **Why did Walt Disney's star actor, Mickey Mouse, have to wait until 1935 to appear in a color cartoon when the Silly Symphonies were done in color as early as 1932? G.G., St. Cloud, MN**

A —It was significantly more expensive to produce cartoons in color, so in the early days of the process, when he was experimenting, Walt Disney decided to reserve use of color for the Silly Symphonies. That series was his training ground, and he felt that color would add to its popularity. The Mickey Mouse cartoons were so popular, they did not really need a boost.

Q The Silly Symphonies were my favorite series as a child. How many of them were made? T.H., Tyler, TX

A —There were a total of seventy-five Silly Symphonies, from *The Skeleton Dance* in 1929 to *The Ugly Duckling* in 1939. Based on musical themes, classic stories, and unique characters, this series was used by Walt Disney to give his animators practice so they could eventually turn their skills to making animated feature films.

Q We know that Clarence Nash did the voice of Donald Duck in the cartoons, but who voiced that hilarious chicken Clara Cluck? L.H., Seattle, WA

A —The voice of the Disney barnyard nightingale was singer and film character actress Florence Gill. Watch the feature film *The Reluctant Dragon*, which contains classic and rare footage of Nash and Gill actually recording the voices of their cartoon characters. Some other faces to watch for in the movie: actor Frank Faylen (remember him from the old *Dobie Gillis* show?) in the sound effects lab; Alan Ladd, in one of his first film roles, telling the story of "Baby Weems"; and even Walt Disney himself. Even though many years have passed since *The Reluctant Dragon* was made, it serves as a nostalgic and fascinating look at the Disney Studios. Many of the animation processes and techniques shown in the film are still in use today.

Q Did I hear actor Ronald Colman's voice in the Donald Duck cartoon *Donald Double Trouble*? L.G., Fresno, CA

A —In that cartoon, where Donald tries to impress Daisy with a double who has a perfect voice, we used actor Leslie Denison doing a Ronald Colman–like voice. Oftentimes, Disney cartoons included caricatures of stars, but their voices were always provided by imitators. In fact, in *The Autograph Hound*, Peter Lind Hayes did the voices of Robert Taylor, Charlie McCarthy, Groucho Marx, Edward G. Robinson, Joe E. Brown, Ronald Colman, Gary Cooper, Lionel Barrymore, Stepin Fetchit, Bing Crosby, Bob Burns, Hugh Herbert, Charles Laughton, and Clark Gable.

Q How tall is Mickey Mouse? K.B., Boise, ID

A —The animators themselves wondered that for many years. During the recording of the dialogue for *The Pointer* (a 1939 Mickey Mouse cartoon), the animators wanted to film Walt doing the voice, hoping to capture a sense of the gestures and body attitudes he had expressed during story conferences. Walt hadn't appeared in front of a camera much before, and he was nervous, but the animators prevailed. The camera was positioned far enough away from Walt so that he wouldn't be aware of it; he wore his baggiest, most comfortable clothes, and the recording proceeded. At the point in the recording where he said, "I'm Mickey Mouse . . . y'know? Mickey Mouse?" Walt instinctively reached out with his hand to denote the height of a little kid. It was the only time his animators ever knew just how big Walt considered Mickey to be.

Q Many years ago, when I was very young, I remember seeing a cartoon called *The Little House* that was based on a popular children's book of the same title by Virginia Lee Burton. Was this a Disney film? Anita, Philadelphia, PA

A —*The Little House* was a Disney cartoon released on August 8, 1952. It tells the story of a little house that begins its life in the country, is encroached upon by developments and the big city, and is eventually moved back to the country by a concerned family. Wilfred Jackson directed the cartoon.

DISNEYLAND

Q On a visit to Disneyland when I was a kid, my parents bought me a forty-seven-page softcover book on the Pirates of the Caribbean attraction. Can you tell me when this book was printed and if they made these books for any other attractions? I seem to remember having one on It's a Small World. Paul, South Pasadena, CA

A —The Pirates booklet was first published in 1968, shortly after the attraction opened at Disneyland. A second edition was published in 1974, after a Pirates attraction opened at Walt Disney World. You are correct that there was also a booklet for It's a Small World. That one was actually printed first, for the New York World's Fair in 1964, but the later editions were published for Disneyland. These were the only two attractions that had such booklets, and they were sold at the Parks well into the 1970s.

Q I go to Disneyland three or four times a year. On my last trip, my mother and I rode the Disneyland Railroad quite a lot. We're wondering about the telegraph sounds at the New Orleans Square station. Does the telegraph actually spell out something in code, or are they just random sounds? Jeff, Reno, NV

A —The code spells out Walt Disney's speech on the Opening Day of Disneyland, on July 17, 1955, which consisted of him reading the dedication plaque.

Q Ever since I was a small boy, I've loved the monorail, and as an adult, I still do. I grew up with the monorail Mark IIIs and just loved the look of those. I was wondering, are there any Mark IIIs still intact, and if not, what happened to them? Anthony, Berwyn, IL

A —The Mark III monorail trains that made their debut at Disneyland in 1969 no longer exist. The last one, deemed "Old Red," had its front car reincarnated into "Mickey's Mouseorail" in 1990, touring the country for Disneyland's thirty-fifth anniversary. It was later put on display in the Rocket Rods queue area (1998–2000) before being dismantled. (Disneyland had gotten new Mark V monorail cars to replace the Mark IIIs beginning in 1986.)

Q There is an Arabic inscription on a wall right before making the final left turn (to the docks) on the Jungle Cruise at Disneyland. What does it say? I have asked perhaps fifty people over the years and no one knows. Tom, Camarillo, CA

A —The Arabic inscription reads "Fine Food, Fine Dining, Fine Entertainment." I understand that it was put in that location as a plug for Aladdin's Oasis, which took the place of the Tahitian Terrace in 1993.

Q On our last trip to Disneyland, we noticed all the new "mouse ears" hats that are available that can be custom-made— super idea! And we started asking around as to who was the first person to suggest the mouse ears and what year they started. I have a small collection from way back, but was just wondering. Jeanne, Banning, CA

A —The mouse ear hats were originally the idea of Roy Williams, who was a Disney story man and the "Big Mooseketeer" on the *Mickey Mouse Club* TV show. The original licensee, the Benay-Albee Novelty Co., began producing and selling the hats, after their popularity on the show, at Disneyland, and in stores everywhere.

Q What is the name of the ride in Tomorrowland at Disneyland that took you through *Tron*? Do I remember another ride that shrank you down to the size of a molecule? Both are gone now. Herlin, Ontario, CA

A —In 1977 the PeopleMover in Tomorrowland at Disneyland added a Superspeed Tunnel, where film elements gave Guests the feeling of speeding up. *Tron* footage replaced the original footage in 1982. The PeopleMover closed in 1995. It was in Monsanto's Adventure Thru Inner Space that Guests were made to feel as though they had shrunk; it closed in 1985.

Q **I've seen over the years at Disneyland a cage that held the hag from *Snow White and the Seven Dwarfs*. When the cage was rattled, she would come to life and try to bribe folks to let her out by promising to show them how to "turn water to gasoline." Who made this, and what was the reason? Reid, Ben Lomond, CA**

A —The Witch in the cage was originally made by the former WED Display and Design department at Walt Disney World, under Jim McNalis, for use in 1975 Emporium windows in the Magic Kingdom Park promoting *Snow White and the Seven Dwarfs*. When the Disneyana Shop opened on Main Street, U.S.A., at Disneyland in 1976, the Witch, animated and with added audio, moved west to become a major display piece in that shop. Later on it was used in the Villain's Lair shop in Fantasyland and Le Bat en Rouge in New Orleans Square.

Q **In the Celebrate parade at Disneyland, there is a female chipmunk character and a female cow character. Who are these characters? I've asked many people, and nobody seems to know where they originated. Also, why were they chosen to be used in this parade? Jeff, Burbank, CA**

A —The cow is Clarabelle Cow, who appeared in early Mickey Mouse cartoons. The female chipmunk is Clarice, who played a nightclub singer in the 1952 cartoon *Two Chips and a Miss*. We always like to bring back some of the lesser-known Disney characters for nostalgia's sake.

Q I have the Anaheim, CA, Disneyland parking ticket #11109 for 50 cents. What year was this created? Laurie, Kansas City, MO

A —Disneyland charged 50 cents for parking from 1968 to 1982, but we cannot tell you a particular year for yours. When the Park opened in 1955, parking was 25 cents.

Q My first birthday was celebrated in 1960 at Disneyland, and there are pictures of me on a donkey. My father says it was part of the mule-train ride/attraction, but my mother thinks there was a petting zoo at that time. Can you help us figure it out? Jane, Minot, ND

A —The Mule Pack was an original attraction at Disneyland. In 1960, when you were there, it was known as Pack Mules Through Nature's Wonderland. The mule ride remained in the Park until 1973; there was no petting zoo at that time.

Q There's a classic Disneyland T-shirt design with Mickey Mouse standing on his left foot and looking off to the side. How did that particular image become associated with Disneyland, and how long has it been around? Danny, San Francisco, CA

A —The classic Mickey Mouse design on T-shirts came in the late 1960s and early 1970s during a rebirth of interest in nostalgia in the U.S.

Q We have a Cast Member in the family who has been properly trained to give directions and point with two fingers. She tells us it's because this gesture is the most polite and least offensive. Another Cast Member recently told us the reason is that Walt used to point while holding a cigarette between his two fingers! What's the truth? Rand, Reseda, CA

A —To some people, in this country and in others, it is considered rude to point with the index finger, especially to point at someone. Thus, Disneyland decided that its Cast Members should point, or gesture, with two fingers (the index and middle finger). In the U.S., this is fairly unique to Disney Parks, and if you see someone point that way, you can say, "I bet you once worked for Disney." The pointing has nothing to do with Walt Disney's smoking—he never smoked when he was in Disneyland.

Q How often does Disneyland change its fireworks show? I have had the privilege of seeing *Remember Dreams Come True*, *Believe in Holiday Magic*, and *Magical*, and all are great shows. I am anxious to see when a new fireworks show will premiere! Travis, Gibbon, NE

A —There is no specific schedule. The original show was known as *Fantasy in the Sky*, and it continued with few changes for over four decades. In recent years, Disneyland has started creating new fireworks shows for special events, such as a significant Park anniversary. This started with *Believe . . . There's Magic in the Stars* for the Park's forty-fifth anniversary in 2000. The Walt Disney World Magic Kingdom first changed its *Fantasy in the Sky* show in 2003, to *Wishes: A Magical Gathering of Disney Dreams*.

Q I've heard so much about the lead horse on the King Arthur Carrousel. What's so special about "Jingles"? Chris, Houlton, ME

A —He is just one of the more elaborately decorated horses on the Disneyland attraction, and thus one of the most popular. For the Park's fiftieth anniversary, he was painted gold. In 2008 he was redecorated and dedicated to actress Julie Andrews. On the saddle are Julie's initials and a silhouette of the flying Mary Poppins.

Q **My kids are excited about a new ride scheduled for Cars Land in 2012 where the ride cars float on air. I recall a flying saucer ride at Disneyland years ago where they had air-suspended saucers that operated like a bumper car ride, and my memory places it where the teacup ride is now. They say I'm old and crazy, but I remember riding on that ride and how cool it was. Help! Merlin, Winlock, WA**

A —Flying Saucers was at Disneyland from 1961 to 1966. It was located in Tomorrowland. Because of problems with the technology, still unproven at the time, the attraction had constant maintenance issues and was often broken down.

Q **Someone recently told me that Main Street at Disneyland once included an operating pharmacy. Was any medicinal merchandise ever sold there? Alex, Hartford, CT**

A —Upjohn Pharmacy was on Main Street, U.S.A., from 1955 to 1970. It was primarily a display of what an old-fashioned drugstore might look like, with old medicine bottles and other accoutrements on exhibit. They never sold anything there, but they did hand out free miniature bottles of vitamins.

Q **As part of the queue for Disneyland's Rocket Rods, you entered a room filled with full-size PeopleMover cars, Space Mountain cars, and other vehicles. A screen on the wall showed an animated film about life in the future. What was that film? I enjoyed seeing it, and I miss it now that the ride is closed. Brett, Newport Beach, CA**

A —The short film about futuristic transportation you remember from the Rocket Rods preshow was a segment from a 1958 television show called *Magic Highway, U.S.A.* Unfortunately, *Magic Highway* has never been released on DVD.

Q How many trash cans do the Disney Parks own, and how many of them are in Disneyland? As pass holders, my family goes to the Park quite often, and we're curious as to how many there really are. Scott, Yorba Linda, CA

A —The Parks in California and Florida have approximately 5,400 trash cans, 1,250 of which are at the Disneyland Park. These numbers do not include the trash cans elsewhere, such as in the parking lots, at the resorts, or at Downtown Disney. As you are no doubt aware, Imagineers carefully theme the trash cans for the areas in which they are located, so that ones in Adventureland might be painted to look like bamboo, while ones in Frontierland might look like rustic logs.

Q In Disneyland's early days, there was an exhibit of the set from 20,000 *Leagues Under the Sea* at the entrance to Tomorrowland. I know that the organ from the *Nautilus* salon was later installed in the Haunted Mansion. What happened to the rest of the set and props? Are there any other pieces on display in California or in Florida? Jerry, La Mirada, CA

A —The only other existing set pieces I am aware of are from Captain Nemo's salon: a specimen display cabinet, which for years was in the One-of-a-Kind shop at Disneyland; the organ bench; and a settee. The settee remained in the Disney Studios' prop department and was used in 2003's *Haunted Mansion* movie. Walt Disney Imagineering has a box of prop gauges and machinery fittings from the film. An underwater rifle, plus a diving helmet and boots, from the Archives' collection, are currently in the One Man's Dream attraction at Disney's Hollywood Studios.

Q How many dolls are in Walt Disney World's It's a Small World, and how many countries are represented? Christian and Julie, Atlanta, GA

A —It's a Small World at Walt Disney World contains 289 dolls. Walt Disney World publicity does not list countries; the attraction is simply divided into areas of the world, such as North America, Africa, and Polynesia.

Q I recently noticed a flag at the New Orleans Square station at Disneyland waving from the top of one of the buildings. It had a dark blue background with what looked like a duck or swan on it. What is this flag? Brett, Corona, CA

A —The flag you saw is the Louisiana state flag. Its design consists of a group of pelicans that also appears on the state seal and a white ribbon bearing the state motto, "Union, Justice, Confidence," against a solid blue background.

Q I once saw a black-and-white movie about the building of Disneyland. The movie compressed the whole process into just a few minutes. Do you know where I could find a copy of this film? Linda, Livermore, CA

A —There were two TV shows that featured the sped-up action of the construction of Disneyland. They were *A Progress Report* (aired on February 9, 1955) and *A Further Report on Disneyland* (aired on July 13, 1955). These shows have not been released on video or DVD, so they are not currently available.

Q When the Haunted Mansion opened at Disneyland, were there live people who jumped out at you? I remember going on the attraction as a little girl and having to leave via an emergency exit because I was so frightened. Tracie, San Jacinto, CA

A —From time to time, the Haunted Mansion at Disneyland added people to the attraction. One was in a suit of armor. These Cast Members scared even the most jaded Disneyland Guests who had been through the Mansion many times and thought they knew all of the special effects.

Q **A Cast Member informed me that the old Disneyland sign reading "The Happiest Place on Earth" was taken down when they built Disney California Adventure. Is this sign still in one piece somewhere? Scott, San Antonio, TX**

A —Disneyland auctioned off that sign in 2000; actor and Disneyland fan John Stamos was the winning bidder.

Q **There used to be a pirate ship next to the whale in Disneyland's Fantasyland. It was attractively built and had painted woodwork. We really miss it. What happened to it? Bob and Bev, Belmont, CA**

A —The ship, which housed a restaurant and was first known as the Chicken of the Sea Pirate Ship, was originally constructed entirely of wood, but sitting in water for many years, some of the wood rotted and had to be replaced by concrete. When it was removed during Fantasyland's total remodeling in 1982, it could not be saved.

Q **I have a 1972 map of Disneyland purchased in the Park. The show buildings housing the Haunted Mansion and Pirates of the Caribbean are shown in detail, and where the attractions' highlights are located inside is notated. Is this intentional? Mike, Albuquerque, NM**

A —Show buildings were always indicated on early Disneyland maps. The Grand Canyon Diorama on the Santa Fe and Disneyland Railroad had its segments labeled on the first map in 1958, setting the precedent. Pirates of the Caribbean followed on the 1966 map, and the Haunted Mansion was added in 1969. In 1978 a new map design did not detail the show buildings; maybe the Disneyland people realized that they had indeed been giving away some of the illusion.

Q **I found a copy of *The Disneyland News* Vol. 1. No. 1, dated July 1955. I compared the newspaper's front page to the copy in *The Disney Treasures*. The articles, mastheads, and photos are identical, but the book version's headline reads, "50,000 Attend Gala Park Opening" while mine reads, "E.J. Visits Disneyland." Did the Park make custom versions for Guests? Peter, San Diego, CA**

A —Yes, you could have your name printed on the paper to commemorate your visit to the Park. The original cost was 25 cents, or 35 cents if you wanted to mail it back home. The newspaper was a monthly publication and continued for several years.

Q **As occasional patrons of Club 33 at Disneyland, my family and I have always been curious about the origin and significance of the club's name. My hypothesis is that the numeral "33" turned sideways resembles the lowercase initials of a certain familiar animated celebrity. Curtis, Davis, CA**

A —The reason for the club's name is very simple: Numbers were placed on the buildings on Royal Street, and "33" happened to be the number assigned to the building that houses the club. There is a common misconception that this number refers to the original number of participant companies in Disneyland.

Q **In going through my father's estate, I came across a set of tickets for the Santa Fe and Disneyland Railroad. They are canary yellow with six stubs attached. In what years were these used? My mom figures they're from around 1957. Suzy, Groton, MA**

A —There were more than a dozen different versions of these early Disneyland souvenir railroad ticket strips. They were first used when Disneyland opened in 1955, and the Park continued to use them for about three or four years. Unfortunately, none of the tickets was dated, and we have no information on exactly when each was issued.

Q I have noticed P. J. Collins's signature on many TWA Rocket to the Moon flight certificates, even ones that are otherwise blank. Did he sign them all, and more important, who is P. J. Collins? When were these flight certificates discontinued? Stephen, San Diego, CA

A —In the early TWA Rocket to the Moon attraction at Disneyland, the fictitious captain on the voyage was named Captain Collins. So it is his name that appears on the certificates, which were given away free to Guests. I don't know when these certificates were discontinued, though it could have been in 1961, when TWA ceased its sponsorship of the attraction.

Q We went to Disneyland every year for my birthday when I was little. On one occasion Disneyland gave away pins at every land. We managed to keep two: Donald in an astronaut costume and Mickey on an old-fashioned bicycle. Why was the Park giving out pins? Charlotte, San Diego, CA

A —Those pins were gifts that people won from the Gift-Giver Extraordinaire Machine during a continuation of the thirtieth anniversary promotion in 1986. Every Park Guest that year won a prize, ranging from individual pins to televisions, airline tickets, and cars. In addition to your pins, there were others for Adventureland, Frontierland, Bear Country, Fantasyland, and New Orleans Square, plus a pin of Mickey beating a drum.

Q Our family loves the attractions at Disneyland, but the landscaping is equally interesting. In many areas of the Park there is a type of tree with purplish flowers and blade-shaped green leaves that blooms in spring and early summer. What is this tree called? I'm also curious about the Park's landscape crew. Brad, Las Vegas, NV

A —I checked with the Horticulture department at Disneyland, and the trees you noticed are jacarandas. They are popular in Southern California. The department itself began work before Disneyland ever opened, when Walt Disney hired landscape expert Morgan "Bill" Evans to plan the Park's landscaping.

Q I just won an auction for a Disneyland Skyway bucket. Can you tell me how many buckets are in existence, and how many are owned by the public rather than by Disney? Also, are any of the original round buckets still around? Tracy, Costa Mesa, CA

A —My guess is that Disney still has about ten of the gondolas. We have no record as to where the others have gone or how many are owned by the public. There were forty-two gondolas when the attractions closed in 1994. As far as we know, none of the original round gondolas are still at the company. The gondolas were made by Von Roll, a company that had similar skyways all around the world.

Q When did Cast Members start to wear name tags? How have they changed over the years? Jonathan, Guilderland, NY

A —Disneyland Cast Members wore metal ID tags, which had numbers, not names, from the Park's first day, in 1955. Name tags were introduced in 1962. The first were gray with white lettering and smaller than those worn today. There have been many changes through the years, including name tags that were worn only during a special event or for an anniversary.

Q **I bought an old Disneyland tray stamped with a price of 10 cents and "Walt Disney Productions." It shows a circus-tent area to the right of Main Street; some buildings behind the right side of the street look accessible to the public. A covered bridge to the right of the castle leads to a path up a hill. I saw Disneyland in 1956, and I don't remember these areas. Sue, Centralia, WA**

A —This tray was made by the California Metalware Corporation in 1955. It used conceptual artwork created before Disneyland was completed, so it shows a number of scenic elements that were never in the finished Park.

Q **I'm sure you're familiar with the scene near the end of Pirates of the Caribbean where the prisoners are trying to get the jail-cell key from the dog's mouth. I have always wondered why they don't simply walk out of the open cell door not more than ten feet away from them. Is there an explanation for this? Tino, Mission Viejo, CA**

A —According to Rhonda Counts, a show producer at Walt Disney Imagineering, "This is an example of Imagineer Marc Davis's sense of humor. The pirates in the cell are not very bright! They are so focused on getting the key that they are not aware of the exit next to them."

Q **I read that the King Arthur Carrousel in Disneyland at one time had a menagerie of animals. Are any of the carousel animals in the Treasures in Paradise store in Disney California Adventure original figures from the Carrousel? Kendra, Rancho Santa Margarita, CA**

A —When Walt Disney bought the original Carrousel, an antique one that he found in Toronto, he replaced various animals on it with horses, refashioning their legs because he wanted them all to be leaping. We spoke with Bethann Brody, one of the Imagineers who worked on the décor for Treasures in Paradise. She reports that the carousel animals in the shop are actually new ones that have been made to look old. Some of the other carousel pieces in Treasures in Paradise were originally fashioned for the non-Disney movie *Fear and Loathing in Las Vegas* (1998). The Walt Disney Company eventually acquired these fantastic pieces and used them as decorations in the shop.

Q **I've always wondered how many candles are on the birthday cake in the ballroom of the Haunted Mansion. Also, is the decaying portrait in the entrance hall a depiction of the Ghost Host? Daniel, Milwaukie, OR**

A —The National Fantasy Fan Club (now Disneyana Fan Club) had your first question on a scavenger hunt once, and I found it difficult to count the candles because the candle lights were blinking on and off and the Doom Buggies moved too fast. According to Walt Disney Imagineering, there are thirteen candles on the cake. I have not heard that the Ghost Host is pictured anywhere; he is just the narrator.

Q **As a seven-year-old child on my first trip to Disneyland in 1970, I was so terrified by the Adventure Thru Inner Space ride that I snuggled tight by my mom and wouldn't open my eyes. I did open my eyes on a trip about two years later and was fascinated by the ride. I especially loved the dioramas previewing the adventure and the tiny cars going into the microscope. Whatever became of the dioramas, giant snowflakes, and Atomobiles? I hope they are safe somewhere out there (*in* there?). Matt, Fremont, CA**

A —Adventure Thru Inner Space, sponsored by Monsanto, was a very popular attraction at Disneyland from 1967 to 1985. When the attraction was removed, only some of the miniature Atomobiles were kept by The Walt Disney Company; one was auctioned on a Disney Auctions section of eBay in October 2000. (It sold for $5,100.) Several of the miniature Atomobiles are now in the Walt Disney Archives. The giant microscope could be glimpsed for years at the beginning of the Star Tours journey, commemorating the attraction that used to occupy that space.

Q **I have a friend who says that one of the Space Mountain attractions used to have a hole in the roof so that it felt like the cars were going to shoot off into space. I've never heard of such a thing, and I don't believe him, but he won't back down. Who's right? Peter, Minneapolis, MN**

A —Perhaps your friend is thinking of Space Mountain at Disneyland Paris, where the cars are shot upward on the outside of the attraction as if out of a cannon. Neither of the American Space Mountain attractions ever had a hole in its roof.

Q **When was Disneyland first called a "Magic Kingdom," and who coined the term? Robert, Pikeville, KY**

A —The term "Magic Kingdom" was applied to Disneyland when the Park opened in 1955. The name of the publicity or marketing person who had the idea for the designation is not known.

Q **When Pirates of the Caribbean was remodeled, two new pirates were added at the end. They are trying to push and pull treasure up a ramp. Inside the treasure trove is a painting of Blackbeard that looks exactly like the painting on the wall in *Blackbeard's Ghost*, starring Dean Jones. Might this be the actual prop from the movie? Keith and Jayne, Port Orchard, WA**

A —A framed picture of Blackbeard's ghost, as portrayed by Peter Ustinov in the 1968 Disney movie, is indeed located in the treasure trove in Pirates of the Caribbean at Disneyland, added during the recent rehab. It is not the actual prop from the film.

Q Could you tell me who came up with the idea of Splash Mountain? We spent a vacation at Disneyland and it was my favorite attraction. D.S., Fairbanks, AK

A —Splash Mountain was the idea of Disney Imagineer Tony Baxter, who came up with the idea in 1983 while stuck in his car during rush-hour traffic. The attraction opened at Disneyland in 1989. It is based on Disney's 1946 feature *Song of the South*. New versions opened at Walt Disney World and at Tokyo Disneyland in 1992.

Q During a recent trip to Disneyland, my four-year-old son noted that the short segment of music played during the railroad journey through Primeval World is from the 1961 film *The Mysterious Island*. Can you tell us how this bit of music came to be used on this attraction? Lane, Winnetka, CA

A —Disney often licenses music from other sources for use in its movies and Parks. The designers of Primeval World obviously thought that this particular piece fit with the mood they were trying to convey in the attraction.

Q In the summer 1996 issue of *Disney Magazine*, you answered a question about a bear named Rufus who sleeps in a cave on Splash Mountain. Didn't Rufus run the lights at the Country Bear Jamboree show? Scott, Mesquite, NV

A —Rufus has been around ever since Bear Country was created at Disneyland in 1972. There was a snoring bear in a cave near the entrance to Bear Country, and he was named Rufus. When a Christmas version of the Country Bear Jamboree show was added in 1984, Rufus was used as the name of a not-quite-all-there stage manager. The name has since been used for other bear characters.

Q **I remember the ride America Sings in Tomorrowland at Disneyland. I noticed that some of the animals on Splash Mountain look like the ones that were on America Sings. Did the critters from America Sings move? Monica, Temple City, CA**

A —They did indeed. Many of the Audio-Animatronics characters from the closed America Sings attraction were renovated and placed in Splash Mountain. Some new ones were added also, namely Brer Bear, Brer Fox, and Brer Rabbit from *Song of the South*, making a total of 103 characters.

Q **The petrified tree is my favorite thing displayed at Disneyland. Can you tell me more about it? Billy, Mount Laurel, NJ**

A —The tree is the oldest item at Disneyland—all of 75 million years. When Walt Disney saw a petrified tree for sale on private land in Colorado, he knew he had to have it. He purchased it as a gift for his wife, Lilly, for their anniversary in 1956, but rather than keep it at their home, he had it installed next to the Rivers of America at Disneyland.

Q **I was cleaning out a file cabinet in my father's basement and came across an envelope. It contained a little book called *The Story of Disneyland*. The copyright on the front says 1955, by Disneyland, Inc. The book is in mint condition, with not even a bent corner. The text written by Walt in the front of the book says that the pictures in the book are sketches because they wanted to have a souvenir book ready when the Park opened. Can you tell me more about this book? William, St. Louis, MO**

A —That is the first guidebook for Disneyland. It originally sold for 25 cents. As soon as the Park opened and photography was possible, a new guidebook was prepared, which was released later that year.

Q **On a recent visit to Disneyland, I noticed the names Jess and Bess on two horse stalls in the Fire Station on Main Street. Do these names have any significance? Christopher, Granada Hills, CA**

A —The twin horse stalls originally housed the horses that pulled the fire wagon when the Park opened in 1955, but because of the congestion on Main Street, the wagon was permanently retired to the Fire Station and the horses were stabled in the backstage Pony Farm (now called the Circle D Corral) in 1960. It is likely that Jess and Bess were the names of the first horses to pull the fire wagon.

Q **I've always wondered about the small woman you see when exiting the Haunted Mansion at Disneyland. You know, the one who says, "Hurry baaaack, hurry baaaack," and "Next time, don't forget your death certificate." I'd love to know any information about the woman. Mark, Mountain View, CA**

A —The woman is Lee Toombs, who worked at Walt Disney Imagineering. Leota Toombs Thomas began her career at the Disney Studios in the Ink and Paint Department. At WED Enterprises, Toombs worked in the Model Shop. It was then that she was cast to be the face in the crystal ball in the Haunted Mansion as well as the tiny woman one encounters at the exit (known as Little Leota). As an expert painter and featherer of WED animals and birds, she later went to Walt Disney World for five years to help maintain the show quality of the figures there. She died in 1991.

Q All of the trivia facts I have read about Disneyland refer to the Matterhorn as the largest and tallest structure in the Park. Why wouldn't Walt Disney want the Sleeping Beauty Castle to be the most prominent structure seen? Anne, Wilmington, DE

A —Walt did not want a large castle at Disneyland because he felt that the medieval European tyrants had built huge castles to intimidate the peasants. Walt wanted a small, friendly castle instead. The Matterhorn was built to the scale of the original mountain, about one-hundredth of the size. The Matterhorn was built during Walt's lifetime, so obviously he approved the size.

Q What became of the shows that Disney created for the 1964–65 New York World's Fair? H.W., Las Vegas, NV

A —At the close of the fair all four shows were transported to Disneyland, where they became popular attractions: Great Moments with Mr. Lincoln, General Electric's Carousel of Progress (later moved to Walt Disney World), It's a Small World, and Primeval World.

Q What happened to the "live" mermaids that sat and waved in the water of Submarine Voyage? C.D., Citrus Heights, CA

A —The mermaids who sat on rocks in the lagoon where the submarines traveled at Disneyland were only around for a short time in the early to mid-1960s. They were removed as entertainment priorities at the Park changed, but also because the chlorine in the water was affecting the young women portraying the mermaids.

Q Who provides the speaking voice of President Lincoln in Great Moments with Mr. Lincoln? L.W., Nephi, UT

A —The voice of Abraham Lincoln at both the Great Moments with Mr. Lincoln at Disneyland and the Hall of Presidents at Walt Disney World was provided by character actor Royal Dano. Dano occasionally portrayed Lincoln in films. He bore an uncanny resemblance to the sixteenth president. As an aside, Hutch Dano, the young man who stars in *Zeke and Luther* on Disney Channel, is the grandson of Royal Dano.

Q In *Walt Disney Treasures: The Chronological Donald, Volume One*, Leonard Maltin says that there is a penny arcade in Disneyland. Where is it? Did that arcade inspire Donald's cartoon *A Good Time for a Dime*? Brady, Winslow, IL

A —The Penny Arcade at Disneyland is on Main Street, U.S.A. *A Good Time for a Dime* was made in 1941, long before the Disneyland arcade was built, in 1955. Penny arcades were popular in the 1940s, making them a timely subject for a cartoon.

Q In the late 1950s or early 1960s, I watched a *Walt Disney Presents* show that dealt with natural wonders such as geysers, Death Valley, balancing rocks, and natural bridges. I think they showed a balancing rock that actually tottered, with the explanation that the rotation of the Earth kept it in place so it wouldn't fall. Does this rock still exist, and does it actually totter? Donna, Calgary, Alberta, Canada

A —You may be thinking of the tottering rock that was in the painted desert area of the original Rainbow Caverns Mine Train attraction at Disneyland. It was shown on one of the early television shows about the Park. The attraction also included geysers and natural bridges.

Q Why are all the horses on the King Arthur Carrousel, at Disneyland, white? Maia, Baton Rouge, LA

A —The original King Arthur Carrousel at Disneyland in 1955 had horses in repeating rows of six different colors (black, gray, chestnut, white, tan, and amber). In the mid-1970s, Disney Imagineers decided to change the color scheme to achieve "an airier, softer feel," and the horses were all painted white.

Q I am sure that lots of interesting things have happened at Disneyland. Has anyone ever given birth there? And if so, how many times has that happened? Marianne, Hilliard, OH

A —Sometimes a baby is ready to be born at an unexpected time, and there is no opportunity to get the mother to a hospital. There actually have been three babies born at Disneyland, the latest in April 2002.

Q Who was the first athlete to say "I'm going to Disneyland!"? And when did he say it? Mary Kate, Tucson, AZ

A —The first was Phil Simms of the New York Giants at the Super Bowl in 1987, answering the question, "Now that you've won the Super Bowl, what are you going to do next?" Almost all of the television commercials were filmed twice—once for Disneyland and once for Walt Disney World.

Q I heard a rumor that when the Matterhorn Bobsleds ride was being completed at the Disneyland resort, the city of Anaheim had a city ordinance prohibiting the building of structures over a certain height. So I heard that Walt Disney installed a basketball court so he could claim that it was an arena and avoid the city ordinance. Is this true? And can I play there? Michael, Tarzana, CA

A —Well, this is not exactly correct. There is a basketball hoop (not an entire court) inside the Matterhorn, and it was put there so that the mountain climbers could have something to occupy themselves with during their breaks. There was no problem with a city ordinance.

Q **How did Ronald Reagan get picked to host the opening ceremonies at Disneyland? Monica, Allentown, PA**

A —Ronald Reagan, Art Linkletter, and Bob Cummings were selected for their host duties at the opening of Disneyland by Walt Disney himself. All three were friends of his.

Q **Did Walt Disney start adding new attractions to Disneyland as soon as it opened, or did it take a while to catch on? W.W., Redding, CA**

A —Indeed he did, because Disneyland was an immediate success. Within seven weeks, the Park saw its one millionth Guest. Walt knew he had to quickly add attractions to increase the capacity of his popular Park, so in 1956 he added such attractions as Tom Sawyer Island, the Skyway, and Storybook Land. These were relatively inexpensive attractions, but as soon as Walt was able to set aside some money, he started work on three major attractions that would open in 1959—the Matterhorn, the Submarine Voyage, and the monorail.

Q **How many U.S. presidents have been to Disneyland? What about Walt Disney World? Cindy, La Puente, CA**

A —We are aware of the following presidents visiting Disneyland: Truman, Eisenhower, Nixon, Reagan, George H. W. Bush, Carter, Kennedy, Ford, and Obama. Clinton and George W. Bush have been to Walt Disney World (as have Disneyland attendees Reagan, Nixon, George H. W. Bush, Ford, and Obama). The only president since Truman who did not visit a Disney Park was Lyndon B. Johnson.

Q How was Tom Sawyer Island at Disneyland created? Is it a "real" island made of mostly earth, or is it made of something artificial like concrete? Glenn, Tacoma, WA

A —I would imagine that Tom Sawyer Island was created primarily with the dirt that was excavated to create the Rivers of America. It is not concrete or anything like that.

Q Is it true there is a hidden Mickey Mouse symbol located somewhere in every ride at Disneyland? Peter, Buffalo, NY

A —No. The idea of hiding Mickey images did not begin until the late 1980s, and then primarily at Walt Disney World.

Q I heard that Liz Taylor once "rented" Fantasyland for a private party. Is this true? Shelly, Omaha, NE

A —Liz Taylor took over Disneyland for an after-hours sixtieth birthday bash on February 27, 1992. Through the years, in the off seasons, areas of Disneyland were available for rental to private companies so they could hold parties there, but it was rare for an individual to have such a private party.

Q One of my early favorites at Disneyland was the House of Tomorrow. Can you tell me who the architect was? Beverly, Burbank, CA

A —The House of the Future was designed by architects at Monsanto, its corporate sponsor. It was not a work of Disney Imagineers. The House could be visited at Disneyland from 1957 to 1967.

Q Is it true that the parking structure at Disneyland is the biggest parking structure in the world? How many cars can it hold? Ellen, Montebello, CA

A —With space for over ten thousand cars, the Mickey and Friends parking structure is one of the largest in the world.

Q I heard Walt had an office in Sleeping Beauty Castle at Disneyland. Is this true? If so, where in the castle was it? David, Monterey, CA

A —There was no office in Sleeping Beauty Castle, but Walt did have a small apartment over the Fire Station on Main Street, U.S.A., where he relaxed and entertained VIP visitors.

Q Throughout Disneyland, there seems to be the same man's voice on many of the rides and attractions. Who is this voice-over talent? Owen, St. Louis, MO

A —For many years, the "voice of Disneyland" was Jack Wagner, and many people still recognize his voice. Jack, who died in 1995, was named a Disney Legend posthumously in 2005.

Q What year did ticket coupon books get introduced at Disneyland, and when were they discontinued? Victor, Northridge, CA

A —Ticket books for Disneyland attractions were used from October 1955 (just a few months after the Park's opening in July) until 1982. At that time, the Park switched to an all-inclusive passport.

Q I'm watching the *Disneyland Secrets, Stories & Magic* DVD and just saw the footage with the original Mickey and Minnie costumes (the ones that looked a lot like Halloween costumes, as the narrator noted). I wanted to know if Disney still has these costumes saved, or are they lost to history? Ryan-Philipp, North Hills, CA

A —The odd-looking character costumes used in the parade at Disneyland on Opening Day were borrowed from the Ice Capades, which had a Disney segment in its show. I would doubt that they still exist.

Q **Did Walt Disney have any problems acquiring the land he needed to build Disneyland? J.A., San Diego, CA**

A —Walt's choice of the land next to the Santa Ana Freeway in Anaheim almost didn't work out, because there were seventeen different parcels of land involving as many landowners. You can imagine how hard it is to get two landowners to sell their land at the same time—seventeen owners created almost insurmountable problems. But with the aid of the Anaheim Chamber of Commerce and the city fathers, property negotiations proved to be successful.

Q **Has Disneyland ever closed, and if it has, when? Daniel, Chicago, IL**

A —Disneyland was closed on Mondays during the off-season from 1955 to 1957 and on Mondays and Tuesdays from 1958 to 1985. The Park closed full days for rain eleven times between 1956 and 1992, for the national day of mourning for President Kennedy in 1963, and in 2001 at the time of the terrorist attacks on September 11. There have been a number of other days when the Park closed early because of inclement weather.

Q **I've just read that the Sherman Brothers now have their own window on Main Street, U.S.A. (as well they should—after all, they're Disney Legends!). I was wondering, however, if you knew exactly which Park it's in (Disneyland or Magic Kingdom), where exactly it's located, and what type of business it's disguised under? Kaitlin, Bolton Landing, NY**

A —The window is located on Main Street, U.S.A., at Disneyland Park, where it was dedicated on March 11, 2010. It is on a door at the 20th Century Music Company shop and reads:

Two Brothers Tunemakers
Richard M. Sherman and Robert B. Sherman, Proprietors
"We'll write your tunes for a song!"

Q I have some old A–E tickets from Disneyland. Is there a way to tell what year they are from? Also, what year did the characters start appearing in the Park? Paula, The Colony, TX

A —The old ticket books usually had coded dates on them, but the tickets inside did not. If you have only the tickets, sometimes you can narrow down the years because of the attractions listed on them. There have been Disney characters in the Park since Opening Day.

Q One of the main birds in the Enchanted Tiki Room is José. There is also a José in *The Three Caballeros*. Is the José in the Enchanted Tiki Room the same as José in *The Three Caballeros*? Also, who is the voice of José in both the Enchanted Tiki Room and *The Three Caballeros*? They both seem to have the same personalities. Bethany, Woodland Hills, CA

A —These are different birds named José. In *The Three Caballeros*, it is a Brazilian parrot, José Carioca, whose voice was provided by José Oliveira. In the Enchanted Tiki Room, the macaw, José, was voiced by Wally Boag, who was the original comedian in the Golden Horseshoe Revue.

Q If the Carrousel at Disneyland is named for King Arthur, and the sword in the stone is in front of it, why is all the artwork on the Carrousel from *Sleeping Beauty*? Paul, Riverside, CA

A —Well, I guess the Imagineers felt that since the Carrousel is inside Sleeping Beauty Castle's walls, they would use artwork to theme it to our *Sleeping Beauty* film. We had the same problem for years at Walt Disney World, where King Stefan's Banquet Hall was inside Cinderella Castle while King Stefan was in *Sleeping Beauty* (the hall has since been renamed Cinderella's Royal Table).

Q **Did the Mark III monorails at Disneyland have a fourth color? I remember red, blue, and yellow, but I heard there was a fourth vehicle that was hardly used except when one of the others was in for repairs. Brett, Newport Beach, CA**

A —There were four colors for the Mark III version of the monorail, which began service at Disneyland in July 1969—red, blue, gold, and green. The Mark III monorails were replaced by Mark V models beginning in 1986; their four colors were purple, orange, blue, and red. (If you wonder why they skipped Mark IV monorails, it is because they were only at the Walt Disney World Resort.)

Q **I am a fan and supporter of the twenty-sixth animated feature, *The Great Mouse Detective*. What can you tell me about any events that occurred at Disneyland in honor of the film's premiere? A Cast Member said that a special parade happened on July 2 for its U.S. theatrical release, but there are no online sources to prove this. For 1986, I cannot find any parades that feature the larger-than-life characters, Basil and Ratigan, nor can I pinpoint any exact meet-and-greet appearances. Did Basil and Ratigan ever appear to Guests at Disneyland, and if so, are there any photos or video footage in existence? This is aside from personal experiences from Guests. Sabrina, Escondido, CA**

A —The show schedules for Disneyland for July 2, 1986, only show two parades that day—*Totally Minnie* and the *Main Street Electrical Parade*. There were indeed costumes created for Basil and Ratigan, but I do not have records on how they were used.

Q **Was the Golden Horseshoe Saloon used as the set of the Doris Day movie *Calamity Jane*? The set used looks identical to the Golden Horseshoe. Alicia, San Francisco, CA**

A —A lot of people notice that. Actually, Harper Goff, the movie-set designer who designed the *Calamity Jane* saloon set, was the same person Walt Disney called upon a couple of years later to design the Golden Horseshoe. According to *Disneyland: The Nickel Tour* by David Mumford and Bruce Gordon, "It turns out that Harper had been working as a set designer over at the Warner Bros. Studios, where he had designed a saloon for . . . *Calamity Jane*." After he had gone to work at the Disney Studios, Walt told him he wanted a saloon for Disneyland just like the one in *Calamity Jane*, not realizing he was talking to the movie's set designer, "so Harper got hold of a copy of the blueprints of the movie set, reduced them to the smaller Disneyland scale, and finished up one of the quickest design projects in the Park's history."

Q **In the Disney Sing Along video *Disneyland Fun*, there is a song called "Walkin' Right Down the Middle of Main Street, U.S.A." I believe at the end it's credited to Stu Nunnery, with a much earlier copyright date than the video. What has this song been used in before the Sing Along? Craig, Phoenix, AZ**

A —According to Stu Nunnery on ClassicRockMusicBlog.com, "I wrote words and music to 'Main Street, U.S.A.' in 1978 while writing for a 'jingle house' in New York. Disney bought the song, and there was supposed to be a rollout of the song in 1980 when Disneyland was to celebrate its twenty-fifth anniversary. The song did not appear publicly until 1985, when Disneyland celebrated its thirtieth anniversary, and it was sung on a TV special by none other than Marie Osmond and a cast of characters. Since then, the song remains a parade theme at the Parks and is sung by the barbershop a cappella groups walking down Main Street at the Parks."

Q **Who bought the first tickets to Disneyland and the Magic Kingdom: the company or Guests? Alex, St. Augustine, FL**

A —Ticket number one for Disneyland, the Magic Kingdom, and Epcot, as well as for Hong Kong Disneyland, are in the Walt Disney Archives. Roy O. Disney bought the original Disneyland ticket; the others were provided to the Disney Archives by the Parks.

Q **Isn't it true that Walt Disney specifically said he never wanted his Parks to have a Ferris wheel or a carnival atmosphere, and yet there is a Ferris wheel in Disney California Adventure that has just been redone? Katie, Escalon, CA**

A —In speaking about the concept of Disneyland, Walt wrote, "Although various sections will have the fun and flavor of a carnival or amusement park, there will be none of the 'pitches,' game wheels, sharp practices, and devices designed to milk the visitor's pocketbook." He did not specifically preclude Ferris wheels. Disney California Adventure is not Disneyland; it has its own concept, which includes the Paradise Pier section mirroring California's seaside amusement parks in decades past, where a Ferris wheel was usually included.

Q **The Disneyland Main Street Electrical Parade debuted in 1972 and continues to make performances over the summer (however, it's now at Disney California Adventure). I am curious, what changes has the performance seen over the years since its opening? Ryan-Philipp, North Hills, CA**

A —The original twenty-minute parade in 1972 featured twelve floats. Because of America on Parade, the special parade done for the U.S. Bicentennial, the Electrical Parade did not run in 1975 or 1976. Then, because of its popularity, it was brought back in 1977, with all new larger floats, including Elliott the Dragon. A Mickey Mouse fiftieth birthday cake float was added in 1978 and a 108-foot patriotic finale float in 1979. A pirate ship float and Pleasure Island float were added in 1985. The parade ended on Main Street in 1996 before returning to Disney California Adventure in 2001. A new Tinker Bell float was created to lead the parade in June 2009; then the parade concluded regular performances two months later, henceforth to operate seasonally until April 2010, when it moved to Walt Disney World.

Q I know that many of the Audio-Animatronics characters from Disneyland's America Sings attraction were later "recast" for Splash Mountain (and that two became droids in the Star Tours queue), but there were a few characters from America Sings that were not used in Splash Mountain. What became of those critters? Fred, Placentia, CA

A —Some of the America Sings characters not featured in Splash Mountain include Eagle Sam, Mr. Owl, and a rock-and-roll crane. These figures were sent back to Walt Disney Imagineering both for training purposes and so their parts could be used in other shows.

Q In Disneyland's Pirates of the Caribbean, there is a painting in the room where it says "store ye weapons" done by Marc Davis titled *A Portrait of Things to Come*. It is a legendary piece of art and has been seen by millions. I have always wanted a copy of it to hang in my house. Why can't I find a copy anywhere? How come Disney has not made it a part of their gallery? Christopher, Chino, CA

A —Although this piece is not currently available for printing, the Disney Parks often release prints of concept art through an on-demand system. Kiosks can be found at the Disneyland Resort's World of Disney and Disneyana Shop, as well as in several Art of Disney locations throughout Walt Disney World.

Q **What is currently inside the space that was once Walt's apartment above the Disneyland Fire Station? Justin, Los Angeles, CA**

A —Walt's apartment above the Disneyland Fire Station is still there and is still used occasionally by Disney family members and Disneyland executives. It is still furnished similarly to the time when Walt used it. One major change—there used to be a fire pole from the apartment down into the fire station below that is no longer there.

Q **While walking along the Rivers of America in Disneyland, there is a part of the wall that's been closed off by brick. It looks as if it were a tunnel but for really small kids. It's no wider than three feet. There is also a year on it—1472, I think. What is this bricked off "tunnel," and what does the year stand for? Chris, Chino, CA**

A —We get a lot of questions about this. What looks like a bricked-in tunnel is actually just an architectural detail added to the wall to make it look more authentic for the period. The year used on the keystone of the arch, 1764, was simply chosen by Imagineer Matt McKim as being two hundred years prior to his birth year of 1964.

Q **Why is Disneyland's Pirates of the Caribbean different than the one in Walt Disney World? Karen, Chesapeake, VA**

A —Pirates of the Caribbean at Disneyland is set in southern Louisiana, whereas the Florida version is set in an ancient

Spanish citadel in the Caribbean. The attraction in Disneyland is several minutes longer, primarily due to an extended haunted grotto experience, though the queue experience is longer and more thematically rich in Florida. Also, Florida's high water table could only permit one waterfall to be constructed; two waterfalls were a necessity at Disneyland, where the flume drops send Guests to a lower level in order to pass underneath the Park's railroad tracks.

Q **One of my favorite attractions growing up as a kid in California was Disneyland's PeopleMover in Tomorrowland. I can still hear the music in my head that played in the cars. I heard once that this music was from a generic production music catalog. Is this true, or was the music actually created by Disney for the attraction? Don, Seattle, WA**

A —The PeopleMover music was composed by Disney Legend Buddy Baker (1918-2002), the prolific composer who provided the music for many Disney Park attractions.

Q **Each year the Candlelight Processional is one thing that really makes Christmas for our family. Can you tell me how, when, and where it started? Scooter, Avon Park, FL**

A —The Candlelight Processional began as a Christmas holiday tradition at Disneyland in 1958 with a concept developed by Dr. Charles C. Hirt of the University of Southern California School of Music. It has continued every year since that time, usually with a different guest narrator. A Florida version of the Candlelight Processional began at the Magic Kingdom in 1971, moving to its present location at Epcot in 1994.

Q **I recently rode Disneyland's Pirates of the Caribbean attraction and recognized Paul Frees's voice as the pirate**

auctioneer. He's known for giving Professor Von Drake his voice, and I was wondering which other Disney-related characters and attractions he's breathed life into? Lisa, Long Beach, California

A —Paul was quite a prolific voice talent at Disney. Besides doing most of the pirate voices in the Pirates of the Caribbean attraction, he voiced the Ghost Host at the Haunted Mansion, a farmyard horse in *Mary Poppins*, and Dirty Dawson in *One Hundred and One Dalmatians*. You can also hear him in several animated shorts produced in the 1950s.

Q **Do the canoes in Disneyland run on a track? Or are they free to maneuver how participants wish? Adam, Orange, CA**

A —The canoes do not run on a track; they are steered by the Disney Cast Members on board, with Guests helping out with the rowing.

Q **How are celebrities handled when they go to Disney Parks with their families? Greg, Bay Minette, AL**

A —It has always been the philosophy that every Guest is a VIP, so celebrities experience the attractions waiting in the regular queue. Walt Disney used to wait in line with his Guests. When there are high-profile Guests, such as top-ranking government officials and entertainment celebrities, they can draw large crowds of onlookers and take away from the "show." Sometimes it is necessary, therefore, to expedite their entry onto attractions to avoid safety and security risks to themselves and other Guests.

Q **For as long as I can remember, when we would go to Disneyland one of the highlights would be when my parents would get me a "Mickey balloon." That's the one with the ears that they still sell today. How long have they been around? Wendy, Napa, CA**

A —The Mickey Mouse balloons were created by Disneyland licensee Nat Lewis in 1956. Lewis was a circus veteran when he came to Disneyland. The first balloons were black and white, but Lewis continually changed them, adding color and refining the shape.

Q **What was the origin of It's a Small World in Disneyland? Was that Walt's idea? Harold, Boise, ID**

A —Walt had long had a wish to create an attraction about the children of the world, so when Pepsi-Cola requested Disney's help in designing their New York World's Fair pavilion as a salute to children and UNICEF, the United Nations Children's Fund, Walt set his Imagineers to work on the project, and they came up with one of the most popular Disney attractions of all time.

Q **When was the statue of Walt Disney and Mickey Mouse at Disneyland made? Was it there for the Park's opening? Did Walt model for it? Richard, Galveston, TX.**

A —The statue is called *Partners,* and it was created by sculptor Blaine Gibson to commemorate the sixty-fifth birthday of Mickey Mouse, in 1993. The sculptor used photographs of Walt Disney for reference. Identical statues were later installed at other Disney Parks and at the Disney Studios in Burbank, California.

Q **When Disneyland first opened, none of the attractions were roller coaster–type thrill rides. What was the first fast ride at a Disney Park? Shauna, Midland, TX**

A —The Matterhorn Bobsleds was the first roller coaster–type ride created for Disneyland, in 1959, just four years after the Park opened. Walt had enjoyed visiting the Matterhorn in Zermatt, Switzerland; he felt his Park could use a mountain, and a bobsled ride seemed an ideal fit.

Q **So many great attractions have been retired from the Disney Parks. Do you have a favorite former ride? Sheila, San Diego, CA**

A —I really miss America Sings at Disneyland, though I can still see many of the critters from that show when I ride Splash Mountain. Another favorite, gone from Disneyland but now at Walt Disney World, is the Carousel of Progress. Both shows occupied the carousel theater at Disneyland.

Q **When did the Blue Bayou open at Disneyland? Was it there on Opening Day? Bill, Reseda, CA**

A —The Blue Bayou Restaurant was added to Disneyland with the opening of Pirates of the Caribbean, in 1967, and has been a popular dining spot ever since. There is another Blue Bayou in Tokyo Disneyland and a similar one called Blue Lagoon in Disneyland Paris.

Q **Where do the horses that pull the carriages on Main Street live? Are there stables on-site? Cindy, Patterson, NJ**

A —When Disneyland opened in 1955, there were mule rides, stagecoach rides, wagon rides, and other attractions that featured horses and other animals. The Pony Farm on the property covered ten acres and had two hundred head of livestock. As those attractions closed over the years, the Pony Farm, now known as the Circle D Corral, shrank somewhat in size, but it still cares for the Park's livestock. At Walt Disney World, horses are stabled at the Tri Circle D Ranch, located at Fort Wilderness.

Q Has the candy store on Main Street in Disneyland always been there? Bobby, Nashville, TN

A —The Candy Palace (originally called Candyland) opened at Disneyland just six days after the Park opened, and it has been catering to the sweet teeth of Guests ever since. It expanded into part of the Penny Arcade in 1997. Guests enjoy watching candy, to be sold in the shop, actually being made.

Q Have movies ever used Disneyland or Walt Disney World as a location? Linda, Victoria, BC, Canada

A —The first non-Disney motion picture to use Disneyland as a location was Universal's 1962 release *40 Pounds of Trouble*, starring Tony Curtis. *That Thing You Do* (Twentieth Century Fox, 1996) had some scenes in Disneyland, and that same year *Marvin's Room* used Walt Disney World locations.

Q Did Disneyland have Christmas theming starting from the opening year? Lionel, Berkeley, CA

A —Yes, Disneyland has had a holiday theme every year it has been open. In 1955, the "Christmas at Disneyland Festival" ran from November 24 to January 8, 1956. Included was a Christmas Show Parade and a Christmas Bowl, where visiting groups performed.

Q I learned that Cast Members named the yeti in the Matterhorn "Harold." Are there other icons in the Park, such as animals from the Jungle Cruise, that Cast Members have named? Tyler, Camarillo, CA

A —Cast Members occasionally name some of their favorite characters, and those unofficial names get passed down from year to year. Besides Harold, some others at Disneyland include Bertha (showering elephant on the Jungle Cruise) and Bucky (the dragon in Fantasmic!).

Q **I'm remembering a time (early sixties) when my mother took me and my older brother to Disneyland for a dog show of dalmatians. Am I dreaming, or was such a show actually held? Hayes, Farmersville, CA**

A —Beginning in 1958, Disneyland held an annual Kids Amateur Dog Show one day each spring for about a decade. Dogs were judged in various categories, like largest, smallest, and shaggiest. Perhaps one of these is what you are remembering, though I do not recall a show just for dalmatians.

Q **When Fantasyland was remodeled into a Bavarian village, was that the first (and only) major remodel of the Peter Pan ride? Did that remodel involve changing the overhead track path or length? Did the time for a ride remain the same? Nick, Los Osos, CA**

A —There had been major additions to Peter Pan's Flight in 1961, but the entire ride was gutted and rebuilt in 1982–83. The parts that did not change were the overhead track, except for smoothing a sharp turn, and the boats, so, indeed, the length of the ride is essentially the same today as it was in 1955.

Q **Waiting in line for the short-lived Rocket Rods at Disneyland, music would play in the different waiting rooms. One of the songs sounded a lot like "Detroit" from *The Happiest Millionaire*. I was wondering if that was intentional, or just a coincidence. Sarah, Las Vegas, NV**

A —"Detroit," about the Motor City, was indeed used in the preshow area, which was an homage to automotive design and our love of the automobile. Steve Bartek, the composer on the project, created a new arrangement of the song for the Imagineers.

Q **Were there ever other names considered for Disneyland before it opened? Michael, York, PA**

A —In 1948, Walt Disney presented ideas for what he was calling Mickey Mouse Park. That name soon changed to Disneyland. In Florida, Walt had thought to call the project Disney World, but after Walt died, his brother Roy insisted that it be Walt Disney World in honor of the man who conceived the plan.

Q **Where or how did Walt obtain the funds to build Disneyland? Mike, Tustin, CA**

A —Disneyland ended up costing $17 million, a lot of money in 1955. To get the project started, Walt sold his vacation home in Palm Springs and hocked his insurance policies, but eventually he received funding from the ABC Television Network and from Western Publishing, the company that published most Disney books at the time.

Q **I'm a big fan of Tinker Bell, and I recently learned that a Tinker Bell shop actually existed during the early 1960s. Does such a shop still exist? If so, where is it located, and when was it first opened? Marisol, Bronx, NY**

A —The Tinker Bell Toy Shoppe was in Fantasyland at Disneyland from 1957 to 2002, when it changed its name to Once Upon a Time. That shop closed in 2009, and the area now houses the Bibbidi Bobbidi Boutique. There was a separate shop at Disneyland called Tinker Bell and Friends from 2005 to 2007. The Magic Kingdom at Walt Disney World had a Tinker Bell Toy

Shop until 1992, when it became Tinker Bell's Treasures and later Tinker Bell's Fairy Treasures. It closed in 2010.

Q **Are there any of the original Cast Members still working at Disneyland Park, or, if not, still working around the complex in Anaheim? How long has the next longest one been there? David, Peoria, AZ**

A —None of the 1955 Cast Members remain, but Oscar Martinez, a dinner cook at Carnation Café, started in 1956, and in 2006 he celebrated his fiftieth anniversary with Disneyland.

Q **I heard that Main Street, U.S.A., in Disneyland was modeled after a real city. Is it true? If so, what city is it? Penny, Fort Collins, CO**

A —There are two towns that can claim a relationship with Main Street, U.S.A., at Disneyland—Marceline, Missouri, where Walt Disney spent several years of his childhood, and Fort Collins, Colorado, where Main Street designer Harper Goff grew up.

Q **When I was in high school, around 1957 or 1958, we would dress up and go to Disneyland on weekends to dance to great band music. I can't remember where the dances took place. Can you help with details? Karen, La Quinta, CA**

A —In 1957, Disneyland began sponsoring Date Nites on Friday and Saturday nights during the summer and fall, with over 300,000 teens participating in the dancing at the Golden Horseshoe, Plaza Gardens, and the Yacht Club in Tomorrowland until midnight. Teens danced to Disneyland's own Dance Band, as well as a five-man combo and guest groups. Date Nites were expanded to every night of the week during the summer of 1958.

Q When was Carousel of Progress replaced by America Sings? Charmaine, San Diego, CA

A —The Carousel of Progress closed at Disneyland on September 9, 1973, and moved to Walt Disney World, where it opened in the Magic Kingdom on January 15, 1975. America Sings opened in the carousel theater at Disneyland on June 29, 1974.

Q I remember as a very small boy seeing model airplane demonstrations in a caged-in area in the old Tomorrowland, over by the Rocket to Mars ride. What was the purpose of the flight exhibit? I remember the flyer was quite good at his skill. Jon, Santa Ana, CA

A —That fenced-in area in the center of Tomorrowland was there from 1955 to 1966, first called Hobbyland, then Thimble Drome Flight Circle, and finally Disneyland Flight Circle. Cast Members demonstrated model airplanes by flying them around in circles. Walt had been at somewhat of a loss as to what he could put in Tomorrowland, so he thought the flight circle would fit the theme and be something fun to watch. He must have enjoyed it (despite the noisy airplane engines) because it lasted for over a decade.

Q In Disneyland's Pirates of the Caribbean attraction, what's the name of the ship attacking the fort? Jacquelynn, Orange, CA

A —The ship is known as the *Wicked Wench*.

Q During a visit on my thirteenth birthday, I remember a store on Main Street that had an ice cream/soda fountain bar in it. I saw an old-looking telephone on the counter, so I picked up the receiver. To my delight, there were women talking in a gossipy way. From the way the women spoke, it seemed to take place in the early days of the telephone. I have been to the Magic Kingdom several times since, and I can't seem to find it. Is it still there, and if so, at which store? Angela, Fayetteville, NC

A —The Market House on Main Street, U.S.A., at Disneyland, patterned after a general store from the turn of the century, has always had the old-fashioned telephones, and you can still pick up the receiver and listen in on the party line. There was also a Market House at the Magic Kingdom at Walt Disney World beginning in 1971, but it closed in 2007.

Q When Walt purchased the property for Disneyland, how many acres were bought? How many does the Park encompass today? Liz, San Jose, CA

A —The original property purchased for Disneyland in 1954 consisted of seventeen different land parcels totaling 140 acres. Today, the Disneyland Resort encompasses 510 acres—461 are owned by Disney, and forty-nine are under long-term lease.

Q At the end of the bayou portion of the Pirates of the Caribbean ride, there is an old man in a rocking chair on a dock with a pipe. My wife claims he used to say something or sing. I say all he ever did was rock, with a banjo playing in the background. Who is correct? My status as a Disneyland geek is at stake! Gary, San Jose, CA

A —You win! The man in the Disneyland attraction never sang nor spoke. Fun fact: the same character from the Bayou can be seen along the Rivers of America in the Magic Kingdom at Walt Disney World.

Q How were the miniatures in the Storybook Land ride at Disneyland designed and made? Corena, Las Vegas, NV

A —Members of the Model Shop at WED Enterprises (now Walt Disney Imagineering), under the supervision of designer Ken Anderson, made the buildings primarily of plywood, though covered with fiberglass to add to their durability. Detailing was added with plaster, plastic, thatch, glass, stone, and various metals, and wiring was run for lights and audio.

Q **Did a woman by the name of Alice Davis dress President Lincoln, among other characters around the Parks? Wasn't she also married to an animator? Diane, Galena, OH**

A —Alice Davis is the widow of Marc Davis, one of Walt's Nine Old Men. She's best known for researching, designing, and dressing the Audio-Animatronics figures in It's a Small World and Pirates of the Caribbean. Alice told me that she did not create Abraham Lincoln's costume (which was, in fact, done by a company named Western Costuming) because she was not accomplished at men's tailoring. Alice was named a Disney Legend in 2004.

Q **Didn't the Disneyana Shop at Disneyland sell old Disney memorabilia at one time? B.C., Rialto, CA**

A —When the Disneyana Shop opened in 1976, it carried Disney collectibles from the past, but after a few years, the focus of the shop was changed when it became too difficult to keep the shop stocked with interesting pieces. Now the Disneyana Shop specializes in current Disney collectibles, including some items produced exclusively for that shop. There was also a Disneyana Shop at the Magic Kingdom at Walt Disney World from 1983 to 1996, and one opened at Disneyland Paris in 1992.

Q **I seem to remember that Mickey's Detective School had three or four rules. One was "follow the clues." What were the other rules? Bill, Chino, CA**

A —There were three rules in this 2002 Fantasyland Theater stage show at Disneyland Park: 1. Call for a pro, 2. Look high and low, and 3. Follow that trail wherever it goes.

Q **Is the golden marker under Sleeping Beauty Castle really the center of Disneyland? C.J., Bakersfield, California**

A —No, that's an urban legend. It was used to measure visual intrusion around Disneyland.

Q **Does the drop at Splash Mountain in Disneyland go straight down from five stories? V.C., Phoenix, AZ**

A —The drop is at a forty-seven-degree angle. The fifty-two-foot drop (equivalent to a five-story building) was, at Splash Mountain's opening, the longest flume chute in the world.

Q **I am a big fan of Disneyland, and I have always wondered why Walt decided to build the Park in Anaheim. It was a pretty sleepy little town back in the mid-1950s. Do you know? K.W., Elko, NV**

A —Actually, Walt had first thought about building Disneyland adjacent to his motion picture studio in Burbank, California. On March 27, 1952, the *Burbank Daily Review* ran a story that Walt Disney was planning to build his Disneyland there. But as Walt developed his plans, he came to realize that the studio land was simply not large enough to hold all his dreams. Therefore, he hired the Stanford Research Institute (SRI) to do a survey to find a new site for his proposed Park. By studying traffic patterns, population centers, accessibility, climate, and other factors, SRI narrowed the search down to what it considered the ideal location—a site just off the then-under-construction Santa Ana Freeway in Anaheim. Anaheim beat out three other possible sites, in La Mirada, Buena Park, and Santa Ana.

Q In Splash Mountain at Disneyland there is a cave with a sign saying "Rufus," and you can hear snoring inside. Who is Rufus, and is he in any other part of the ride? L.K., Anaheim, CA

A —Before Splash Mountain was built, there was a cave on the site, at the entrance to Bear Country, out of which came the snoring sounds of a hibernating bear, Rufus. The designers of Splash Mountain decided to continue the popularity of this never-seen bear by giving him a home in the new attraction. Rufus does not appear anywhere else in the attraction.

Q What happened to the House of the Future and the smaller version of Autopia that used to be at Disneyland? L.G., Moreno Valley, CA

A —The House of the Future was removed from Disneyland in 1967, by then it was ten years old and no longer quite so "futuristic." Midget Autopia was removed in 1960 because space was needed for other things. Walt Disney donated that ride to his childhood town of Marceline, Missouri, where it was installed in a city park.

Q What happened to the mine train at Disneyland? J.D., Antioch, CA

A —The Mine Train Through Nature's Wonderland in Frontierland was removed in 1977 so that Big Thunder Mountain Railroad could be built in its place.

Q When I was a child my parents took me to Disneyland, and I seem to recall an area for the Mickey Mouse Club. Roy Williams did a drawing for me of Mickey Mouse. Where was this club area? E.F., Dayton, OH

A —The Mickey Mouse Club Headquarters was located at Disneyland in the Main Street Opera House from June 1963 to September 1964, and kids visiting the headquarters were made honorary Mouseketeers. The area was decorated with sets from the television series. Big "Mooseketeer" Roy Williams, by profession a Disney story man and sketch artist, loved drawing for Disneyland Guests.

Q **After all these years, the Jungle Cruise at Disneyland is still my favorite. Was it popular when the Park first opened? S.S., Oklahoma City, OK**

A —When Disneyland opened, the Jungle Cruise was actually the most eagerly anticipated attraction. In the year leading up to the opening, Walt Disney had produced a couple of TV shows showing the construction going on in Anaheim in order to prepare viewers for what they might experience when they visited the Park. Frames of buildings told little about what might be built inside, but construction on the Jungle Cruise was already well along. Trees, shrubs, and other landscaping had to be planted early so that the area would resemble a jungle as soon as the Park opened. Walt was very proud of his upcoming attraction, and, in fact, in one show he drove a car through the unfinished river channel pointing out where animals would be located. Viewers were so intrigued by Walt's vivid descriptions that they were anxious to experience the Jungle Cruise in person.

Q **On one of the *Walt Disney Presents* episodes, Walt Disney mentioned a 1776-era street to be constructed at Disneyland. What happened to it? E.R., Guthrie, OK**

A —In 1956, Walt Disney announced plans for a Liberty Street at Disneyland, to be located behind the east side of Main Street. Included would be a Hall of Presidents. But this was long before

Audio-Animatronics figures were invented, so the presidential figures would have been mere mannequins. Other projects occupied Walt's time, while eventually the Audio-Animatronics process was perfected and deemed ideal for the planned Hall of Presidents. However, Liberty Street was never built at Disneyland; instead, it made its debut as Liberty Square at Walt Disney World's Magic Kingdom in 1971. The Hall of Presidents show has become one of the most inspiring ever produced by Disney Imagineers.

Q **Can you tell me the meaning of the phrase "An E ticket ride"? T.C., Cocoa, FL**

A —The E tickets, part of the ticket books sold at Disneyland and later at Walt Disney World's Magic Kingdom, were for the most elaborate attractions. When Disneyland first issued ticket books, in October 1955, there were only A, B, and C tickets. D tickets were added in 1956, and finally the E tickets in 1959. It was not long before "E ticket ride," meaning the ultimate thrill, became a part of American slang. And that is why astronaut Sally Ride described her first excursion into space as a real E ticket ride. Ticket books were phased out in favor of all-inclusive "passports" in 1982.

Q **In his earliest TV shows, Walt Disney displayed a large painting of what Disneyland, then under construction, would look like. Who painted it, and is it still around? A.L., St. Paul, MN**

A —That painting was done by Peter Ellenshaw, who also did matte paintings for many of the Disney feature films. Rather than use a canvas, Ellenshaw did his work on one of the regular four-by-eight-foot storyboards that were normally used by the animation staff at the Studio. Later it was discovered that the painting was highlighted with fluorescent paint, so that under black light it became a beautiful picture of Disneyland at night. The painting is part of the art collection of Walt Disney Imagineering.

Q **Is the castle at Disneyland based on Neuschwanstein Castle in Germany? M.A.H., Prescott, AZ**

A —Sleeping Beauty Castle's design is a composite of various medieval European castles, and is primarily of French and Bavarian influence. While there are elements of Neuschwanstein included, it is not the sole model for the castle. The Disneyland castle was constructed during 1954-55 for Opening Day on July 17, 1955. To make the castle seem larger than it is, the walls and battlements were constructed of "stones" cut in graduated sizes, with the largest ones at the foundation and the smallest ones at the topmost sentry posts.

Q **When did the Mouseketeers first perform at Disneyland? M.O., New Orleans, LA**

A —The Mouseketeers performed briefly on the Park's Opening Day television show. During Disneyland's first holiday season, in 1955, a Mickey Mouse Club Circus was held under a big top between Fantasyland and Tomorrowland. Besides regular circus acts—featuring performers doing acrobatics and stunts—there were the Mouseketeers, whose TV show had premiered a couple of months earlier.

LIVE-ACTION FILMS

Q *Summer Magic*'s credits list a "Jimmy Mathers," although the actor looks like Jerry Mathers, of *Leave It to Beaver* fame. Is it actually Jerry? Patti, St. Francis, WI

A —Jimmy Mathers is correct. He is Jerry Mathers's younger brother. Jimmy was eight years old when he made the film; his big brother was fifteen.

Q I was searching for *Almost Angels* (1962) and *Emil and the Detectives* (1964) for purchase and found that Disney does not offer them. Why is this, and is there any chance they may be offered in the future? Patrick, East Setauket, NY

A —Disney features are usually released for a period of years, then returned to the vault for a rest. *Almost Angels* was released on VHS from 1986 to 1987; *Emil and the Detectives* was available from 1987 to 1991. Neither has yet been released on DVD.

Q My girls and I absolutely adore the *Princess Diaries* movies, especially the first one. Where were the Genovia scenes filmed? Where are the beautiful gowns worn at the ball by Julie Andrews and Anne Hathaway? Janice, Cumberland, RI

A —The scenes of Genovia were actually filmed in Southern California using matte paintings and a combination of actual locations, including Disney's Golden Oak Ranch. The back of the palace, with its gardens, was filmed at a palatial estate in Pasadena. The palace interiors were filmed in five soundstages at Universal Studios. Surprisingly, some interior shots were filmed at the same Disney Studios soundstage where Julie Andrews filmed *Mary Poppins*. We have the elegant ball gowns in the Archives.

Q What football field was utilized in *Son of Flubber*? D.N., Miami, FL

A —Exterior shooting for the football game sequence was prohibitive because of the special effects and trick shots involved. So a section of stadium and a major part of the field were reproduced on one of Disney's largest soundstages. It was exact in every detail, from the transplanted green sod and the goal posts to the cheering spectators and the enthusiastic cheerleaders. Since the team opposing Medfield College was composed of professional football players and not actors, the players were surprised to be asked to play indoors.

Q Back in the 1970s, when *The World's Greatest Athlete* was made, we didn't have computer special effects. So how was Tim Conway shrunk so effectively to miniature size in that film? B.Y., Detroit, MI

A —In the film, Tim Conway, playing Milo, shrinks to a three-inch size and tumbles into a lady's purse. So a purse with its usual contents had to be built to scale—in other words, huge. Lipstick, comb and brush, hairpins, compact, needle and thread, safety pins, reading glasses, keys, pills, matches, and a camera were all constructed twenty-four times their normal size to film this hilarious scene—at a cost in 1972 of $15,000. In other scenes, Milo encountered many other giant props, including a huge telephone and a cocktail glass that was seven feet tall and held a 1,245-gallon old-fashioned cooled by ice cubes two feet square. A Disney press release promoting the film quipped, "At 40 shots to a quart, consider the possibilities!"

Q I remember a Disney film from my childhood about a New York family who inherits a run-down hotel in Colorado and attempts to reopen it as a ski resort. I believe that Dean Jones was one of the stars in the film; he may have played the father. What was the title of this movie? Is it available to own? Debra, Tampa, FL

A —Dean Jones and Nancy Olson starred in the 1972 Disney movie *Snowball Express*. This film was released on videocassette in 1982 and 1995, and more recently on DVD.

Q Keith Hamshere, who plays Hayley Mills's younger brother in *In Search of the Castaways*, is really cute. Where did Walt Disney find him? O.R., Boulder, CO

A —Keith was actually discovered by Disney talent agents while he was playing the title role in the original London production of the well-known musical *Oliver*.

Q Does the film from *America the Beautiful*, the movie in the round, reside in the Archives? Are there plans (somehow, using Disney magic) to make it into a DVD for sale? I will be the first in line! We love that movie, and viewing it now would be a walk through cultural history! Laurel, Long Beach, CA

A —There is no current technology that would enable the release of a 360-degree CircleVision movie on DVD, and just viewing the film from one camera would not be satisfactory. You would be left wondering what you were missing all around you. That happened to me when I started at Disney. I wanted to get some idea what some early CircleVision films looked like, so I had the film from one camera (one ninth of the total) sent to a screening room at the Studio so it could be projected for me. I did get a very narrow view of the entire film, and while for archival purposes I guess it was okay, it certainly would not have been entertaining for DVD purchasers.

Q In the movie *Superdad*, released in 1974, there's a song called "These Are the Best Times," by Bobby Goldsboro. Has this song ever been released on any Bobby Goldsboro albums or on any Walt Disney sound tracks? Connie, Medford, OR

A —There was a promo record (Disneyland Records FS61) of Bobby Goldsboro's recording of the song released when the movie came out, but I am unaware of it being on any albums. There was no sound track album for the movie. The song was released on sheet music because it was frequently requested for use as a wedding song.

Q In *The Parent Trap,* Hayley Mills's character(s) went to a summer camp in New England. Do you know the name and location of the camp where it was filmed? Pamela, Ipswich, MA

A —The exteriors of Camp Inch were actually filmed at a camp on Big Bear Lake, in Southern California.

Q I've read about the Disney back lot, where they filmed movies and TV shows like *Zorro, The Apple Dumpling Gang,* and *The Absent-Minded Professor.* When was the first time that they ever used the back lot? Justin, Appling, GA

A —The front part of the lot was actually the first part of the Disney Studios used as a movie set—for Robert Benchley's tour of the Studio in 1941's *The Reluctant Dragon.* The back lot was first used for a beach scene in *The Three Caballeros,* but the first permanent sets were built there for *Zorro* (1957). A Western set used for various television productions was added in 1958, followed by a residential street for *The Absent-Minded Professor* in 1960 and a business street for *The Ugly Dachshund* in 1965.

Q Where was *Treasure Island* (1950) filmed? David, Douglas, Isle of Man, UK

A —The movie was filmed in soundstages and on the back lot at Denham Film Studios in England. The same studio served as the location for *The Story of Robin Hood and His Merrie Men* two years later; that was the last film ever shot at Denham.

Q I'm curious about Dorothy McGuire, the actress who played the mother in *Old Yeller*. Is she still living? Robert, Wilmington, NC

A —Dorothy McGuire died in September 2001 at the age of eighty-five. She appeared in the Disney films *Swiss Family Robinson* and *Summer Magic*; she also narrated part of the *Wonderful World of Disney* episode *The Best Doggoned Dog in the World*, which aired in November 1957.

Q Who directed the masterful 20,000 *Leagues Under the Sea*? G.G., Austin, TX

A —Richard Fleischer. He was the son of an early competitor of Walt Disney's. His famous father was Max Fleischer, who created the *Out of the Inkwell*, *Betty Boop*, and *Popeye the Sailor* cartoons and the animated feature *Gulliver's Travels*. Supposedly, Richard asked his father if he would mind if he directed a film for Walt Disney. Max had no problem with that and even came to the Disney Studios to have lunch with Walt.

Q Was there a recipe for the famous Flubber that Fred MacMurray created in *The Absent-Minded Professor*? K.D., Lincoln, NE

A —There was never one mentioned in the film, but when the film was released, *Time* magazine published this recipe (with tongue firmly planted in cheek): "To one pound of saltwater taffy add one heaping tablespoon polyurethane foam, one cake crumbled yeast. Mix till smooth, allow to rise. Then pour into saucepan over one cup cracked rice mixed with one cup water. Add topping of molasses. Boil until it lifts the lid and says, 'Qurlp.'"

Q **Hadn't Jane Wyman and Agnes Moorehead, who appeared in** *Pollyanna*, **worked together before? T.P., Kansas City, MO**

A —Indeed they had. When the two ladies joined the cast of *Pollyanna*, they fondly recalled the previous time they had appeared in a motion picture together. The film was *Johnny Belinda*, and both were nominated for Academy Awards. (Wyman won the Oscar.)

Q **When I watched** *All My Children*, **the character of Phoebe (Ruth Warrick) reminded me of someone. Am I correct in thinking she played the mother in the 1946 movie** *Song of the South*? **Kathryn, Bear, DE**

A —Ruth Warrick, who made her screen debut in *Citizen Kane* (1941), played the mother in *Song of the South*. She passed away in 2005.

Q **In the Minions Recovery Group meeting at the end of** *Inspector Gadget*, **one of the men looks a lot like Mr. T. Is that him? Has Mr. T ever appeared in any other Disney specials or features? Guy, Plainsboro, NJ**

A —Yes, that is Mr. T playing himself in *Inspector Gadget*. He also appeared as a helicopter pilot in Disney's *Spy Hard*.

Q **Is the "Swisskapolka" in** *Swiss Family Robinson* **a traditional polka, or did somebody write it for the film? Eric, Methuen, MA**

A —Disney staff composer Buddy Baker wrote "Swisskapolka" specifically for *Swiss Family Robinson*. Baker came to Disney in 1955 to help George Bruns write music for *Davy Crockett*. He is best remembered for the music he created for Disney attractions at the 1964–65 New York World's Fair and the Disney

Parks. When he retired in 1983, he was the last staff composer at any major studio.

Q **How many Disney features has Jodie Foster appeared in? E.L., Albany, NY**

A —Five: *Napoleon and Samantha*, *One Little Indian*, the first *Freaky Friday*, *Candleshoe*, and *Flightplan*. She also appeared on Disney's 1970 two-part TV show *Menace on the Mountain*.

Q **I once saw a scary Disney movie that had to do with a fair or carnival. What is the title of this film? Matthew, Savoonga, AR**

A —You're probably thinking of 1983's *Something Wicked This Way Comes*, based on the novel by science-fiction author Ray Bradbury. It was directed by Jack Clayton and starred Jason Robards, Jonathan Pryce, and Pam Grier.

Q **I seem to remember a Disney movie about dachshunds. If there is such a film, is it available for purchase? N.R., Wheeling, WV**

A —You're probably remembering 1966's *The Ugly Dachshund*, starring Dean Jones and Suzanne Pleshette, about a Great Dane who thinks he's a dachshund. It was released on DVD in 2004.

Q **I once saw a movie about a German family who makes a hot-air balloon from scraps of material and escapes from East Germany at night. Can you tell me the title of the movie and whether it is available for purchase? Debbie, South Huntington, NY**

A —*Night Crossing*, which was based on a true story, was a 1982 Disney feature starring John Hurt, Jane Alexander, and Beau Bridges. It was directed by Delbert Mann. *Night Crossing* was released on DVD in 2004.

Q In the 1960s or 1970s, I saw a movie about Lipizzan horses being smuggled out of Austria. I cannot remember the name of the movie, and I have been wondering if it is available to the public. Fran, Lancaster, CA

A —You're thinking of 1963's *Miracle of the White Stallions*. The film tells the true story of how the director of Vienna's renowned Spanish Riding School smuggled out the school's white Lipizzan horses to save them from the bombing of the city during World War II. This movie has been released on DVD.

Q I was wondering about the unique and beautiful house in the original version of *The Parent Trap* that the character of Mitch, the father, lived in. Is it still standing? Where is it located? Sara, Algona, IA

A —It was only a movie set. Some of the exterior was built at Disney's Golden Oak Ranch; the interiors were built on a soundstage at the Disney Studios in Burbank.

Q During the big race in *The Love Bug,* David Tomlinson drives a very potent-looking yellow roadster called the Thorndyke Special. What was the actual make of this car? William, Bedford, IN

A —The car that David Tomlinson's villain drove, the Thorndyke Special (after his character's name), was an Apollo GT.

Q One of my favorite actors is Kevin Spacey. Can you give me a rundown of his film work for Disney? Patricia, Tucker, GA

A —Kevin Spacey has appeared in three Hollywood/Disney/ Touchstone films—*Consenting Adults, Iron Will,* and *The Ref*—and he provided the voice for Hopper in *a bug's life*.

Q When I was in high school, my gym teacher showed us an educational film about steroids that I've never forgotten. I could swear that it was a Disney film. Am I right? What is it called? Frank, Houston, TX

A —*Benny and the 'Roids (A Story About Steroid Abuse)* was a Disney educational film from 1988 in which a high school football player learns about the dangers of steroid abuse.

Q What Disney pirate movie (not *Treasure Island*) was shown as a double feature with *The Apple Dumpling Gang*? Phil, New York, NY

A —The movie was *Treasure of Matecumbe* (1976), a Disney adventure starring Robert Foxworth, Joan Hackett, and Peter Ustinov. The film tells the story of two boys in the post–Civil War South looking for buried treasure.

Q I have a storyboard for *Victory Through Air Power* with sixteen sketches, each about two by two-and-a-half inches in size. Who were the storyboard artists for this film? Donna, McHenry, IL

A —The credits list the story crew as Perce Pearce (story director), Jose Rodriguez, T. Hee, Erdman Penner, William Cottrell, James Bodrero, and George Stallings.

Q In many Disney films there's a college named "Medfield." Is there such a school? If not, what is the significance of the name? John and Liza, San Francisco, CA

A —There is no such school; it was just a fictitious name thought up by the screenwriters. "Medfield College" was often used in Disney movies, from *The Absent-Minded Professor* (1961) to *Flubber* (1997), including *Son of Flubber* (1963), *The Computer Wore Tennis Shoes* (1969), *Now You See Him, Now You Don't* (1972), and *The*

Strongest Man in the World (1975). But the name of the college in *The Monkey's Uncle* and *The Misadventures of Merlin Jones* is Midvale, and in *The World's Greatest Athlete*, it's Merrivale. Various buildings at the Disney Studios in Burbank, California, frequently were used to portray the college buildings.

Q **I recently saw *The Littlest Horse Thieves* for the first time in decades and noticed the name Jeremy Bulloch in the credits. Is this the same actor who appeared in the Star Wars films as Boba Fett? Linda, Yatesville, PA**

A —Yes. Jeremy Bulloch also had a small part as a nightclub owner in Hollywood Pictures' *Swing Kids*, released in 1993.

Q **My three-year-old daughter's favorite movie is *Mary Poppins*. She must watch a few minutes of it every night before she goes to bed. Needless to say, I've seen it more times than I can count. I ask myself the same question every time I watch one scene: is there a man dressed as one of the nannies applying for the job? I swear that there is a man in a nanny costume in the top left of one of the group shots. Sunny, Winter Haven, FL**

A —Yes, there are in fact many men in the shots immediately before the nannies get picked up by the wind and whisked away. Back in 1964, most movie stunts were performed by men. In *Mary Poppins*, it probably helped that the nannies were supposed to look severe and strict, angular, and mannish.

Q **Two of my favorite Disney movies are *Yellowstone Cubs* and *Charlie the Lonesome Cougar*. Whenever opportunity arises, I break into my best impersonation of Rex Allen saying, "That's just Mother Nature's way . . ." It usually brings a smile to the face of anyone who watched Disney TV in the sixties.**

Where is Rex Allen now, and what other work did he do? Rick, West Salem, WI

A —Rex Allen was named a Disney Legend in 1996, at which point he put his handprints and signature in cement in front of the Disney Studios theater. He narrated more than forty Western-themed Disney films, mostly for television. He was primarily known as a "singing cowboy," recording many best-selling country songs. He retired to Tucson, Arizona, and died in 1999.

Q **In my favorite live-action Disney movie, *The Rocketeer*, the character of Neville Sinclair lives in a house that has interior walls of carved concrete. Since this is characteristic of Frank Lloyd Wright's work, was this sequence filmed at the Wright-designed Storer House in Hollywood? Diane, North Ridgeville, OH**

A —The interior rooms of Sinclair's house, including the library, radio room, bathroom, and bedroom, were inspired by the Wright house but built on Stage 1 at the Walt Disney Studios in Burbank, California.

Q **Some time ago I rented the Touchstone video *An Innocent Man*, starring Tom Selleck. Near the end of the film there is a scene that takes place outside at night in which I believe you can hear, in the distance, the Fantasyland band organ from Disneyland playing "Baby Mine" from *Dumbo*. Am I just imagining things? Andy, Burbank, CA**

A —"Baby Mine" is indeed played at the end of *An Innocent Man* (1989), and while we do not have a listing for the performance, it could very well be the band organ at Disneyland.

Q **As a kid, my favorite actor was Roger Mobley. What became of him? Chuck, Moore, OK**

A —Mobley actually made his first Disney appearance as part of the Mobley Trio on a Talent Roundup Day show on the *Mickey Mouse Club* in 1958. He returned for *Emil and the Detectives* in 1964, *The Treasure of San Bosco Reef* in 1968, and *Gallegher* from 1965 to 1968. After *Gallegher* he became a paratrooper and later a police officer in Texas. He returned to Disney years later to play bit parts in *The Apple Dumpling Gang Rides Again* (1979) and *The Kids Who Knew Too Much* (1980). In 1985 he became an ordained minister. When I heard from Roger in 1999, when he was still ministering in southeastern Texas rural churches, he wrote, "It's always nice to know that my work is still remembered."

Q **On the album *Classic Disney, Volume II*, there is a song called "On the Front Porch," sung by Burl Ives. What movie is this from? Jessie, San Diego, CA**

A —The song is from 1963's *Summer Magic* and was written by Richard M. and Robert B. Sherman. The movie, about a widow and her family starting a new life in a rural Maine town, starred Hayley Mills and Burl Ives.

Q **When I was little I used to love any movie with the youngest son from *Old Yeller* in it. What was his name? He was also in a movie about running away and joining the circus. What was the name of that movie? Celeste, Springfield, MA**

A —The actor you are talking about is Kevin Corcoran, who starred in *Toby Tyler, or Ten Weeks with a Circus*. In the movie, twelve-year-old orphan Toby Tyler (Corcoran) runs away from his aunt and uncle, joins the circus, and finds friendship with a chimp named Mr. Stubbs. Toby gets a shot at being in the equestrian act, which, with the help of Mr. Stubbs, becomes a huge success. Toby is happily reunited with his more understanding guardians.

Corcoran appeared in a number of Disney features and television shows, including *Swiss Family Robinson*, *Pollyanna*, *The Shaggy Dog* (1959), *Babes in Toyland*, and *Savage Sam*.

Q Could you tell me where *Pete's Dragon* and *Bedknobs and Broomsticks* were filmed? Martin, Glasgow, Scotland

A —Both films were shot at the Disney Studios in Burbank, California, with *Pete's Dragon* having a few location scenes at Disney's Golden Oak Ranch and on the California coast near Morro Bay.

Q I recently saw the complete version of *The Reluctant Dragon*. There's a scene in which Robert Benchley visits the Disney Studios, and he browses a table filled with character statues. I thought I saw Captain Hook and Tinker Bell from *Peter Pan* and Aunt Sarah and her Siamese cats from *Lady and the Tramp*. I know it takes several years to produce an animated film, but would those characters, whose films wouldn't be released until the mid-1950s, have been developed as early as 1941? Christopher, Kennewick, WA

A —Yes, there were indeed characters from *Peter Pan* and *Lady and the Tramp* in the Model Shop sequence of *The Reluctant Dragon*. Work had begun on both of these films in the 1930s. World War II caused production on many of Disney's planned features to be postponed.

Q I enjoy the films of Bobby Driscoll. Can you tell me more about him? Phil, Chardon, OH

A —Bobby Driscoll starred in *Song of the South*, *Melody Time*, *So Dear to My Heart*, and *Treasure Island* for Disney; he also provided the voices of Peter Pan and Goofy Jr. in 1950s cartoons. Besides his films for Disney, Bobby appeared in a number of features and television shows for other producers. He received a special juvenile Academy Award in the year he made *So Dear to My Heart* and the non-Disney film *The Window*. He appeared in the television specials *One Hour in Wonderland* and *The Walt Disney Christmas Show*. He had a troubled life after he outgrew children's roles and died a pauper, of a drug overdose, at age thirty-one in New York City. Bobby was a favorite actor of mine, too, as I was growing up, since we were about the same age, and I knew his mother when I worked at the UCLA Library in the 1960s (she worked there, too).

Q **Where was the airship in *The Island at the Top of the World* built? S.L.E., Durant, OK**

A —The airship *Hyperion* was designed by Peter Ellenshaw, the movie's production designer, and various-sized miniatures were built for the filming of the flying sequences by the special-effects department at the Disney Studios. For the segments featuring the cast in the gondola, a full-size gondola was built with only the very bottom part of the balloon. This was filmed on Stage 2 at the Studio. A full-scale airship was not constructed.

Q **In Disney's remake of *That Darn Cat*, the film takes place in the fictional town of Edgefield, Massachusetts. Where was the film actually shot? Chris and Julie, Somerville, MA**

A —The 1997 *That Darn Cat* remake was filmed in and around Edgefield, South Carolina, which doubled for Massachusetts. In fact, the filmmakers were so taken with the town, they changed the name in the script to Edgefield so the town's signs would not have to be altered for filming.

Q **I remember seeing *The Black Hole* as a child. Was this Disney's first PG-rated movie? David, Spokane, WA**

A —Yes. It premiered in the U.S. on December 20, 1979. However, earlier films, such as *Treasure Island* (1950), might have been rated PG if the rating system had been around then. This and other Disney films received PG ratings when released on video.

Q **What breed of dog played White Fang in the 1991 Disney movie of the same name? Was he a real wolf-dog hybrid? Lauren, Milwaukee, WI**

A —White Fang was played by Jed, half-dog, half-wolf, trained by Clint Rowe. There is a statement in the credits, signed by Defenders of Wildlife, Washington, D.C.: "Because wolves were systematically eliminated throughout most of the United States during our early history and continue to be persecuted today, a nationwide effort is under way to reintroduce wolves into wilderness areas and ensure their survival for generations to come."

Q **I saw my first Disney movie in the sixties. I think it was titled *Tomasina*, and it was about a young girl in Wales or Scotland and a cat. Do you have any information about this movie? Pam, Etobicoke, Ontario, Canada**

A —The movie you remember is *The Three Lives of Thomasina*, which was released nationwide on June 6, 1964. It starred Patrick McGoohan, Susan Hampshire, Karen Dotrice, and Matthew Garber, with Elspeth March as the voice of Thomasina. The movie is about Thomasina, a big ginger cat that comes to live with widowed veterinary surgeon Andrew MacDhui and his five-year-old daughter, Mary, in a village in Scotland. When the cat is hurt, Andrew "puts her to sleep." Mary is so heartbroken she accuses her father of killing her beloved pet. But Thomasina is discovered, still breathing, by Lori MacGregor, a mysterious woman who has an almost supernatural ability to heal animals. Lori brings Thomasina back to life and becomes Andrew's wife and a mother for Mary. But it is Thomasina, back at home with the MacDhuis, who rules the family.

Q **When I saw *Almost Angels*, I fell in love with one of the pieces of music sung by the choir. The scene was set in a church during Mass and featured a solo performance by a choirboy. Can you tell me the title of that music? M.L., Columbia, SC**

A —We get many inquiries about that particular piece of music. It is "Omnes de Saba Venient," with words and music by Joseph Leopold Eybler.

Q **What kind of cat was used in *The Cat from Outer Space*? P.B., Amarillo, TX**

A —Jake, the cat, was an Abyssinian. Actually, two cats—Rumple and Amber—played the role. The producers chose Abyssinians because they thought the breed looked more "alien."

Q **Whatever happened to Tommy Kirk? He was a terrific actor when he was in Disney programs. Is he still alive? K.S., Elk Grove, CA**

A —Tommy Kirk continued in films for a number of years after his Disney movies, but he is now retired. He lived in Tennessee for a while and now lives in Northern California. In 1995, he appeared on a panel that I moderated at the Disneyana Convention at Walt Disney World. He occasionally attends celebrity autograph shows.

Q **The first movie my late mother ever took me to (it was probably 1956 or 1957) was Walt Disney's *The Littlest Outlaw*. The only thing I remember about the movie is that it was**

about a young Mexican boy and his burro. I have never heard about it again. Please tell me what you can. Ed, Waxhaw, NC

A —*The Littlest Outlaw* is the story of a young boy, Pablito, in Mexico, who has a great love for a horse named Conquistador, owned by a general. After Pablito manages to save the horse's life, it is presented to him as a gift by the general. The movie was released on Christmas Day in 1955; it was released on video in 1987 and 1995; it has never been released on DVD.

Q Where was Hayley Mills's movie *In Search of the Castaways* filmed, and who did the great special effects? J.S., San Diego, CA

A —*In Search of the Castaways* (1962) contained some of the most elaborate special effects of any Disney film up to that time, with the set designers building a live volcano; part of the Andes Mountains; reproductions of the ports of Glasgow, Scotland, and Melbourne, Australia, from the 1870s; and a complete New Zealand Maori village. All of this was accomplished at Pinewood Studios in England. The special-effects team was headed by Syd Pearson and Peter Ellenshaw.

Q I recall a Disney movie about a would-be superhero called Condorman. Was he Disney's first live-action superhero, and who animated the cartoon *Condorman* credits sequence at the start of the movie? Mario, Monterey Park, CA

A —*Condorman* was released in 1981. You could probably say he was Disney's first superhero. Title animation was done by Disney animator Michael Cedeno.

Q I'm sure that many versions of Herbie were used in shooting the original film, but was there a primary car, and does it still exist someplace? Richard, Lake Champlain, IL

A —No primary Volkswagen car was ever saved by Disney, though some copies have been used in parades, and one was for a time displayed at the then Disney-MGM Studios. One was also presented to actor Dean Jones. There were dozens of different Herbies used, each built to perform a particular trick, for the various films starting with *The Love Bug* (1969).

Q I've always wondered why Dick Van Dyke played Mr. Dawes Sr. in *Mary Poppins*. I understand why in *The Wizard of Oz*, for instance, Margaret Hamilton played the dual roles of the Wicked Witch and Miss Gulch, and why Christopher Reeve played Clark Kent and Superman; the roles are integral and connected to the stories. But I've never been able to figure out the meaning of the dual Van Dyke roles. Steve, Rochester Hills, MI

A —Supposedly, Dick Van Dyke very much wanted to play Mr. Dawes Sr. and even prepared a screen test to show Walt Disney that he could believably portray the old man. In 2010 at a special one-night D23 performance of the stage version of *Mary Poppins* at the Ahmanson Theater in Los Angeles, Dick did a cameo as Mr. Dawes Sr., a character that ordinarily does not appear in that show; needless to say, the audience was thrilled.

Q I watched the remake version of *Escape to Witch Mountain*, renamed *Race to Witch Mountain*, and had a question about the reporter at the beginning. Is she the same actress who played Natty Gann in *The Journey of Natty Gann* back in the eighties? I loved that movie and probably drove my parents crazy by watching it over and over as a child. I was curious because the actress says something like, "This is Natalie Gann, reporting for . . ." and I rewound the movie to make sure that I had heard her right. Hopefully, you can clear this up for me. Danae, Arroyo Grande, CA

A —Good catch! That was indeed Meredith Salenger, who starred in *The Journey of Natty Gann*, in a cameo portraying "Natalie Gann" in *Race to Witch Mountain* twenty-four years later. I wonder how many other *Natty Gann* fans noticed.

Q **I thought there was a Disney film called *Double Trouble*, but I can find no listing of it. Are you familiar with it? Louise, San Francisco, CA**

A —*Double Trouble* was the working title for the film that was finally released in 1976 as *No Deposit, No Return*, starring David Niven, Darren McGavin, Herschel Bernardi, Barbara Feldon, and Don Knotts.

Q **I am an avid Disney movie watcher, and I own all the Disney animated classics. What I have not been able to figure out is if the film *The Reluctant Dragon* is considered one of these classics. Although it is stated to be in a variety of sources, it seems too short to qualify as a feature-length film. Was it originally released as a combo film, or is this just a special circumstance where a short is considered a movie? Dylan, Los Alamitos, California**

A —*The Reluctant Dragon* was actually a seventy-three-minute motion picture released in 1941. It featured, in live action, a tour of the Disney Studios with humorist Robert Benchley, along with cartoon segments such as *How to Ride a Horse*; *Casey, Jr.*; and *The Reluctant Dragon*. (This segment was also released separately years later, and, since it was the same title as the feature, this is probably the reason why you are confused.)

Q **I had the pleasure of watching Laurel and Hardy's *March of the Wooden Soldiers* this past weekend and was totally fascinated to find Mickey Mouse in the movie (played by a monkey). Are there**

any really clear pictures of this incarnation of the character? Any background you could give on Mickey's (one and only?) live-action appearance? Scott, Royal Oak, MI

A —The Hal Roach Studios obtained permission from Disney to use Mickey Mouse and the Three Little Pigs in *March of the Wooden Soldiers* (1934). We do not have photos of their appearances in that film in our Archives, but I have seen the film and chuckled over the "Disney" characters.

Q I am searching for a feature that I think was on *The Wonderful World of Disney*. It described the Coast Guard training school and boat rescue at Cape Disappointment in Astoria, Oregon. It may have been filmed to coincide with the release of *The Boatniks*. Can you give me any more information, and is it available for purchase? Marian, San Pedro, CA

A —Perhaps you are thinking of *Cruise of the Eagle*. Here is the entry from my *Disney A to Z* encyclopedia: "People and Places featurette; released on March 19, 1959 . . . The varied and important services of the U.S. Coast Guard are glimpsed. They warn ships of dangerous shoals, keep sea lanes open with icebreakers, face gale and hurricane to accurately forecast the weather in remote areas of the Atlantic and Pacific, and perform rescue services to ships and downed aircraft. We are also told of a training program of men of the Coast Guard and their many hardships. Filmed in CinemaScope. 18 min." The film is not available for purchase.

Q I remember seeing a movie that had to do with deaf children. It was about a teacher coming to the deaf school and helping one of the students learn to speak. What is the name of the movie, and who were the main characters? Jaimie, Santa Fe Springs, CA

A

—You are remembering *Amy* (1981), which starred Jenny Agutter, Barry Newman, Kathleen Nolan, and Nanette Fabray. Agutter played a young mother who had recently lost her deaf son and goes to work at a school attempting to teach deaf kids to speak in an era when sign language was considered the only feasible means of communication. The roles of the deaf children were played by students from the California School for the Deaf.

Q

I can't seem to find any information about a Disney movie called *Mr. Hobbs Takes a Vacation*, with Fred MacMurray and Jane Wyman. Was it a Disney movie? Marie, Branchville, NJ

A

—*Mr. Hobbs Takes a Vacation* was a 1962 movie from Twentieth Century Fox starring Jimmy Stewart and Maureen O'Hara. You are probably thinking of another 1962 film, *Bon Voyage*, which was indeed from Disney and starred MacMurray and Wyman.

Q

I have long been a fan of *Swiss Family Robinson*. Where was the movie filmed? Andrea, Spokane, WA

A

—*Swiss Family Robinson* was filmed on the island of Tobago in the Caribbean.

Q

I once saw a show about the legend of an Indian boy who was trying to demonstrate his bravery by attempting to get an eagle's feather. As legend goes, the boy was falling, and he turned into an eagle. What was the name of this story, and will this ever be shown again on TV or be available to purchase? James, Tyler, TX

A

—The film, titled *The Legend of the Boy and the Eagle*, was originally released as a featurette in movie theaters in 1967, then shown on TV in 1968. It was rerun a number of times and released on video in 1986, but it has not been available for many years.

Q **Was Patrick Dempsey's secretary in the movie *Enchanted* played by the actress who supplied the voice of Ariel in *The Little Mermaid*? Anonymous, Wilmington, NC**

A —Yes, that was the same person—Jodi Benson. Paige O'Hara, voice of Belle, and Judy Kuhn, singing voice of Pocahontas, also had cameo roles in the movie.

Q **Were the sixties family comedies, like *The Shaggy Dog* and *That Darn Cat!*, mostly filmed on the Disney lot? Gina, Bingham, MA**

A —By the end of the 1950s, we had four soundstages at the Disney Studios, two of them among the largest in Hollywood. We also had a number of back lot sets, so, yes, most of our films at that time were indeed filmed at the Studio.

Q **Do any of the Disney family members have cameos in Disney films? Linda, Missoula, MT**

A —Actually, there are a few. Sharon Disney, Walt's daughter, appears briefly in *Johnny Tremain*; she and her sister, Diane, appear on television in *One Hour in Wonderland*; and Diane's son Walter appears as a baby in *Son of Flubber* (in a TV commercial).

Q **Did Disney ever collaborate with other movie studios? Sheila, Ann Arbor, MI**

A —Back in the 1930s, Disney made cartoon inserts for a couple of Fox and MGM movies, but actual coproductions of movies did not come until the 1980s, when Disney partnered with Paramount on *Popeye* and *Dragonslayer*. Buena Vista Distribution Co. has occasionally distributed films made by other companies.

Q **Where were the outdoor portions of 20,000 *Leagues Under the Sea* filmed? Some of the locations are beautiful, such as the cannibal island. Madison, Tampa, FL**

A —The tropical scenes in 20,000 *Leagues Under the Sea* were filmed at various locales in the Bahamas and Jamaica.

Q **Where is the bed knob from *Bedknobs and Broomsticks* now? Betty, Roanoke, VA**

A —That magic bed knob resides in the Walt Disney Archives—we have it in a display case in our reading room. The prop was created so that it would glow when a light was shown through it from below. We also have on display a couple of prop books from the film—the Isle of Naboombu book and the two parts of the ancient book from which the spells originated. In our warehouse, we have Professor Emelius Brown's suitcase of trinkets and Eglantine's flying broom, in the original packaging in which it arrived in the mail.

Q **Where was *The Haunted Mansion* movie with Eddie Murphy filmed? Sandee, Concord, NH**

A —The exterior of the mansion was built at the Sable Ranch in Canyon Country, California, with the interiors created at Barwick Studios in Glendale, California. Scenes of the drive to the mansion were filmed in Savannah, Georgia.

Q **Has Disney ever made a foreign-language film? Talia, Philadelphia, PA**

A —While we have dubbed or subtitled most of our theatrical films for release abroad, I can think of only one early occasion where we made concurrent versions in Spanish and English, and that was *The Littlest Outlaw* in 1955. For that film, we purposely hired bilingual actors. In recent years, Disney has cooperated in making foreign-language films primarily for audiences in China, India, and Russia.

Q **What is the full name of the bank in *Mary Poppins*? The song is a bit jumbled with the names. Also, was a replica of the St. Paul's snow globe ever created? Edye, Lexington, KY**

A —According to the song in *Mary Poppins*, the bank is the Dawes, Tomes, Mousley, Grubbs Fidelity Fiduciary Bank. Yes, there was a replica of the St. Paul snow globe done for the Disney Catalog—it was based on photos taken of the original globe in the Archives.

Q **I saw a movie as a child that I believe was a Disney movie. The story line was about some children and their quest to save some miniature ponies from working in a coal mine. Am I right? Laurie, Hazel Green, AL**

A —The movie, *The Littlest Horse Thieves* (1977), is about the "pit ponies" that worked in the coal mines of Yorkshire, England.

Q **Where is the "yellow house" from the Disney film *Summer Magic*? Was it a real house, or a set? I am trying to draw it, because I want to build my new house as close to it as possible! Linda, Accident, MD**

A —The house was just a set, built on the back lot at the Disney Studios in Burbank, Callifornia, but it no longer exists. Interiors were filmed on a soundstage.

Q **I seem to remember additional scenes in the original *Parent Trap* movie with Hayley Mills that do not appear on the video**

or on TV. Were there some additional scenes that were cut (and lost)? Susan, Lancaster, NY

A —When *The Parent Trap* was shown on TV, additional footage was needed to fill out the time slot, so some filmed but unused scenes (originally "left on the cutting room floor") were added back into the movie. You may be recalling these scenes.

Q I saw a movie as a child—I know it was a Disney movie—called *Tonka*. I remember the main character, Sal Mineo, and Tonka was his horse. With such vivid memories of this movie, I couldn't be making it up . . . am I crazy? No one can seem to find it, and I saw it three times, so I loved it, obviously. Lois, Woodbury Heights, NJ

A —*Tonka* came out in 1958. It was released on video briefly in the 1980s, but is not currently available. Perhaps you can find a used copy somewhere.

Q The bonus features on the DVD of *Swiss Family Robinson* include clips of other Disney films produced during the same era that this film was made. One of the films was simply titled *Japan* and showed fishermen in Japan. Can you tell me what this film's about and if it's available on DVD? Keith, Hamburg, NJ

A —*Japan* was one of the last of seventeen People and Places travelogues Disney produced for movie theaters. Filmed in CinemaScope, it ran twenty-eight minutes and was released on April 6, 1960. The film, now dated, showed colorful Japanese customs and manners of the past, contrasting them with what was then present-day Japan. It is not currently available.

Q I'm a huge fan of Disney's *Return to Oz* film. I saw the Tik-Tok and Tin Man characters from the feature film in a *102 Dalmatians* behind-the-scenes attraction at Disney-MGM Studios in Walt

Disney World. Are these characters still being preserved by your Studio? Will these characters be making an appearance any time in the future? Scott, Chicago, IL

A —Yes, we are very proud to have a comprehensive representation of artifacts from *Return to Oz*, including Dorothy's costume, complete with her ruby slippers, and her lunch pails. We also have the Tin Woodsman, Jack Pumpkinhead, and even the Gnome King's ruby slippers. Tik-Tok was on display for many years at Disney's Hollywood Studios; Disney archivist Rob Klein is currently restoring him, as there are plans to use him in an upcoming Archives exhibit.

Q **Where was *Bedknobs and Broomsticks* filmed? Travis, New York, NY**

A —It was filmed on soundstages and on the back lot at the Walt Disney Studios in Burbank, California. It was shortly after I came to Disney, and I was lucky enough to be able to watch some of the filming on my lunch hours. The Portobello Road set was especially intriguing—I had fun "shopping" in all of the antique stalls. The battle scene with the armor from the museum was also amazing to watch.

Q **In *Pollyanna*, what building was used for the exterior and interior filming of Aunt Polly's house? M.S., Lancaster, CA**

A —The exteriors were filmed on location in Santa Rosa, California, at what was then the residence of a Mrs. Juilliard McDonald. The chosen house, known as Mableton, occupied a full block in the center of town and was surrounded by spacious lawns and gardens. It was built in 1877 as a replica of an old Natchez, Mississippi, antebellum house. Mableton still stands as a town landmark in Santa Rosa, though it had to be extensively rebuilt after a disastrous fire in 1977. The home of Mr. Pendergast was filmed some forty miles away in the Napa Valley. All of *Pollyanna*'s interiors were filmed at the Disney Studios in Burbank, California.

Q

A friend in England mentioned a Disney film to me called *Hill's Angels*, but I recognized it as one released over here under the title *The North Avenue Irregulars*. What's the reason for the different titles? J.K., Tampa, FL

A

—Sometimes marketing people abroad feel a different title would be stronger in their territory, so the title is changed. Besides the example you cited, I can list a few others—*Unidentified Flying Oddball* became *The Spaceman and King Arthur*; *The Littlest Horse Thieves* became *Escape From the Dark*; *Almost Angels* became *Born to Sing*.

Q

Can you tell me anything about a metal disc I found labeled "Sons of Liberty" and "Priscilla Lapham"? Since my great-grandmother was a Lapham, I wonder if this girl might be an ancestor of mine. M.R., Spartanburg, S.C.

A

—The medal you have is a "Secret Medal" that was issued as a promotion for our 1957 film *Johnny Tremain*. There were six different medals released by Armour Star Franks, one in each package, each one depicting a character or an event from the film. Priscilla Lapham was the character portrayed by Luana Patten in the film, which was adapted from Esther Forbes's novel.

Q

In the movie *Summer Magic*, the brother, Peter, is played by Jimmy Mathers. Is he any relation to Jerry Mathers of *Leave It to Beaver*? S.W., Battle Creek, MI

A

—Jimmy Mathers was Jerry Mathers's younger brother. He appeared in a 1961–62 CBS situation comedy called *Ichabod and Me*.

Q **Where was *Condorman* filmed, and how did they make Michael Crawford (the original Phantom in the smash musical *Phantom of the Opera*) fly? I am a big Michael Crawford fan. J.O., New Orleans, LA**

A —*Condorman* was filmed at Pinewood Studios in England, as well as on location in France, Monaco, and Switzerland. Colin Chilvers was in charge of special effects, but he will not divulge his secrets.

Q **I loved *Who Framed Roger Rabbit*. Weren't the man who did Roger's voice and Christopher Lloyd on a TV series together in the 1970s? What other movies has Bob Hoskins done? R.H., Oklahoma City, OK**

A —You have a good memory. Charles Fleischer, Roger Rabbit's alter ego, was on *Welcome Back, Kotter* during the 1978-79 season, playing the role of Carvelli, and on a brief summer series in 1975 called *Keep on Truckin'*. Christopher Lloyd was on *Taxi* as Reverend Jim from 1979 to 1983. Bob Hoskins has been in many movies, including *Zulu Dream*, *The Cotton Club*, *Brazil*, *Sweet Liberty*, *Super Mario Bros.*, and *Mona Lisa*.

Q **Where did Walt Disney get the two locomotives used in *The Great Locomotive Chase*? H.H., Altadena, CA**

A —While the two original locomotives, the *Texas* and the *General*, were still in existence, they were museum objects and not available for filming. To double for the *General*, Walt borrowed the *William Mason* from the Baltimore and Ohio Railroad, and for the *Texas*, he was loaned the *Inyo* by Paramount Pictures.

Q **How many True-Life Adventures did Walt Disney make? Who was the narrator for the series? J.P., Red Lion, PA**

A —There were thirteen True-Life Adventures in the award-winning nature series released between 1948 and 1960. Seven of the films were featurettes and six were full-length features. Eight of these films won Oscars for Best Documentary. The narrator, veteran Disney writer Winston Hibler, later became a Disney producer. He passed away in 1976.

Q **Didn't Kurt Russell have a brother who acted in several Disney films? J.K., Springfield, IL**

A —I think you must be referring to Bryan Russell, who was not related to Kurt. Bryan was featured in *Babes in Toyland*, *Emil and the Detectives*, *The Adventures of Bullwhip Griffin*, and, on television, in *Gallegher* and *Kilroy*.

Q **Where did Disney film the firehouse that was used in *Herbie Rides Again*? K.H., Louisville, KY**

A —The firehouse featured in *Herbie Rides Again* was built on the back lot of the Disney Studios in Burbank, California. Movie magic did all the rest: the street scenes of San Francisco were matted in around the firehouse.

Q **As Maine residents, we have searched for the lighthouse used in the movie *Pete's Dragon* but have had no luck finding it. Could you tell us where it is? D.H., Bucks Harbor, ME**

A —You will search in vain for the Passamaquoddy lighthouse in Maine. Even though *Pete's Dragon* was set in Maine, it was filmed in California. The lighthouse was built specifically for the film on a point above Morro Bay. In fact, the lighthouse worked so well, the film crew had to get special permission from the Coast Guard to operate it. The town of Passamaquoddy was constructed on the back lot of the Disney Studios.

Q *Summer Magic* is a favorite of mine. I consider it a musical, but don't often see it on a list of Disney musicals. What Disney films do you consider musicals? K.W., Silver Lake, OH

A —Of the early Disney films, I would list *Summer Magic* as a musical. Besides the animated classics, many of which could be called musicals, I would include in such a list *Song of the South, So Dear to My Heart, Babes in Toyland, Mary Poppins, The Happiest Millionaire, The One and Only, Genuine, Original Family Band, Bedknobs and Broomsticks*, and *Pete's Dragon*. However, music was always important in Disney productions, and many films featured from one to several Disney songs.

Q How did Walt Disney choose Julie Andrews to star in *Mary Poppins*? R.F., Wilmington, NC

A —Walt had heard of Julie's success on Broadway in *Camelot*. When Walt saw the show, he was taken by her performance and realized she was the one to portray the flying nanny.

Q I have noticed the name Cotton Warburton, listed as a film editor, on the credits of many Disney movies. Is this the same Cotton Warburton who was a famous football player? J.M., Santa Ana, CA

A —Warburton, a film editor at The Walt Disney Studios for twenty-two years (after spending nineteen years with MGM), was indeed the well-known football star. He went to the University of Southern California in 1931. During his years there Warburton became an all-American quarterback. He led the USC Trojans during a twenty-seven-game winning streak, which remained a school record until 1980. Besides his many football awards, Warburton also won an Academy Award for his editing of *Mary Poppins*.

Q Who composed the music for the Disney film *Night Crossing*? I loved it. G.L., Hays, KS

A —The composer was Jerry Goldsmith, who won an Academy Award in 1978 for his musical score for *The Omen*. The sound track for *Night Crossing*, featuring the National Philharmonic Orchestra, conducted by Goldsmith, was released by Intrada on vinyl and CD.

Q In the film *The Biscuit Eater*, what kind of dog was Moreover? D.F., Eleele, HI

A —Moreover was a rare breed, a German wirehaired pointer. His real name was Rolph Von Wolfgang, and he was discovered playing with his master, who was working as a tree trimmer at Disney's Golden Oak Ranch, the last big movie ranch in California. Scenes from the movie were filmed at the ranch.

Q At the beginning of *Pete's Dragon*, the brothers fall in a mudhole, and one gets mud in his mouth. Do moviemakers use real mud, or pudding? S.W., Tega Cay, SC

A —When we use mud in a movie, we make it out of fuller's earth mixed with water and vermiculite. This mixture works better than ordinary mud because it's lighter, is easier to clean off, and photographs better. It also stays as mud for days, so the filmmakers don't have to keep making new batches of mud each day they're shooting. It's no taste treat—mud of any sort doesn't taste good—but it's not harmful.

Q Could you list the movies for which Disney won Academy Awards for special effects? I.S., Evansville, IN

A —Oscars for best special effects (and in the later visual effects category) went to Disney's *20,000 Leagues Under the Sea*, *Mary*

Poppins, Bedknobs and Broomsticks, Who Framed Roger Rabbit, and *Pirates of the Caribbean: Dead Man's Chest.*

Q **Where was *Mary Poppins* filmed? J.D., Mount Vernon, IA**

A —*Mary Poppins,* even though set in London, was filmed on soundstages at the Disney Studios in Burbank, California. In order to control the elements, even the outdoor street scenes were constructed on soundstages.

Q **After enjoying *Follow Me, Boys,* I wondered if Scoutmaster Lem Siddons had been a real person. W.D., Columbus, GA**

A —No. Siddons was a fictional character created by MacKinlay Kantor for his award-winning novel *God and My Country,* on which our film was based.

Q **Even though most of the Disney feature films were in color, weren't there a few that were in black and white? H.B., Amarillo, TX**

A —Yes, but so few you can count them on one hand: *The Shaggy Dog, The Absent-Minded Professor, Son of Flubber,* and *The Sign of Zorro.*

PUBLICATIONS

Q I have several books published by Disney Press. When did the Disney Press imprint begin publishing books? Robert, Wilmington, NC

A —Disney Press published its first title, *101 Dalmatians: A Counting Book*, on May 31, 1991. Before that, Disney licensed other publishers, such as Random House, Golden Press, and Grolier, to print their books.

Q When I was a child back in the eighties, my parents gave me an older set of Disney books that I absolutely loved. There were four books in the set; they had dark green covers and each book had a different color binding (red, yellow, blue, or lighter green, I think). One book had nursery rhymes and fairy tales featuring great illustrations of Disney characters, and another had stories like *Pollyanna*, *Old Yeller*, and *Darby O'Gill*, etc. I don't know what these books were called, but I would love to get copies of them. Do you know the titles, when they were printed, and if it is still possible to find these books? I would love to purchase them for my daughter! Elaine, Orlando, FL

A —This was a popular mail-order set called The Wonderful Worlds of Walt Disney, published by Golden Press in 1965, with four books titled *America*, *Fantasyland*, *Worlds of Nature*, and *Stories from Other Lands*. More than a million of the sets were sold. Copies can be found through used-book dealers or on eBay.

Q Does Disney still publish the magazine *Vacationland*? If it doesn't, when was the last issue? Kathy, El Cajon, CA

A —*Vacationland* was a marketing magazine that was published in both Disneyland (1957–1984) and Walt Disney World (1971–1977) editions. It was distributed free in local hotels and motels, but is no longer being published.

Q Many years ago I purchased a book on *Snow White and the Seven Dwarfs*. It was published through Circle Galleries. I bought it because that was always my favorite Disney movie. My grandson asked about it, and I do not really know much of its background or history. Can you help me? Sam, Pasadena, CA

A —Circle Fine Arts Press published the limited-edition Snow White book, bound in white leather and sold in a red cloth slipcase with gilt lettering, in 1978, in a print run of 9,500. It included four serigraphs. A trade edition, without the serigraphs, was published in 1979 by Viking Press.

Q One of my all-time favorite Little Golden Books is *Mickey Mouse Goes Christmas Shopping*. Mine has a copyright of 1953 and a price of 29 cents. Something about the artwork in this book seems different from most Disney art, but I just can't put my finger on what it is. Can you tell me if this story was ever a short film, or was it produced only in book form? Tina, Tulsa, OK

A —The illustrations in that Little Golden Book were done by Bob Moore and X Atencio. Although both worked for Disney, they were hired as freelance artists by Golden Press to illustrate this book. It is not based on any cartoon. Moore was more of a marketing and publicity artist (movie posters, Christmas cards, etc.). Atencio is known for some stop-motion animation in the 1950s and for his later work as an Imagineer.

Q How many issues of the old *Walt Disney's Mickey Mouse Club Magazine* were printed? Bob, North Wales, PA

A —The *Mickey Mouse Club Magazine* (later called *Walt Disney's Magazine*) was available by subscription from 1956 to 1959; originally, it was $1 for four issues and later $2.50 for six issues. There were twenty-two issues in all.

Q I just received several copies of *Disneyland Magazine*, all from the early 1970s. Each cover depicts a different Disney movie scene, and inside are comic book stories involving Disney characters. Can you tell me more about this publication? Geri, Dallas, TX

A —*Disneyland Magazine* originated in England. It was so popular that Disney licensed the American company Fawcett Publications to publish a weekly edition in the States. The periodical began in February 1972 and ran until July 1974.

Q I have a copy of an old book about the Haunted Mansion called *Magic from the Haunted Mansion in Disneyland*. Is this a collectible item? Justin, Deep Springs, CA

A —*Magic from the Haunted Mansion in Disneyland* was published in 1970 and sold only at Disneyland. It was one of the few publications, other than guidebooks, created for exclusive sale at the Park. It is not especially valuable but is becoming hard to find.

Q When was the comic book character Gladstone Gander phased out? Jerry, Cambridge, OH

A —Gladstone Gander debuted in 1948 in *Walt Disney Comics and Stories*. He has also appeared on the TV series *Ducktales*. I don't think he's been phased out; he's just never been as popular as some of the other Disney characters.

Q One of the first books I ever read as a child chronicled the cross-country adventures of Mickey, Donald, and their friends. I believe the friends traveled by car and trailer to Yellowstone National Park, the Rocky Mountains, and other such places. Can you tell me the title of this wonderful book? Victor, Wellington, FL

A —This book is a D. C. Heath and Co. reader entitled *Mickey Sees the U.S.A.* There were twelve Disney books in the series, geared to different reading levels; the first volume appeared in 1939.

Q I stumbled upon a great find at a charity book sale: a hardcover book titled *Disney Magic: The Launching of a Dream*, about the cruise ship. How was this book distributed? The opening page says it was for "promotional use only." I've been on her sister ship, the *Disney Wonder*, so imagine my excitement on finding this treasure! Theresa, Marietta, GA

A —This limited-edition book by John Heminway was never actually for sale. It was available on one occasion—the *Disney Magic's* maiden voyage. The *Magic* sailed across the Atlantic Ocean in July 1998 from the Italian shipyard where it was built. The book was presented to passengers and members of the press as a souvenir. I was on that trip and received a copy.

Q I recently obtained a *Disney Magazine* that appears to be several decades old. It was issued in October and was free with a purchase of Mr. Clean or Camay. The issue contains articles on *One Hundred and One Dalmatians*, Debbie Reynolds, and Cinderella's brave mice. I would love to know what year it was printed. Jennifer, Lyons, OR

A —About twenty issues of this particular Disney magazine were published from May 1975 to April 1977. (It has no direct relation to the later *Disney Magazine* from the 1990s and 2000s.) The magazine was produced by Disney in conjunction with Procter & Gamble. Each month a new issue appeared in participating grocery stores, and it was free with the purchase of the designated product for that month—such as Downy, Comet, Camay, and Spic and Span. Your particular issue is from 1976.

Q From approximately 1971 through 1976, my mother bought me copies of *Disneyland Magazine*, published by IPC Magazines in Great Britain. The magazines contained comic strips based on a variety of Disney movies. In addition, children's literature such as *The Water Babies* was serialized. I still have a collection of more than one hundred editions. Are these magazines still being produced in Great Britain? (The other great comic book of my childhood, the German edition of *Micky Maus*, is still produced weekly in Germany.) Sabin, Vancouver, BC, Canada

A —*Disneyland Magazine* was published weekly in the United States by Fawcett beginning in 1972 and ending in 1974. The Walt Disney Archives has copies of the British version of the magazine from 1971 to 1976; we don't know if the magazine was published after that period, but since your set also ends in 1976, it would seem that this was the last year of publication. The *Micky Maus* comic book has been published in Germany since September 1951.

Q My grandmother gave me the *Disney's Wonderful World of Knowledge* encyclopedia from the 1970s. In Volumes 17 and 20 there are references to Rockerduck, the second-richest duck in the world and Scrooge's bitter enemy, but everyone knows that the second-richest duck and Scrooge's rival is Flintheard Glomgold. Also, in Volume 20, it says that Piglet worked with Donald Duck in *The Wise Little Hen*, but I thought it was Peter Pig. Could you clear these two things up? Nate, North Wales, PA

A —Since many writers have written comic stories for Disney, it is possible that someone else could have created a "second-richest duck" to go with Uncle Scrooge. Since the character has been around for sixty years, it's hard for a new writer to research all previous stories. And yes, the pig in *The Wise Little Hen* was named Peter Pig. He was nothing like Piglet in the Pooh films.

Q I picked up some drawings that were in or supposed to be in a World War II Disney production for the boys in the service. It was a small booklet called *Pin-ups for Service Men from Walt Disney*. The artist was Robert "Bob" Grant. A copy of the front pages of the booklet says, "Robert Grant, 1st Motion Picture Unit, Army Air Force, Culver City, Calif." Can you give me any information on Bob Grant? Tom, Centreville, VA

A —The only wartime pinups of which I am aware were ones done by artist Fred Moore on a sheet inserted in *Dispatch from Disney's*, a brochure done in 1943 for the Disney artists who were in the service. Bob Grant was an artist at the Disney Studios from 1935 to 1964, less four years of service during World War II. He worked primarily on comic strips and book illustrations. He passed away in 1968. This booklet of pinups may have been done during the period when he was away from the Disney Studios.

Q What year did Scrooge McDuck first appear in a Disney comic, and what was its title? Ryan, West Hills, CA

A —Uncle Scrooge first appeared in a comic story in a Donald Duck comic book called *Christmas on Bear Mountain* in December 1947.

Q Was there a Goofy comic book? H.P., White Plains, NY

A —Until the 1990s, there was no regular series of Goofy comics, but between 1953 and 1962 there were sixteen "one-shot" Goofy comics. In 1990 and 1991 there was a series of seventeen "Goofy Adventure" comics.

Q When I was a kid (late seventies and early eighties) we had a book with Mickey, and he was on a train that was taking him to Walt Disney World. I have fond yet vague memories of this storybook. I remember that the train looked like the monorail and that they got orange juice. Any idea what this book was? Sarah, Burlington, Ontario, Canada

A —Former Disney artist and book collector Russell Schroeder helped me with this answer: the book is *The Mouseketeers' Train Ride*, a Golden Shape Book published by Golden Press in 1977.

Q I had a wonderful Donald Duck comic in which he traveled through space and went to stars. He was largest on Betelgeuse (I think) and smallest on another star. Imagine my surprise when I found out that both of the stars he visited were real stars. Do you know what the comic issue was, and is it anywhere I can read it again? Erica, Brooklyn, NY

A —That is the lead story in *Walt Disney's Comics and Stories* #199 (April 1957). You might be able to find the comic in a used comic book store or on eBay (there are a number of copies available there as I write this).

Q I have a book that belonged to my father titled *Mickey Mouse in Giantland*, copyright 1934 by Walt Disney Enterprises, Ltd., with story and illustrations by the Staff of Walt Disney Studio. Can you tell me a little bit about this book? Cathy, Fort Myers, FL

A —Though perhaps the story is loosely based on a 1933 Mickey Mouse cartoon titled *Giantland*, it is more or less an original narrative written specifically for the book, which was published by David McKay in Philadelphia. The book is uncommon, so you have a nice item for your Disney collection.

Q When I was a young boy in the 1950s, Disney comic books were among my favorites. There was a particular one which was my all-time favorite in which Mickey Mouse was a detective, and, if I recall correctly, there were clues with a round black spot on them. What can you tell me about this? Story name? Year published? Anything else? Bob, Clermont, FL

A —*Mickey Mouse Outwits the Phantom Blot* was actually the first Mickey Mouse comic book, published in 1941. It is very rare; a recent price guide listed it at $13,000 in very fine condition. There was later, in the 1960s, a series called "The New Adventures of the Phantom Blot."

Q I recently came across the original artwork for a Sunday newspaper comic strip from March 3, 1983 (or so is noted on the art itself): *Walt Disney's Treasury of Classic Tales: Snow White and the Seven Dwarfs*. It is beautifully illustrated and bears the Disney copyright on the art, but neither the artist nor the inker are credited. Can you tell me who the artist was? Matt, Burbank, CA

A —That comic strip was run in newspapers to tie in with a 1983 reissue of the film. It was written by Carl Fallberg and drawn by Richard (Sparky) Moore.

Q As a child, I had a Golden Book story of Mickey and Donald taking a spaceship to the moon. They found they had a stowaway, and it was PegLeg Pete. I haven't heard PegLeg Pete referred to in a generation. Is that children's book still in print? Was it even written by Disney writers? Becky, Lanett, AL

A —That book is long out of print. The title was *Mickey Mouse and His Space Ship*, published as Little Golden Book D29 in 1952; it was reprinted in 1963 as D108. The author was Jane Werner (1915-2004), an employee of Western Publishing and Lithographing, the company that created a lot of the Disney children's books.

Q As a Robin Hood fan, I have heard that there was a Mickey Mouse newspaper comic strip about the famous outlaw. Can you tell me when it appeared? P.L., North Hollywood, CA

A —Besides the 1952 live-action feature *The Story of Robin Hood and His Merrie Men* and the animated feature *Robin Hood* (1973), there was a Robin Hood story that appeared in the Sunday newspaper comic pages beginning April 26, 1936, and running until October 4. Mickey collectors feel this was Mickey's finest Sunday adventure. Called *Mickey Mouse Adventures with Robin Hood*, the strip was later reprinted in *Walt Disney's Comics and Stories* (1941) and in the book *Mickey Mouse in Color* (Pantheon, 1988). In the story, Mickey is accidentally miniaturized (*Honey, I Shrunk the Mouse?*) and he takes refuge in a Robin Hood book, where he joins Robin's band.

Q Why haven't I seen more of Gladstone Gander in comic books or films? D.W., Milwaukee, WI

A —Gladstone was a character in the comic books but never in films. He had such an abrasive personality that the creators of the comic books soon ran out of interesting situations in which to use the character. It is interesting to note that the publisher of one line of Disney comics took the Gladstone name for his company.

Q What was the first Disney book? I remember the Little Golden Books from my childhood and wonder if it could have been one in that series. M.R., Eugene, OR

A —The Disney publications go back much further than the Golden Books. The first one, titled *Mickey Mouse Book*, was published in 1930 by Bibo and Lang in New York. It was a curious piece, containing a story written by the eleven-year-old daughter of the publisher, a game, cartoons, and a song, all in sixteen pages. It was available for about a year, and a total of 97,938 copies were printed in four editions. In 1930, the suggested retail price was 15 cents; a first edition of the book today in fine condition would fetch several thousand dollars.

Q **Which Disney artists originally drew the Mickey Mouse and Donald Duck newspaper comic strips? T.L., Andover, MA**

A —The original artist for the daily Mickey Mouse strip (1930) was Ub Iwerks, who had been the designer of Mickey Mouse for Walt Disney. He drew the strip for a month, followed by Win Smith for three months. When Smith left, Floyd Gottfredson was asked to take over the strip for a few weeks until they could find a replacement. But Gottfredson continued to draw the strip for forty-five years, until the day he retired. The Donald Duck strip (1938) was drawn by Al Taliaferro, who continued until 1969. Over the years these artists were aided by various writers and inkers.

Q **In what cartoon did Daisy's nieces, April, May, and June, first appear? J.K., Riverdale, MD**

A —Daisy's nieces were characters in comic books; they never appeared in a cartoon. Their first appearance was in *Walt Disney's Comic and Stories* #149 (February 1953).

Q **When did Disney begin producing newspaper comic strips? R.S., Youngstown, OH**

A —The first Disney comic strip was the daily Mickey Mouse strip, which debuted on January 13, 1930, distributed by King Features Syndicate.

Q **In how many languages are Disney books and comics published, and which countries have been the most prolific? R.T.J., Greenwich, CT**

A —In the Archives, we have Disney publications in forty-three different languages from fifty-four countries. The largest output has come from France, Italy, and Japan.

Q **When I was a kid back in the 1930s, my friends and I used to collect Big Little Books just as today's kids collect comic books. I still have some of the Disney titles. Were there many? B.E., Dallas, TX**

A —There were several dozen Disney Big Little Books published by Whitman Publishing Company from 1933 to 1950. The later ones were called Better Little Books. The original cost was a dime.

TELEVISION

Q Who wrote "The Ballad of Davy Crockett"? A.B., Franklin, NC

A —*Davy Crockett*, the runaway hit of the first season of *Disneyland* TV shows, was supposed to take up three hour-long segments, but when the film was completed it ran short. One morning Walt visited the office of a new studio composer, George Bruns, and mentioned the problem of bridging the sequences. Half an hour later, Bruns had composed a song that fit lines from Tom Blackburn's script: "Born on a mountaintop in Tennessee . . ." "The Ballad of Davy Crockett" was number one on *Your Hit Parade* for thirteen weeks and sold ten million records.

Q When I saw the "This Day in Disney History" on the D23 Web site for September 13, I was so excited to see a picture of Danny Kaye with Minnie on the Dumbo ride! However, there was no mention of him specifically in the write-up. Can you shed a little light on the Disney-Danny connection? I am a huge fan of both! Janice, Seattle, WA

A —The inimitable Danny Kaye—a favorite of mine, too—was the host of two Disney television specials—*Kraft Salutes Disneyland's 25ᵗʰ Anniversary* in 1980 and *Epcot Center: The Opening Celebration* in 1982.

Q I remember a series on TV called *Scarecrow*. Was this made by Disney, and is it available? Ron, Frederick, MD

A —*Dr. Syn: The Scarecrow of Romney Marsh* was released on DVD in 2008. The two-disc set included both the original three-part television show from 1964 and the feature film that was compiled from those three parts.

Q Does Disney ever plan to release *Tiger Town* on DVD? I loved that movie as a kid in the eighties. Adam, Orange, CA

A —This film, which had only a limited theatrical release in Detroit in 1984, was actually the first television movie produced for Disney Channel. It was released on DVD in 2004.

Q I was recently talking to my mother about my childhood toys, and we came up with Fluppy Dogs. I know it was a cartoon, and there were plush toys. I was hoping you could help me locate the *Fluppy Dogs* movie on either DVD or VHS. I think it was a Disney cartoon. Victoria, Orlando, FL

A —Disney's *Fluppy Dogs* was a television special from 1986 about five colorful, magical talking dogs who entered the life of a ten-year-old boy and his snobbish neighbor. It has never been released on VHS or DVD.

Q I have read that in the 1950s President Eisenhower asked his top military brass to watch the Tomorrowland programs *Man in Space*, *Man and the Moon*, and *Mars and Beyond*. I am wondering whether those programs were ever shown to foreign audiences as a way of promoting the U.S. space program, perhaps through the auspices of the United States Information Agency. I am a master of public diplomacy student at the University of Southern California and would really appreciate the information for a paper. Jerry, Los Angeles, CA

A —According to Ward Kimball, who directed *Man in Space*, "Eisenhower borrowed the show to run for the brass in the Pentagon. He called Walt personally to borrow it." Whether it actually led the president to decide to enter the space race, we do not know. After its TV showing in 1955, the film was later shown in theaters at home and abroad and on television in countries that aired the Disney show. The space films were released on DVD on the *Walt Disney Treasures: Tomorrowland* set.

Q I am too young (I'm in my early thirties) to have seen *The Wonderful World of Disney* TV show. I do remember seeing VHS copies growing up. My favorites were *The Plausible Impossible*, *The Ranger of Yellowstone*, and *Man in Motion* (at least I think that was the title). I loved these shows and would love to show these to my son as he grows up. Are there any plans to bring these out on DVD? Jennifer, Fawn Grove, PA

A —Of the titles you mentioned, only *The Plausible Impossible* has been released on DVD, in 2002, on the Walt Disney Treasures set *Behind the Scenes at The Walt Disney Studio*.

Q What happened to the movie *Run Appaloosa Run* that was shown on *The Wonderful World of Disney* in the late sixties and early seventies? If it is still out there, where can I find it on DVD? If not, why haven't they released it from the vault? Dava, Farson, WY

A —It has never been released on DVD, but it did come out on a *Wonderful World of Disney* VHS in 1986 and 1995. Perhaps you can find a copy on eBay (there are several copies offered there as I write this).

Q I love the old Disney TV show *The Scarecrow of Romney Marsh*. Did Patrick McGoohan actually wear the Scarecrow's costume? Did he provide the Scarecrow's voice? Tammy, Brandon, FL

A —That was all Patrick McGoohan. Makeup expert Harry Frampton created the look of the Scarecrow by stitching and painting an ordinary dishcloth to fashion an eerie mask. To complete the costume, a board was strapped to McGoohan's shoulders, and he wore a tattered coat and shapeless hat. McGoohan came up with a raspy, deep-throated voice and maniacal laugh—quite different from the voice he used as the vicar in the film.

Q Is it possible to view or purchase *Walt Disney's Wonderful World of Color* TV episodes from the late 1960s? My wife and mother-in-law were in the episode *Brimstone, the Amish Horse*. My wife, then an infant, and my mother-in-law were in a few scenes. They were part of the Amish faith, so little to no photos of the family are available. Any help or suggestions would be greatly appreciated. Joseph, Lancaster, PA

A —*Brimstone, the Amish Horse* was a television program airing in October 1968. It has never been released on VHS or DVD, so it is currently unavailable. If you write the Walt Disney Archives at the Disney Studios in Burbank, perhaps they can check to see if there are any still photos of your wife and mother-in-law.

Q I would really like to see the old two-part Moochie films that were shown long ago on *Walt Disney Presents*. What were their exact titles? Are they available on video? Paul, Batavia, NY

A —*Moochie of the Little League* aired on October 2 and 9, 1959. (It also had a 16 mm release for rental to schools and community organizations as *Little League Moochie*.) *Moochie of Pop Warner Football* aired on November 20 and 27, 1960. Neither film has ever been released on videocassette or DVD.

Q I'm curious about John Lovelady, who created the puppets and performed the role of Dormouse on Disney Channel's *Disney's Adventures in Wonderland*. He was also involved in the creation and performance of several Muppets. Did Lovelady work on any of the full-size puppets on the Disney Channel shows *Welcome to Pooh Corner* and *Dumbo's Circus*? Crain, Holbrook, NY

A —We find no Disney credits for John Lovelady other than his work on the Emmy-winning *Disney's Adventures in Wonderland*

in the early nineties. As you noted, he had earlier worked on *The Muppet Show* for Jim Henson, performing the characters of both Crazy Harry and Nigel.

Q There's an eighties Disney movie called *Sultan and the Rock Star* that I've been wondering about. Was it made for TV? Can you tell me any other trivia about this film? Tammy, Bangor, ME

A —*Sultan and the Rock Star* was made for *Disney's Wonderful World*, airing first in April 1980. Besides Sultan, a large Bengal tiger, the film starred a young Timothy Hutton. During production, Hutton spent two weeks at Disney's Golden Oak Ranch just learning to act around Sultan; for the first few days he was reportedly scared out of his wits.

Q What is the music at the beginning of *Disneyland After Dark*? It reminds me of the music played on the monorail. Louise, Easthampton, MA

A —You may be thinking of a piece called "Monorail" by Buddy Baker, who wrote numerous background scores for films and TV shows, as well as music for the Disney Parks. He cowrote "Grim Grinning Ghosts" with Imagineer X Atencio for the Haunted Mansion.

Q I recall a show from my childhood that featured Jim Henson's Muppets going to Walt Disney World. I can't remember if it was an actual movie or a special on *The Wonderful World of Disney*. Is it available to own? Cody, Salinas, CA

A —*The Muppets at Walt Disney World*, directed by Peter Harris, was a television show that aired in 1990. In it, Kermit and his friends go to Paradise Swamp in Florida and then decide to visit nearby Walt Disney World, where Mickey Mouse welcomes Kermit as an old friend. Unfortunately, the show has not been made available on video.

Q   **I have a vague memory of a Disney film I saw as a child on Disney Channel about the young Harry Houdini. Does this ring a bell? Alfonso, Fullerton, CA**

A   —Disney made a two-hour television show that aired in March 1987 called *Young Harry Houdini*. It starred Wil Wheaton as the young magician and escape artist, who runs away from home to join a traveling carnival.

Q   **We have been huge fans of Disney Channel since the beginning. Early on there was a "mommy and me" type of show. What was it called? Sarah and Jim, Sarasota, FL**

A   —The show was called *You and Me, Kid*. It first aired on Disney Channel on April 18, 1983.

Q   **I recall a Disney program called *The Mouse Factory*. The show was a thirty-minute compilation of various cartoon segments, and each episode had a guest host. Would you please tell me more about it? Mike, Lombard, IL**

A   —*The Mouse Factory*, produced and directed by animator Ward Kimball, aired for two seasons beginning January 26, 1972, with a total of forty-three shows. Guest hosts, such as Bill Dana, Wally Cox, Don Knotts, John Astin, and Kurt Russell, introduced classic animated clips that followed a different theme each show. The program was syndicated on different stations around the country and aired at different times of the day.

Q   **In the Disney Trivia board games, Gosalyn is said to be Drake's (Darkwing Duck's) niece. But the television show and comics**

called her his adopted daughter. Did he adopt his niece, or are the games wrong? Stephanie, Long Beach, CA

A —According to the television show's producer, Tad Stones, Gosalyn is Drake's adopted daughter. So if a game says she is his niece, it is incorrect.

Q I have a picture of Mickey holding on to a rocket from a Disney Days tear-off calendar. I don't remember when it appeared, but I'd guess 1997 or 1998. Do you know anything about this image? Debbie, Huntington Beach, CA

A —The illustration was created for an invitation to a Disney Channel launch party in 1983.

Q At Disneyland in the mid- to late 1950s, I purchased a celluloid image of a lion. On the back it states, "This is an original celluloid drawing actually used in a Walt Disney Production." The return address section of the envelope reads, "A souvenir from Disneyland." We are interested in knowing what lion this is. Mr. and Mrs. A.K., St. Augustine, FL

A —Your cel was used for *The Great Cat Family*, a 1956 Disney television show that told the history of cats, illustrated with Disney film clips. Some animation, including your lion, was created just for the television show.

Q Do you remember an old Disney show about a character named Dick Turpin? Debbie, Bear, DE

A —Yes. The two-part TV show *The Legend of Young Dick Turpin* first aired in February 1966. Turpin was a legendary eighteenth-century English highwayman, portrayed in the film by David Weston.

Q In what movie or short did Jiminy Cricket teach us how to spell "encyclopedia"? Kathy, Wheeling, IL

A —Jiminy Cricket's *Encyclopedia* was a separate little cartoon that appeared a number of times on the *Mickey Mouse Club* television show beginning in 1956.

Q About twenty years ago on Israeli television, there was a great Disney animated series called *The Wuzzles*. Not more than ten episodes were broadcast. Were more episodes made? Does *The Wuzzles* still get shown in the U.S.? Were collectibles made of the characters? Hila, Safed, Israel

A —The main characters' names are Eleroo, Bumblelion, Hoppopotamus, Rhinokey, Moosel, and Butterbear. Only thirteen episodes were aired in the United States. *Disney's Wuzzles* aired on CBS in the 1985–86 season and on ABC during the 1986–87 season. There was some merchandise available at that time.

Q I was a big Zorro fan in the 1950s. One day my mother saw an ad in the newspaper that gave a phone number to call to "speak to Zorro." She called while I waited nervously at the kitchen table. She finally got through, handed me the phone, and I heard Zorro saying, "Hello . . . hello . . . this is Zorro . . . is anyone there?" I couldn't speak. My seven-year-old tongue was tied in a knot. I ran to my room and shut the door. It really sounded like Zorro to me. Was that Guy Williams, or one of many people acting the part at a battery of phones? And if this gets published, I have a message for Zorro: "Hello, my name is Keith." Keith, Brooklyn, NY

A —While I have not heard of this specific promotion, it is doubtful that Guy Williams would have handled the obviously vast number of telephone calls personally.

Q I remember a show called *The Whiz Kids* that aired on Sunday's *The Wonderful World of Disney*. I believe it was about a few kids who invented things. Can you tell me a little about it? Thomas, Thousand Oaks, CA

A —Disney had a pair of two-part TV shows, *The Whiz Kid and the Mystery at Riverton* (1974) and *The Whiz Kid and the Carnival Caper* (1976). The kids who starred in the show were Eric Shea, Clay O'Brien, and Kim Richards. Some readers may also remember a non-Disney CBS series in the 1983–84 season called *Whiz Kids*, about a group of computer experts. The kids in that show were Matthew Laborteaux, Todd Porter, Jeffrey Jacquet, and Andrea Ellison.

Q At what riding school was 1963's *The Horsemasters* filmed? Also, what were the real names of the horses in the film? Tricia, Cheshire, CT

A —The exteriors of the jumping field and quarry were filmed at Smallbrook Farm, a riding school in Thursley, Surrey, England. Other fields nearby were also used. Longcross House near Chertsey, Surrey, doubled as the exterior for Valleywood House, the riding school in the film, and interiors were shot at Shepperton Studios in Middlesex. Ten horses were named in the production files, though their riders are not designated: Shadow, Little Richard, Forrester, Pennant, Nutmeg, Copper, Cotton Socks, Corney, Claddagh Boy, and Blue Trout.

Q Like most children, I grew up with Walt Disney productions. One of my favorites was the *Zorro* television series. All my life I wanted to have a sword like Zorro's. If it isn't possible for me to buy one of the swords used in the series, can you tell me where the ones used in the series were purchased? Crawford, Waco, TX

A —Sorry, but we have only one Zorro sword in the Archives, and it is not for sale. It is probable that many of the swords used in the production of the series were rented from Hollywood prop houses. Most of the costumes used in early Disney films were rented from such companies as the Western Costume Company.

Q I remember a movie I particularly liked on *The Wonderful World of Disney* that I believe was called *Mr. Boogedy*. If my memory serves me correctly, the movie was about a family who had a ghost problem. Is the movie in the Disney Archives somewhere? Nicole, Doylestown, OH

A —The film *Mr. Boogedy*, which starred Richard Masur and John Astin, was a two-hour television movie that first aired on April 20, 1986. It was followed by a sequel, *Bride of Boogedy*, in 1987. Both films have aired on Disney Channel but have not been released on video or DVD. They are preserved in the Disney film vaults.

Q Years ago, I believe on *The Wonderful World of Disney*, there was a story about a badger. Do you know the title? Fred, Brampton, Ontario, Canada

A —You may be recalling *The Boy Who Talked to Badgers*, a two-part show that aired in September 1975. Christian Juttner played a boy who seemed to prefer animals to people and was even able to communicate with them.

Q What was the Disney movie in which Kurt Russell starred as a young rebel soldier during the Civil War? S.C., San Marcos, CA

A —The film was the three-part television miniseries *Willie and the Yank* (1967). The European theatrical version of it was called *Mosby's Marauders*. When he was in production on this film,

Walt Disney was given an autograph of John S. Mosby, who was a real Civil War cavalry hero, and he had it displayed in his office.

Q **As a young boy in the 1950s, I watched the *Mickey Mouse Club* and particularly enjoyed the adventure serials such as *The Hardy Boys* and *The Adventures of Spin and Marty*. Weren't there some others, like *The Swamp Fox*, *Texas John Slaughter*, and *Elfego Baca*? Who starred in these, and when were they aired? Bruce, Roseville, CA**

A —*The Hardy Boys* and *Spin and Marty* were serials that aired on the *Mickey Mouse Club,* but the other titles you mentioned were miniseries on the TV show *Walt Disney Presents. The Swamp Fox* (eight episodes, aired 1959–61) starred Leslie Nielsen; *Texas John Slaughter* (seventeen episodes, 1958–61) starred Tom Tryon; and *Elfego Baca* (ten episodes, 1958–60) starred Robert Loggia.

Q **Why did Walt call his TV show *Walt Disney's Wonderful World of Color*? Was it to do with color TV becoming more popular, or was it because the show was focused on colorful stories? Austin, Amarillo, TX**

A —Walt moved his TV show, originally on ABC, to NBC primarily because NBC was more proactive in pioneering shows in color, and Walt felt color would really enhance his product. With foresight, he had made almost all of his shows in color, even though they were being shown only in black and white on ABC. Thus, he was able to repeat some of the more popular ones, such as the *Davy Crockett* miniseries, after the show moved to NBC. The show had the *Wonderful World of Color* title only from 1961 to 1969, even though the series was on TV a total of twenty-nine seasons. During this period the popularity of the show helped NBC's parent, RCA, sell a lot of color television sets.

Q Was Annette Funicello one of the first Mouseketeers? And who wrote the song that goes "M-I-C-K-E-Y"? Hank, Taos, NM

A —Annette was one of the original twenty-four Mouseketeers; eventually there would be a total of thirty-nine. She remained the entire time. Jimmie Dodd, the club's adult leader, wrote the "Mickey Mouse Club March."

Q I know that *The Wonderful World of Disney* has had many different titles over the years. When did it become *The Wonderful World of Disney*? Marino, Lake Elsinore, CA

A —The show received that title a few years after Walt's death, in September 1969. Previously, it had been known as *Disneyland*, *Walt Disney Presents*, and *Walt Disney's Wonderful World of Color*.

Q There was a Disney movie in the late seventies about the adventures of a spy from America who was visiting a friend in England. I would love to find out the title and see it again. Can you help? Troy, Apple Valley, CA

A —You may be remembering *The Secret of Boyne Castle*, a three-part television show from 1969 starring Glenn Corbett and Kurt Russell. The plot concerns an American agent trying to meet a defecting scientist in Ireland, with the Russians trying to prevent the meeting. It was repeated in 1978 under the title *The Spybusters*. The film is not currently available.

Q When I was younger, I remember watching a Winnie the Pooh show. It started with the story of the Hundred Acre Wood and an old book opening up. It wasn't a cartoon; the characters were in costume. What was the name of this show? Ana, Oceanside, CA

A —You are probably thinking of *Welcome to Pooh Corner*, with performers in the costumes and masks of the Pooh characters performing in storybook settings. The process was called "advanced puppetronics." The show debuted on Disney Channel on April 18, 1983.

Q **When I was very young in the early 1970s, I used to love to sit and watch *The Wonderful World of Disney* with my dad and my younger brother on Sunday night. There was a movie that I loved and have never seen again. I do not know the title, but it involved a large, mysterious creature in a swamp. It turned out that the creature was really hollow. It was created and run by a person inside. Would you know the title? Is it available anywhere? Lisa, Waddington, NY**

A – You are thinking of *The Strange Monster of Strawberry Cove* (1971). It starred Burgess Meredith and Agnes Moorehead. It has never been released on VHS or DVD.

Q **I remember seeing a short film (I remember the name *The Collector*) back in the 1970s about a collector of Mickey Mouse figures (and possibly other character collectibles) that was filmed in stop-action and featured hypnotic patterns of movement set to a catchy melody by all of the Mickey Mouse figures throughout a man's house. I have had no luck in finding either the film or any reference to it. Does it exist? Is it possible to get a copy of it for home viewing? George, Arlington, VA**

A —*The Collector* was a stop-motion film using Mickey Mouse collectibles (some borrowed from the Walt Disney Archives) made by filmmaker Mike Jittlov for the *Mickey's 50* television show. Jittlov later appeared in the television show *Major Effects* (1979) with two more of his stop-motion films. You may be able to find the film on YouTube.

Q As a child twenty or so years ago, I used to watch Disney Channel all day. I remember a show whose main characters were a short Viking and his less-than-intelligent larger and heavier sidekick. I loved that show but can't remember the name of it. I've searched endlessly on the Internet with no luck. Can you help? Paul, Columbus, OH

A —That was *Asterix*, non Disney animation that aired on Disney Channel in the 1980s and 1990s. Asterix is a very popular cartoon character in Europe; his sidekick is Obelix.

Q I really love *The Golden Horseshoe Revue* episode from the 1960s on *The Wonderful World of Disney* that celebrated the Horseshoe's ten-thousandth performance. It featured the show's talented stars, Betty Taylor and Wally Boag, in addition to guest stars Annette Funicello, Gene Sheldon, and Ed Wynn. Was the saloon stage re-created on a Disney Studios soundstage, or was the episode filmed entirely on location at the Golden Horseshoe in Frontierland at Disneyland? Joseph, San Francisco, CA

A —Interesting question! I had never thought about that before; I assumed that it had been filmed at Disneyland. I checked the film's shooting calls, and I should not have made that assumption. The interior of the Golden Horseshoe was actually built on Stage 2 at the Disney Studios, with filming beginning February 5, 1962. There was one day of audience-reaction shots filmed at the actual Golden Horseshoe at Disneyland, though the only primary Cast Members on call that day were Betty Taylor and Wally Boag.

Q Didn't Disney put out a short called *They Call the Wind Mariah*? While playing the tune, it showed a young couple leaving San Francisco for Reno. On the way they encountered a blizzard, and I think they were driven off the road. Was this Disney, or was it put out by someone else? David, Olalla, WA

A —You are close on the title. Disney did a TV show called *A Storm Called Maria* in 1959. It was based on George R. Stewart's famous book *Storm* and covered the birth and development of a major storm in the Sierra Nevada Mountains and how it put people in danger. Disney also did a television show based on another Stewart book, *Fire*, called *A Fire Called Jeremiah*. It covered the similar theme of the birth and development of a large forest fire.

Q A two-part question—several episodes of the *Wonderful World of Color* have been included in past releases of the Walt Disney Treasures series. Do you know if Disney plans on a special DVD release of selected shows from this program? Also, the theme song of the *Wonderful World of Color*, "The World Is a Carousel of Color," is one of my favorite Disney melodies. I've never been able to find the exact recorded version of this song as it was performed by the Disney chorus at the beginning of the show. Will this version ever be made available? Jame, Winnipeg, Manitoba, Canada

A —I know of no current plans for releasing more of the *Wonderful World of Color* episodes on DVD. The song's actual title is "Wonderful World of Color (Main Title)." It was released in 1991 as part of the three-CD set *The Music of Disney—A Legacy in Song*. A quick glance shows lots of copies of this out-of-print boxed set available on eBay.

Q My favorite shorts when I was a kid always involved this duck who was a scientist/professor with a very unique voice. I can't for the life of me remember his name, and no one knows who I'm talking about! Katie, Lancaster, CA

A —That was Professor Ludwig Von Drake, Donald Duck's erudite uncle, who often thought he knew more than he did. He was created to act as narrator for a number of the Disney television shows, beginning in 1961.

Q When I was a little girl (sometime in the late 1980s), my parents had a video taped off of television with Minnie Mouse singing Elton John and Kiki Dee's "Don't Go Breaking My Heart." I absolutely loved this video. Unfortunately, I gave my dad permission to tape over it, and I lost it. What is it called, and is there any way I can get a copy of it today? Emily, New Brunswick, NJ

A —Minnie Mouse and Elton John sang a duet of "Don't Go Breaking My Heart" on the 1988 television special titled *Totally Minnie*. That special, for Minnie's sixtieth birthday, has not been released on VHS or DVD.

Q I remember a series on the *Mickey Mouse Club* that starred Annette Funicello as a visiting cousin who is falsely accused of stealing a necklace. What was the name of that series, and is it available on DVD? Blair, Fort Davis, TX

A —The twenty-episode serial aired on the *Mickey Mouse Club* during its 1957–58 season, and was simply called *Annette*. Tim Considine and David Stollery of *Spin and Marty* fame also appeared in it. It was based on a book titled *Margaret*, by Janette Sebring Lowrey.

Q Was there ever a Disney wildlife TV show? I seem to remember one. Linda, Little Rock, AR

A —Disney had a wildlife series called True-Life Adventures, mostly made in the 1950s, but these were made for theaters. Some of them were shown on the Disney television series, and many additional shows made for television featured animals.

Q

Besides Annette Funicello, did any of the other original Mouseketeers go on to showbiz success? Ruben, Phoenix, AZ

A

—Annette was probably the primary success story, but others, like Paul Petersen, Don Grady, Sharon Baird, Johnny Crawford, and Bobby Burgess, made names for themselves on television series. Cubby O'Brien became a well-known drummer and Tommy Cole became a proficient makeup artist.

Q

There are two childhood movies I'd like to know the names of: the first is set at a boys' military school named after a Civil War general. The second movie stars Hayley Mills and is set in World War II England. Help! Gretchen, Charlotte, NC

A

—The two TV movies are *The Ghosts of Buxley Hall* (1980) and *Back Home* (1990). The latter was released on VHS in 1993.

Q

I recently found two Jiminy Cricket cels that were purchased between 1956 and 1959 at Disneyland. How can I tell which film they were from? Robert, Lakewood Ranch, FL

A

—It's difficult to identify Jiminy Cricket cels because he appeared in so many films. If the cels were purchased at Disneyland in the 1950s, it's most likely they would have been from one of Jiminy's many educational cartoons for the *Mickey Mouse Club—You and Your Five Senses, I'm No Fool with Fire*, etc.—which were produced during that era.

Q

When I was younger, I used to wake up at 5 a.m. to watch a show on Disney Channel. It was an exercise and dance show with

Mickey and Minnie and their friends. I used to love it, but I can't remember the name of it. Can you help? Warren, MI

A —That show, one of the original shows on Disney Channel premiering in 1983, was called *Mousercise*, with the aerobics led by Kellyn Plasschaert.

Q **Can you give me the names of all the original Mouseketeers from the 1955 to 1957 show? Travis, Citrus Heights, CA**

A —There were thirty-nine Mouseketeers that appeared on the original show from 1955 to 1959 (twenty-four of them were on the first season)—Nancy, Don, Sherry, Sharon, Billie Jean, Bobby, Lonnie, Tommy, Johnny, Dennis, Eileen, Dickie, Mary, Bonnie Lynn, Annette, Darlene, Judy, Cheryl, Linda, Dallas, John Lee, Bonni Lou, Charley, Larry, Cubby, Karen, Paul, Lynn, Mickey, Tim, Mary Lynn, Bronson, Michael, Jay-Jay, Ronald, Margene, Mark, Doreen, and Don.

Q **I saw in "This Week in Disney History" that Karen Pendleton, an original Mouseketeer, was born on July 1, 1946. Is this the Karen of "Karen and Cubby" fame that sang a duet in the closing song of the original *Mickey Mouse Club*? She was always my favorite even though most everyone else was smitten with Annette. What is she doing now? Mary Ellen, North Augusta, SC**

A —She was very popular on the show, receiving the third-highest amount of fan mail of all the Mouseketeers. Karen left show business after the *Mickey Mouse Club* ended. In 1983, she was involved in a bad car accident that left her paralyzed from the waist down, but that didn't stop her. While in a wheelchair, Karen returned to college, received her BA and MS in psychology, and is now working in that field.

Q I'm sure I remember that the opening theme for the *Mickey Mouse Club* show was produced and broadcast in color. However, the only color clips I've seen until now were on TV documentaries. Was the fifties show in glorious black and white? Scott, Captain Cook, HI

A —The original *Mickey Mouse Club* television show was indeed aired in black and white, but Walt Disney, always thinking about possible future uses of his material, filmed almost all of his shows in color. Thus the opening animated segment, originally seen only in black and white, can now be shown in color.

Q We watched *The Wonderful World of Disney* every week when I was growing up, and there's one movie I remember seeing twice. It was about a boy on his own (I don't remember the reason) and he met a Chihuahua who danced. They traveled together. I only remember them eating a raw egg—I don't remember much else—but I would love to see it again. Kathy, La Quinta, CA

A —The film you recall is *Pablo and the Dancing Chihuahua*. It first aired in two parts on television in 1968. It has not been sold on videocassette or DVD, but perhaps someday it will be rereleased.

Q Does Disney have any plans to bring *Mystery at Pirates Inn* to DVD? Anonymous, Farwell, MI

A —Perhaps you are referring to *The Secrets of the Pirate's Inn*, a two-part television show from 1969 starring Ed Begley and Jimmy Bracken. It has never been released on VHS or DVD, and I know of no plans to do so.

Q Wasn't there a serial on the *Mickey Mouse Club* in the 1950s about a boy training as an airline pilot and a girl training as a flight attendant? S.V., Highland Village, TX

A —A serial called *What I Want to Be* began on the very first *Mickey Mouse Club* show on October 3, 1955, and ran for ten episodes. It was filmed at the TWA headquarters in Kansas City and depicted the special training procedures for becoming an airline pilot and flight attendant.

Q **Can you tell me if the star of the Disney Channel series *Adventures in Wonderland*, Elizabeth Harnois, starred in an earlier Disney film? J.T., Cornwall, NY**

A —Elizabeth Harnois appeared in Walt Disney Pictures' *One Magic Christmas* (1985), playing the role of Abbie in a cast that included Mary Steenburgen, Harry Dean Stanton, and Arthur Hill. In 2011 she appeared as Ki in *Mars Needs Moms*.

Q **I loved Disney Channel's *Mickey Mouse Club*. What were the years of the previous Mickey Mouse Clubs? S.S., Gilroy, CA**

A —The *Mickey Mouse Club* on Disney Channel is actually the fourth incarnation of the club. The first Mickey Mouse Clubs were run out of movie theaters around the country in the early 1930s. The first television version began in 1955 and ran for four years. These same shows were syndicated in the early 1960s and again in the mid-1970s, with the latter release being so successful that a new version was developed in 1977. The Disney Channel series ran from 1989 to 1994, starting the careers of such performers as Christina Aguilera, Ryan Gosling, Keri Russell, Britney Spears, and Justin Timberlake.

Q **On Disney Channel's *Mickey Mouse Club* I loved the serials like *Teen Angel*, but my mom tells me the *Mickey Mouse Club* in her day had some great serials, too. Could you tell me what they were? S.T., Silver Spring, MD**

A —The original *Mickey Mouse Club* serials that ran for more than five episodes were *Spin and Marty*, *Corky and White Shadow*, *The Dairy Story*, *The Hardy Boys*, *The Secret of Mystery Lake*, *Clint and Mac*, *Annette*, and *Boys of the Western Sea*. The most popular of these was *Spin and Marty*, which starred Tim Considine and David Stollery as an "odd couple" at a boys' ranch.

Q **Who is the actor who did the voice of Scrooge McDuck on *Ducktales*? P.S., Gansevoort, NY**

A —The voice of Uncle Scrooge was provided by actor Alan Young, best known for playing the role of Wilbur on the classic *Mister Ed* TV series. Young first did the Scrooge voice in *Mickey's Christmas Carol* (1983) and on a record album made eleven years before the cartoon.

Q **In an earlier column, you stated that there was no way to tell Huey, Dewey, and Louie apart. Didn't that change with the *Ducktales* television series? G.A., Indianapolis, IN**

A —You are correct. Because the stories for the TV series are much more complicated than they were for the short Donald Duck cartoons, it was deemed necessary to distinguish between the three nephews. So for that show Huey was always dressed in red, Dewey in blue, and Louie in green. You can remember this by noting that the brightest *hue* of the three is red (Huey), the color of water, *dew*, is blue (Dewey), and that *leaves* Louie, and leaves are green.

Q **Which of Walt Disney's movies were the first to be shown on television? L.A., Austin, TX**

A —During his first season on television (1954-55), Walt aired three of his theatrical feature films—*Treasure Island* and, in somewhat shortened versions, *Alice in Wonderland* and *So Dear to My Heart*. Turning the tables, the big hit of that TV season—three episodes chronicling the life of Davy Crockett—was later released in theaters as the feature film *Davy Crockett, King of the Wild Frontier*.

Q **Since there were three original *Davy Crockett* shows, is much footage missing from the feature film made from them—*Davy Crockett, King of the Wild Frontier*? R.C., Gadsden, AL**

A —The TV shows were about forty-seven minutes each, or a total of 141 minutes for the three shows, so some editing had to be done. The completed feature ran ninety-two minutes. Less editing was needed for the later film, *Davy Crockett and the River Pirates*, since it was taken from two TV episodes.

Q **When I saw *The Million Dollar Collar* on Disney Channel, it reminded me of a Disney TV show I had seen about a dog named Hector. Were they one and the same? M.A., Jacksonville, FL**

A —*The Million Dollar Collar* was the theatrical version of *The Ballad of Hector the Stowaway Dog*, which first appeared in 1964 on Disney's TV series *Wonderful World of Color*. They are virtually the same, though there is usually some editing required to make a feature film out of a two-part television production. The theatrical version never played in the U.S., but it premiered in England in 1967.

Q **Did Walt Disney have to make a pilot film for his *Zorro* series? E.M., Fort Worth, TX**

A —No. Television executives wanted him to, but he was able to convince them that he knew what he was doing, would give them a quality product, and that he need not produce a sample first. The first *Zorro* show aired on October 10, 1957.

Q **Could you give me some information about Jimmie Dodd's Mousegetar? Since it only had four strings, was it actually a bass ukulele, not a guitar? Whatever happened to it? K.G., Nashville, TN**

A —The Mousegetar was built specially for the *Mickey Mouse Club* show and was given to Jimmie by the man who made it. Jimmie always played that guitar on the show. In later years, he continued to always play a four-string guitar; he called it a tenor guitar. When the show ended, Jimmie was able to keep the guitar, and his widow, Ruth Dodd Braun, donated it to the Walt Disney Archives.

Q **Was there a reason for the similarity in the character names of Hayley Mills's daughter in *Parent Trap II* with the role Hayley herself played in *The Moonspinners*? Anonymous**

A —The writer of *Parent Trap II*, Stuart Krieger, purposely sprinkled several bits of Hayley Mills trivia throughout the script. So not only was Nikky Ferris the name of Hayley's character in *The Moonspinners*, but Mary Grand, the daughter's friend, was close to Mary Grant, Hayley's *In Search of the Castaways* character. Sharon's boss is named Walter Elias (from Walter Elias Disney).

Q **Could you settle an argument? My husband says that after the success of *Davy Crockett*, Fess Parker starred in a *Daniel Boone* series. I disagree. Wasn't it Dewey Martin? R.G.H., New Orleans, LA**

A —It is easy to see the source of your confusion. Disney followed *Davy Crockett* with a four-part miniseries on Daniel Boone starring Dewey Martin during the 1960–61 TV season. Fess Parker, however, starred in the popular non-Disney *Daniel Boone* series from 1964 to 1970 on NBC.

Q **Did I recognize the director of the Blind Institute in *Love Leads the Way* as the star of an old Republic Pictures serial in the 1950s? S.K., Yuma, AZ**

A —Yes, that was George D. Wallace, who starred in the *Commando Cody, Sky Marshal of the Universe* serial.

Q **Is it true that Guy Williams is not the actor's real name? K.V., Denver, CO**

A —The star of *Zorro* was actually born Armando Catalano, the son of Italian parents who emigrated to New York. During discussions at the time *Zorro* was going into production, some people questioned whether the Guy Williams name might be confused with then-current Western stars Bill Williams or Guy Madison, and there was talk of changing it. But Walt Disney recommended keeping the name Guy Williams.

Q **How can I find some information about John Clem, from the film *Johnny Shiloh*? M.C., Brazil, IN**

A —Johnny Clem was a real drummer boy during the Civil War; in fact, he remained in the Army and retired as a brigadier general in 1916. Check your libraries for the book *Johnny Shiloh*, by James A. Rhodes and Dean Jauchius, upon which our film was based.

Q **I remember when the twenty-fifth anniversary of the *Mickey Mouse Club* was celebrated in 1980, Disney was looking for some missing Mouseketeers. Were they ever found? M.L., Carrollton, TX**

A —The story that Disney was searching for four missing Mouseketeers was picked up by the wire services and the publicity went nationwide. Amazingly, within twenty-four hours all four Mouseketeers were found; two of them (Larry Larsen and Don Underhill) were near Disneyland in Irvine, California. Charley Laney was located in San Diego and Ronnie Steiner was in Winnipeg. The former child actors all made it to the reunion.

Q **How did Walt Disney choose Fess Parker to portray Davy Crockett? A.O., Brewster, NY**

A —Actually, Fess Parker was not the one who was first considered for the role. James Arness, later best known for *Gunsmoke*, was recommended to Walt Disney. But when he screened a science-fiction film, *Them*, Disney was attracted not to Arness but to another actor in the thriller, Fess Parker. Parker was hired and proved to be perfect as Davy Crockett.

Q **Did I notice Jean Marsh, of television's *Upstairs, Downstairs* fame, in *The Horsemasters* when it was shown on Disney Channel? R.T.W., Birmingham, AL**

A —Yes, Jean Marsh appeared in that TV movie, which Disney made in the early 1960s. She was also in the theatrical release of *Return to Oz*, based on the books of L. Frank Baum.

Q **When did Walt Disney make his television debut? E.R., Cedar Rapids, IA**

A —Walt's very first television show was a special titled *One Hour in Wonderland*, which aired on Christmas Day, 1950. It featured Walt Disney as host, with guests Edgar Bergen and Charlie McCarthy. A second Disney Christmas show followed in 1951.

Q *Spin and Marty* on the *Mickey Mouse Club* has always been one of my favorites. How many episodes were made in all? D.W., Springfield, MA

A —There were three different *Spin and Marty* serials. The first had twenty-five episodes, the second twenty-three, and the third thirty. Thus, there were a total of seventy-eight episodes.

Q I know the *Mickey Mouse Club*'s Annette Funicello made many films while she was under contract to Disney. Where did he discover her? T.H., New Orleans, LA

A —When Annette Funicello was twelve years old, she appeared on an amateur program at the Starlight Bowl in Burbank, California. Walt Disney happened to catch the live performance, titled *Ballet vs. Jive*, and this led to her selection as one of the original Mouseketeers. Her first public appearance as a Mouseketeer was at the opening of Disneyland, on July 17, 1955.

Q How many different Davy Crockett films did Walt Disney make? P.D., Pittsford, NY

A —The *Davy Crockett* show, one of TV's first miniseries, aired as three episodes in 1954–55. Even though Davy died at the end of the series, he was resurrected the following season for two more programs based on Crockett legends. The five shows were then combined, reedited, and released theatrically as two feature films, *Davy Crockett, King of the Wild Frontier* and *Davy Crockett and the River Pirates*.

Q What was the name of Zorro's horse? D.D., Carmel, CA

A —This is a frequently asked question, and the answer is Tornado. Zorro, gallant defender of the poor and scourge of military tyrants in Spanish California, originally slashed his ragged Z symbol for television audiences on October 10, 1957. The popular Disney TV series, starring Guy Williams as the swashbuckling hero, aired for two seasons and a total of seventy-eight episodes.

Q **I am a big fan of Ludwig Von Drake. When did he make his debut? R.J., Franklin, MA**

A —Ludwig Von Drake was one of the first Disney characters to make his debut on television. He was created to host the first color TV show on *Walt Disney's Wonderful World of Color*. The episode was called *An Adventure in Color* and aired on September 24, 1961. The show also featured the TV debut of the immensely popular *Donald in Mathmagic Land*.

Q **I seem to remember a series that was on *The Wonderful World of Disney* about an English (or Welsh?) minister who was a conservative by day, but by night was a Robin Hood-type character known as "The Scarecrow." Am I remembering correctly, or was this something else entirely? No one seems to have any idea what I am talking about! James, Wallingford, CT**

A —This popular series was made in 1964 as *The Scarecrow of Romney Marsh*, and it was later made into a feature film called *Dr. Syn, Alias the Scarecrow* for theaters. Patrick McGoohan starred as the disguised vicar of Dymchurch who fought for justice in eighteenth-century England.

Q **I remember a show on Disney Channel that had bears that lived in a large tree. When they drank this special juice they could**

jump really high. Do you remember the name of the show?
Krystal, Miami, FL

A —The animated cartoon was called *Disney's Adventures of the Gummi Bears*, and it originally aired on NBC beginning in 1985. The juice they drank, which gave them the bouncing power, was called gummiberry juice.

Q I saw a movie when I was a child that I think was a Disney movie. The basic story line was that a couple of boys discovered a girl ghost who had died in a well. She had also lost her doll down the well. I would love to find out its name. Jennifer, Puyallup, WA

A —We probably get more questions about this film, *Child of Glass*, than any other, so it obviously made a big impression on those who saw it. It originally aired on television in 1978 and was available on video from 1987 to 1991. Perhaps you can find a used copy somewhere.

Q I remember a real cute movie about an otter kept as a pet. The two brothers tried to keep the otter in their backyard pool and got into lots of mischief. I'd like my children to see it. What was its name? Kit, Elk Grove, IL

A —I wonder if you are thinking of a seal instead of an otter. There was a 1962 two-part television film called *Sammy, the Way-Out Seal*, in which two brothers bring an injured seal back from their vacation, and he causes havoc at their home.

Q In the early nineties Disney Channel series *Under the Umbrella Tree*, what was the name of the blue jay? Soleil, Anaheim, CA

A —His name was Jacob Bluejay, and his voice was provided by Stephen Brathwaite. This series was produced not by Disney but by the Canadian Broadcasting Corp.

WALT DISNEY WORLD

Q I have always been interested in the history of Walt Disney World. I recently read about an Epcot film that was shown only to Florida residents. Can you tell me more about this? Dennis, Pitman, NJ

A —The film, featuring Walt Disney, was shot on October 27, 1966, just six weeks before he died. It was the last time Walt participated in a filming session. The twenty-minute film aired on Florida television stations and was shown to groups in the state to explain Walt's ideas for his project and to gain their support.

Q Why has Figment left Epcot? I last took a picture with him by the "leaping" fountains in 2006, and now he is gone. There are traces of his history there, but no more Figment or Dreamfinder, for that matter. What happened? Connor, San Antonio, TX

A —Figment is still the mascot of the Imagination pavilion. In 1999, with the premiere of Journey Into Your Imagination, he only had a cameo role. However, after an overwhelming number of Guests pleaded for his return, the attraction was refurbished again, and since 2002, Journey Into Imagination with Figment has featured the playful dragon. Dreamfinder, holding a small Figment, used to pose for photos outside the pavilion until 1998; Figment alone made appearances occasionally after 2004.

Q On my first trip to Walt Disney World, about ten years ago, there was a parade that took the kids off the sidewalk and let them interact and dance with the characters. What was it called, and why don't they let kids be a part of the parade anymore? Bridget, Brooklyn, NY

A —You are likely thinking of the Share a Dream Come True Parade, which premiered with the 100 Years of Magic celebration in 2001. The parade invited Guests to participate with characters along the route in a series of "show stops" for a number of years. The more recent version of the parade, Celebrate a Dream Come True, adopted a new theme that did not incorporate show stops.

Q **While preparing for an all-adult family trip to Walt Disney World, my brother and I were reminiscing about River Country, which was the water park we visited on our first trip in 1987. We were wondering, when did it close, and what was built in its place? Carrie, New Rochelle, NY**

A —River Country closed on September 1, 2001, after having been open for twenty-five years, and nothing has been built in its place. It was essentially superseded by the more elaborate water parks of Typhoon Lagoon and Blizzard Beach.

Q **In 1973 my wife and I visited the Magic Kingdom at Walt Disney World on our honeymoon. We saw and loved an attraction called the Mickey Mouse Revue. If I remember correctly, it was similar to the Country Bear Jamboree. On subsequent visits we could no longer find it. Could you tell us what happened to it? Ronald, Boca Raton, FL**

A —The Mickey Mouse Revue, an Audio-Animatronics attraction featuring Disney characters performing some of the most memorable Disney songs, was created for Walt Disney World, opening in 1971. In 1980 the attraction was removed and sent to Tokyo Disneyland, where it played from 1983 to 2009. Mickey's PhilharMagic is now in the former location of the Mickey Mouse Revue in the Magic Kingdom at Walt Disney World, and the same attraction replaced the Revue at Tokyo Disneyland.

Q **I remember loving a ride called Dreamflight in Tomorrowland at the Magic Kingdom. Why did they close such an**

interesting flight-simulation ride, and when?
Teresa, Chester, NY

A —The attraction opened as If You Had Wings, sponsored by Eastern Airlines (1972–87). When Delta took over as the sponsor, they changed the title to If You Could Fly for nineteen months while they designed a new attraction. That new attraction was Delta Dreamflight, opening in 1989. When Delta discontinued sponsorship in 1996, the attraction was renamed Take Flight until it was removed in 1998 so Buzz Lightyear's Space Ranger Spin could take its place.

Q In 1988, I was in Walt Disney World with my mom and dad. At that time there were only the Magic Kingdom and Epcot. I believe Disney-MGM opened the following year. I thought I remembered Fantasmic! being at Epcot? Is that possible? If so, where was it? Michael, Manassas Park, VA

A —Fantasmic! was never at Epcot. You may be remembering Laserphonic Fantasy, which ran from 1984 to 1988, when it was superseded by IllumiNations. Fantasmic! was created in 1992 at Disneyland and opened at what's now Disney's Hollywood Studios in 1998.

Q In 1989 my family and I visited what was then Disney-MGM Studios, and I convinced everyone to go on the Animation tour rather than The Great Movie Ride. It was late, just before Park closing. I remember it being quite a walk with TVs and video explaining what happened in the area behind large panes of glass. I managed to go on the tour again a couple years ago. This time it was during the day. We were let into a theater and given an intro. We then went on the tour, but it was much shorter than I remember, and there were no large panes of glass showing a large room where the animators worked. I was wondering when the attraction was changed? Amanda, Portage la Prairie, Manitoba, Canada

A —The Magic of Disney Animation tour opened in 1989, and at that time, Walt Disney Feature Animation had a studio there doing actual animation for Disney features. Guests could watch the animators at work through large windows. The Florida studio closed in 2004, so there were major renovations and changes to the tour that year, including the addition of Animation Station.

Q I remember visiting World Showcase in Epcot soon after it opened. I recall seeing a sign saying, "Coming soon: Spain." Why did this never materialize? Have any other countries been considered for inclusion? Does World Showcase have space to expand? George, Atlanta, GA

A —Spain was just one of a number of countries, such as Switzerland, Costa Rica, and Russia, which were considered for inclusion in World Showcase, but Disney was unable to obtain sponsorship. There is still room to expand.

Q Is there a list somewhere of all the animals carved into the Tree of Life? I've searched high and low and can't seem to find one. Kaitlyn, Mount Holly, NJ

A —Disney has not put out a list of the animals because they want Guests to have fun trying to find as many as they can. There are a total of 325 animals, according to the Walt Disney World Web site.

Q Where was the Visitors Center located for Walt Disney World prior to its opening? I remember visiting the center with my grandparents probably around 1969–70. Rick, Richland Center, WI

A —The Walt Disney World Preview Center was open from January 10, 1970, to September 30, 1971, in Lake Buena Vista, just off I-4 and Highway 535. It was there so that Guests could learn all about the resort that was under construction. The building is still there; it is now the national headquarters for the Amateur Athletic Union. The street on which it is located was originally named Preview Blvd.; it later became Hotel Plaza Blvd.

Q **In The Living Seas at Epcot, there was a mural that changed color and morphed into different images when I was there in the nineties. If I remember correctly, someone told me that it was made of "polarized light." I couldn't find it this year when I went back to Epcot. Is it still there and I just missed it, or is it gone? If it's gone, what happened to it? Karen, Santa Ana, CA**

A —Perhaps you are referring to the mural that was in the Work of Art scene at Journey Into Imagination. It was described as a "polage," or "polarized light collage." A system of polarized filters changed the colors of the lights behind Plexiglas panels. There also was a distinctive mural in the Listen to the Land attraction in the Land pavilion. It was 143 feet long by nine feet high, with a colorful and abstract representation of the Earth's rich soil. It also changed colors as you proceeded through the beginning of the attraction.

Q **I've noticed that Disneyland has added some of the attractions that Walt Disney World has. Are there any plans to add some of the attractions from Disneyland to Walt Disney World, like Roger Rabbit's Car Toon Spin, Pinocchio's Daring Journey, Casey Jr. Circus Train ride, Storybook Land Canal Boats, Alice in Wonderland, or Indiana Jones Adventure? Charles, University Place, WA**

A —There are no current plans to add any of the attractions you listed at Walt Disney World. In order to make the Parks special, there are some unique attractions at each Park.

Q Is Team Disney the same as the Casting building at WDW? Was it designed by Robert Graves? Bill, Mount Dora, FL

A —No. Team Disney at Walt Disney World is an administration building designed by Arata Isozaki; it opened in 1991. It is themed around a huge sundial. The Walt Disney World Casting Center, which opened nearby two years earlier, was designed by Robert A. M. Stern.

Q I noticed that Mission: SPACE makes a few homages to Horizons. Are there any other Park rides that reference the attractions that used to be there? Abby, MN

A —This is frequently done by the Imagineers. Thus, for example, The Many Adventures of Winnie the Pooh at Disneyland references the Country Bear Jamboree that it replaced, and the attraction of the same name at Walt Disney World's Magic Kingdom references Mr. Toad's Wild Ride. Star Tours at Disneyland referenced Adventure Thru Inner Space. There is an original World of Motion car in the Test Track queue at Epcot. Back at the Magic Kingdom, Skippy from The ExtraTERRORestrial Alien Encounter makes a cameo appearance in Stitch's Great Escape.

Q After our recent trip to WDW, a friend and I were discussing the Hall of Presidents. She said she misses it from Disneyland, and I told her it was never at Disneyland, only Great Moments with Mr. Lincoln. She said, "I remember seeing all of the presidents in the round building. It was at the end." I have no idea what she's talking about. Was there ever anything like what she describes at Disneyland? Randy, Santa Ana, CA

A —She is mistaking the Hall of Presidents at Walt Disney World, which is the only location that has all of the presidents. You are correct that only Great Moments with Mr. Lincoln was at Disneyland. The "round building" probably refers to the carousel theater, which has been the home to the Carousel of Progress, America Sings, and Innoventions, but no presidents.

Q **During our last visit to Walt Disney World we were looking at a pin set of the countries represented at Epcot and realized that The American Adventure pavilion was not the name of a country, like all the others. No one at the pavilion could explain why it was not named the United States pavilion. Can you explain why? Paul, Auburn Hills, MI**

A —I guess it was a bit redundant to have a U.S. pavilion in the U.S. Having The American Adventure name helps make it special and stand apart from the other country pavilions.

Q **I was at the Magic Kingdom at Walt Disney World recently when my wife noticed the old loading area for the Plaza Swan Boats. I seem to remember them going around the Swiss Family Treehouse and the front of the castle. Is my memory correct? What happened to the boats? Steve, Stoughton, MA**

A —The Plaza Swan Boats began cruising the waterways around the central hub of the Magic Kingdom in 1973, operating only during peak periods. They were taken out of service in 1983. The swans were removed and the boats were sold.

Q **At The Twilight Zone Tower of Terror, Rod Serling, the host of *The Twilight Zone*, appears on a television to give a history of the hotel. Serling died years before the attraction opened; how could this footage have been filmed? Andrew, Staten Island, NY**

A —Rod Serling passed away in 1975. The attraction's designers used film footage of Serling from *The Twilight Zone*; an actor who sounded like Serling added some lines to fit the needs of the attraction. If you listen closely, you can hear the cut between Serling's voice and the new lines.

Q **When was the song played in the Carousel of Progress, "The Best Time of Your Life," changed back to the original one, "There's a Great Big Beautiful Tomorrow"? Dave, Brownsburg, IN**

A —"The Best Time of Your Life" was added when the attraction moved to Walt Disney World in 1975. "There's a Great Big Beautiful Tomorrow" returned to the attraction in 1993.

Q **On my latest trip to Walt Disney World, in 2003, I noticed that the Hall of Presidents has a new narrator, but no one was able to tell me who it is. Do you know? Also, who was the first narrator, before Maya Angelou? Randy, Bay Shore, NY**

A —The new narrator is J. D. Hall. The original narrator was Lawrence Dobkin, who narrated several Disney educational films and a 1961 Disney television show entitled *A Fire Called Jeremiah*. He also recorded narration for other Park attractions in the 1970s and 1980s, such as Great Moments with Mr. Lincoln, Space Mountain, and Submarine Voyage.

Q **I'm a big fan of the retired Epcot attraction World of Motion. What happened to the Audio-Animatronics? Andrew, Shawnee, KS**

A —When Audio-Animatronics figures are removed from an attraction, they're usually used for spare parts. This was the case with World of Motion; some figures ended up as pirates at Disneyland when the Pirates of the Caribbean attraction went through one of its regular rehabs. Set pieces from the attraction were not kept.

Q **Can you tell me how they built the Utilidor system beneath Walt Disney World's Magic Kingdom? I've wondered about this for quite a while. Cameron, Royal Palm Beach, FL**

A —The Utilidor system is a vast network of tunnels connecting many areas of the Magic Kingdom. These tunnels allow behind-the-scenes operations and maintenance to occur without disruption of the Park's atmosphere. The high water table in Florida meant that the system had to be constructed aboveground, and the Magic Kingdom was built right on top of it as a kind of second floor.

Q **Last June I visited Walt Disney World for the first time in years, and I found myself wondering whether they ever clean out the money from It's a Small World. If so, what do they do with it? Connie, Sheridan, IL**

A —Some of the money tossed into the various waterways at Walt Disney World goes to Quest, Inc., a nonprofit organization that employs people with disabilities, and some is placed in our company's Ears to You account. Cast Members who are Disney VoluntEARS apply for grants for the organizations with which they volunteer, and the money is presented to the nonprofit groups each year at a breakfast honoring the volunteers.

Q **I remember a TV show about the opening of Walt Disney World. I think it aired back in 1971, but I can't remember on which network. Are copies of this show available? Ronald, Point Pleasant, NJ**

A —You're thinking of the special *Grand Opening of Walt Disney World*, which aired on NBC on October 29, 1971. It was hosted by Julie Andrews and Glen Campbell and featured numerous celebrity guests, including Buddy Hackett and Jonathan Winters. The show has never been released on video.

Q I have some Pirates of the Caribbean postcards from many years ago. How old are they? Bill, McKees Rocks, PA

A —There were two packs of six different Pirates of the Caribbean postcards issued first in 1966 at Disneyland and again around 1973 at Walt Disney World. The cards featured artwork for the attraction by Marc Davis.

Q I've noticed that the palm trees at Walt Disney World aren't native to central Florida. Where are these trees from? Greg, Newington, CT

A —There are many different species of palm trees around Walt Disney World. For example, there is a large Canary Island date palm (*Phoenix canariensis*) in Mexico at Epcot. Around Spaceship Earth are Mexican fan palms (*Washingtonia robusta*). At the Polynesian Resort, there are hundreds of palms, from the common queen palm (*Arecastrum romanzoffiana*) to the unusual ribbon fan palm (*Livistona decipiens*). Sago palms (*Cycas revoluta*) can be found near the entrance to Tomorrowland in the Magic Kingdom. Disney landscapers have been known to search the world for just the right trees to match the various themes at the resort.

Q Walt Disney World's Pirates of the Caribbean attraction reminds me of a famous fort in San Juan called Castillo de San Felipe del Morro. Just above the turnstiles, "Castillo del Morro" is engraved on the entrance. Is the attraction based on this Puerto Rican fort? Ramon, Cordero Aguadilla, Puerto Rico

A —Nothing in the publicity for Pirates of the Caribbean states that the Castillo de San Felipe del Morro was used by the attraction's designers as a model, but it is pretty obvious that they at least studied photographs of that edifice. Imagineers often get their inspiration from a number of buildings, as was probably the case here.

Q **Who provides the voice for Donald Duck in Mickey's PhilharMagic at Walt Disney World? It sounds like Clarence Nash at times and Tony Anselmo at others. Bernie, Orlando, FL**

A —Tony Anselmo has mentioned in interviews that some lines of dialogue in the film are by the late Clarence "Ducky" Nash and were taken from the film library. The director, George Scribner, loves *The Three Caballeros*, and he wanted to put in a few lines from that film for old times' sake. Tony thought that this was a great idea; he challenges the audience to determine which lines are Clarence's and which are his.

Q **How many triangle-shaped pieces were used to make Spaceship Earth at Epcot? Jeff, Ashland, MA**

A —Spaceship Earth has an inner sphere of 1,450 structural-steel straight beams arranged in a typical geodesic form of giant triangles. The outer sphere is held about two feet away from the inner core by aluminum hubs and contains aluminum support frames for the 954 triangular aluminum panels on the exterior.

Q **A Cast Member in Mickey's Toontown Fair told us that Pluto was Minnie's dog. If so, why is his doghouse in Mickey's backyard at the fair? The Healy family, Grapevine, TX**

A —In Pluto's first screen appearance, *The Chain Gang*, he didn't belong to Mickey or Minnie. He was a bloodhound tracking Mickey, who had escaped from prison. In his next cartoon, *The Picnic*, Pluto was Minnie's dog, but he was known as Rover in that film. He finally became Mickey's dog in his third cartoon, *The Moose Hunt*.

Q I have an old cassette of music from the Disney Parks with a song titled "Magic Journeys." Does this song refer to an older attraction or show in Disneyland? Alyssa, Miller Place, NY

A —The song refers to *Magic Journeys*, a 3-D movie that played at Journey Into Imagination at Epcot from 1982 to 1987 and at the Fantasyland Theater at the Walt Disney World Magic Kingdom from 1987 to 1993. It was also shown at Disneyland from 1984 to 1986.

Q I'm almost always able to recognize the voices of Paul Frees and Thurl Ravenscroft in Disney Park attractions, but I need help with a few others. Three Audio-Animatronics characters in particular have piqued my interest: Country Bear Big Al, and Benjamin Franklin and Mark Twain from The American Adventure. Bob, Whippany, NJ

A —Country crooner Tex Ritter, father of actor John Ritter, originally voiced Big Al and sang "Blood on the Saddle." In later versions of the show, Peter Klimes did the voice. In The American Adventure, Dallas McKennan is Ben Franklin, and John Anderson is Mark Twain.

Q I have a 1979 Walt Disney World vacation guide with a picture in it from the Walt Disney World Village [now Downtown Disney Marketplace]. In the photo is a statue that is very similar to the one in the Italy pavilion at Epcot. Are they the same statue? Timothy, Quincy, IL

A —While both statues depict Neptune, god of the sea, their designs are quite different. The Neptune statue at the village was one of about a dozen classical statues, all eventually removed when the area's fishing-village theme was developed. A Disney art director acquired these sandstone statues in Europe.

Disney designers made the Epcot statue, which was framed with rebar and then sprayed with gunite (a mixture of cement, sand, and water) to look like stone.

Q **I think Billy Barty did Figment's voice in Epcot's Journey Into Imagination, but who voiced Dreamfinder? And what about the robot (S.I.R.) in The ExtraTERRORestrial Alien Encounter? Amanda, Sunrise, FL**

A —Billy Barty did voice Figment. Two people provided the voice for Dreamfinder: Chuck McCann and Ron Schneider. The voice of S.I.R. (Simulated Intelligence Robot) in The ExtraTERRORestrial Alien Encounter was Tim Curry.

Q **Where did Gillespie Street in Disney's Hollywood Studios get its name? George, Sea Isle City, NJ**

A —Ed Grier of Disney's Hollywood Studios reports that the last time Imagineers changed the facades along that block, they wanted to refer to two cities: London (on the first half of the block) and Philadelphia (on the second half). There is a Gillespie Street in northeast Philadelphia that is typical of the row house architectural style that is so common in the City of Brotherly Love.

Q **Are the portraits in the portrait hall in the Haunted Mansion meant to represent anyone in particular? Roger, Brunswick, ME**

A —No, they don't depict anyone in particular.

Q **When my family visited Walt Disney World in 1972, my father took color slides of the Park and the parade. In one of the parade pictures, you can see a banner that reads "50 Happy Years." The question is: fifty happy years of what? Mickey Mouse didn't turn fifty until the late seventies, and the Parks**

are much younger than the Mouse. To what do these banners refer? Joyce and Dennis, Casa Grande, AZ

A —The "50 Happy Years" banner would have been used in 1972–73 to help commemorate The Walt Disney Company's fiftieth anniversary. The company was founded in October 1923. There was a "50 Happy Years" banner in the 1972 Christmas parade. There was also a television special that aired on January 21, 1973, titled *Fifty Happy Years*.

Q I believe that the Starlight Café in Tomorrowland used to be called Tomorrowland Terrace. Is this correct? I used to love to order a Galaxy Burger, Moon Fries, and a Space Coke (or something like that)! What were the menu items named? Am I close? Frank, Wake Forest, NC

A —The restaurant was Tomorrowland Terrace from the opening of Walt Disney World in 1971 until September 26, 1994. On December 9, 1994, it reopened as Cosmic Ray's Starlight Café. A Walt Disney World menu book from the late 1970s shows that you could buy such future-themed foods as an Orbit Burger (hamburger), a Moon Burger (cheeseburger), or a Space Dog. The Orbit Burger was 80 cents, by the way. Later that year, a Gemini Burger (it had two beef patties) was added to the bill of fare.

Q My family rides It's a Small World every time we take a Walt Disney World vacation. However, when we get to the Scottish section, we all cringe at the out-of-tune bagpipes. Why do they not play in tune? Alison, Lanchester, Durham, England

A —According to Russell Brower, who was in Media Design at Walt Disney Imagineering, "The bagpipes play against a 'drone' of two notes, which can seem incongruous at times, depending on the context. Also, the 'chanter,' or melody pipe, on the bagpipes is much like a note on an accordion—always slightly out of tune! It is the nature of the instrument."

Q **While waiting to be seated at Cinderella's Royal Table at Walt Disney World, my dad noticed that one of the coats of arms that hang beside the huge fireplace in the waiting hall is the same as that of his family (Murphy). Is there any way of finding out who or what these shields represent? I thought I read somewhere that they were the coats of arms of some of the Disney Imagineers who helped create Cinderella Castle. Cindy, East Douglas, MA**

A —I am not aware of any Imagineer named Murphy, but in addition to the coats of arms of the Imagineers, it is likely that the designers also picked other attractive coats of arms out of heraldry books.

Q **The Haunted Mansion is one of my favorite attractions at Walt Disney World. The narrator, or "ghost host," has a very distinctive voice. Recently, I saw *Rudolph and Frosty's Christmas in July* on Toon Disney, and the character Winterbolt sounds exactly like The Haunted Mansion narrator. Can you tell me if they are in fact the same person? Diane, Shelbyville, MI**

A —Paul Frees was both the ghost host at The Haunted Mansion and Winterbolt in the 1979 television special *Rudolph and Frosty's Christmas in July*. Frees also did the voice of Ludwig Von Drake for the Disney television shows along with a number of other voices for attractions such as Pirates of the Caribbean. He died in 1986.

Q **At Disney's Hollywood Studios I saw the plane that Walt Disney used when he was picking out sites for the future Walt Disney World. Do you have any information or history about this plane? Was it used after Walt passed away? Roger, Port St. Lucie, FL**

A —The airplane displayed at Walt Disney World is a Grumman Gulfstream I that Walt Disney purchased as a corporate plane in 1963. It was put in service in May 1964 and designated N234MM (for Mickey Mouse). This was one of Walt's three corporate planes; the others were a Beechcraft Queen Air (1963-65) and a Beechcraft King Air (1965-67). The Gulfstream was indeed used by Walt for his scouting trips to Florida, and it also was often used for promotional tours celebrating the release of a new Disney movie or the anniversary of a Disney Park. The plane carried fifteen passengers and remained in service until 1992. At that time, the highway next to Disney's Hollywood Studios was closed temporarily so the plane could land there and then be lifted by crane into the Park to be displayed.

Q **Are the buildings in the England section of World Showcase at Epcot exact replicas of buildings in Europe? Carolyn, Newark, OH**

A —No, they are not based on any particular buildings. Disney designers wanted the England section to present a blend of architectural styles: Victorian, Yorkshire Manor, Tudor, Georgian, and Regency. There is even a Shakespearean cottage. Imagineers spent three years on research, looking at pictures and visiting historic sites throughout England, Scotland, and Wales.

Q **Can you please tell me what actors played the aliens in the X-S Tech lab video in Alien Encounter at Walt Disney World? I know Tim Curry is the voice of the robot, Jeffrey Jones is the chairman, and Kathy Najimy is Dr. Femus. But who were the others? Michael, New York, NY**

A —The other credits we have for The ExtraTERRORestrial Alien Encounter are Kevin Pollack (Spinlok, director of operations) and Tyra Banks (X-S Tech spokeswoman).

Q In my favorite attraction, the Haunted Mansion, there are three hitchhiking ghosts. A Disney employee told me the names of two of them: Gus and Ezra. What is the name of the other ghost? Michael, Baltimore, MD

A —Years ago, Imagineers Bruce Gordon and David Mumford told me that the hitchhiking ghosts had no official names. However, unauthorized fan-created stories came up with the names of Gus, Ezra, and Phineas. Disney has occasionally utilized those names on merchandise items.

Q I recently purchased a cel titled *Icicle Princess*, signed by Marc Davis. The certificate of authenticity says, "This conceptual drawing depicts one of five Snow Queens and Princesses for an attraction entitled 'Enchanted Snow Palace.'" Do you have any more information on this drawing or attraction? Patricia, Mayfield Village, OH

A —The Enchanted Snow Palace was one of many attractions for the Walt Disney World Magic Kingdom that never got past the design stage. The Snow Palace, an inside roller coaster intended for Fantasyland, was conceived by Imagineer Marc Davis in the 1970s, his idea being that visitors to warm and sunny Florida would find a winter-themed attraction intriguing. A similar idea was used years later in creating the ski resort–themed water park Blizzard Beach.

Q My wife and I really enjoy the Carousel of Progress at Walt Disney World. One of my earliest recollections as a child was visiting that attraction at the 1964 World's Fair. I know that the Sherman Brothers wrote a song for the attraction called "There's a Great Big Beautiful Tomorrow." In fact, that is the song that was playing during our recent visit. However, both of us swear that for a while the Carousel had a different tune. The only words we remember are, "This is the time, this is the time, this is the time of your life . . ." Are we crazy, or did the Carousel of Progress once have a different theme? We also noticed this time that the dog was called Rover in each stop, but we recall that the dog was once called Queenie. Mark, Nashville, TN

A —You have a good memory. "There's a Great Big Beautiful Tomorrow" was the theme song of the Carousel of Progress when General Electric sponsored it at the New York World's Fair and later when it was moved to Disneyland. However, when the Carousel was moved to the Magic Kingdom at Walt Disney World in 1975, GE chose to emphasize the present more than the future, so there was a new song, "The Best Time of Your Life." The original song was returned during a 1993 rehab. The names of the dogs in the four sections have changed over the years. In the original show, the names were Rover, Buster, and Sport (the dog in the final scene was not named); other names were used in revisions. When the attraction moved to Walt Disney World, the first dog's name became Rover, the second Queenie, and the last two were both named Sport. Today, all the dogs are named Rover.

Q My wife and I spent our honeymoon at Walt Disney World in August 1999, and we are now Disney fanatics. Our question is, what is the exterior of Spaceship Earth made of? Will and Alea, Springdale, PA

A —The outside "skin" of Spaceship Earth, the world's largest geodesic sphere, consists of 150,000 square feet of highly reflective brushed aluminum.

Q It is my goal in life to work for Disney someday, although I'm not sure what department I want to work in. Someone told me there is a Disney college in Florida—not the Disney Institute,

but an actual college where all Disney Imagineers are trained. Is this true? Tracee, Yakima, WA

A —There is no Disney college for Imagineers; they get their training in regular colleges. You may be thinking of the Walt Disney World College Program, where college students from around the country are selected to go to Walt Disney World to work for several months, earning college credits as well as getting paid. The participants work in many areas of the resort, and many return after college to full-time jobs with Disney. There is a similar program at Disneyland.

Q **All the hurricanes and tropical storms of 1999 had me wondering: what does Walt Disney World do to protect its equipment, animals, plants, and personnel during bad weather? Donna, Pittsburgh, PA**

A —Walt Disney World has many contingency plans in the event of hurricanes or other severe weather conditions. These range from bringing in outdoor furniture, moving animals into secure buildings, and closing some of the outdoor attractions to the complete daylong closing of the Parks, which happened for the first time with the approach of Hurricane Floyd in September 1999. During that storm the Parks were closed, but most of the resorts remained open, except for those in low-lying areas that were in danger of flooding. Guests in those resorts were evacuated to convention centers on the property. All Walt Disney World structures are built to withstand severe weather.

Q **At the new (1998) Tiki Room in the Magic Kingdom at Walt Disney World, the voice of the French bird sounds just like Jerry Orbach, who voiced Lumiere, the candelabra in *Beauty and the Beast*. Is it possible that he is the voice of the bird? If not, who made the French bird come to life? Darlene, Longmont, CO**

A —To answer your question, I checked with Kevin Rafferty, a show writer at Walt Disney Imagineering. Here is his reply: "Yes, the voice of Pierre the French bird in The Enchanted Tiki Room— Under New Management is indeed Jerry Orbach's. He literally stepped off the golf course one Saturday and came over to our [WDI's] Studio A to provide the talent. He was a wonderful guy to work with, and a lot of fun! The reason I asked Jerry to do this is because I loved his Lumiere character (not to mention he's a great singer), and his voice was closest to the original voice of Pierre. As a side note, in our remake of the show, the other three original Tiki Birds (Fritz, José, and Michael) were all performed by the original voice talents: Thurl Ravenscroft, Wally Boag, and Fulton Burley, respectively."

Q **In the late 1970s or early 1980s, I visited the Magic Kingdom at Walt Disney World. Across from the Turnpike car ride was a one-man band called Michael Ice and His Iceberg Machine. It was a future-world band with a silver piano, and the performer wore a silver outfit. Could this have been Michael Eisner? It was about the same time he became a Cast Member. Jeff, Cincinnati, OH**

A —This unusual performer was Michael Iceberg and His Iceberg Machine. Iceberg's real name was spelled Iseberg. He performed his unique style of music at Walt Disney World for a number of years, as well as during the summer of 1982 in Tomorrowland at Disneyland. He used a combination of synthesizers and such odd things as washing-machine parts and bicycle gears to create his signature music and sound effects. Author Steve Birnbaum called him "truly funny, whimsical, and serious . . . a must."

Q **Who does the singing for Teddi Barra and Trixie in the Country Bear Jamboree at Walt Disney World? David, Leesburg, FL**

A —Trixie is listed as Cheryl Poole and Teddi Barra as the Stoneman Family (they also provided the voices for a number of the other bears).

Q **If Space Mountain didn't open at Walt Disney World until 1975, was the actual mountain constructed after the Park's 1971 opening, or was it there from the beginning with nothing inside it for four years? I am guessing that the PeopleMover was an original 1971 attraction, since it was integrated into most of the Tomorrowland attractions. If so, Space Mountain had to have been there too, unless the PeopleMover made a trip through nothing on the east end of the Park. What's the story? Christopher, Gordonville, PA**

A —The WEDWay PeopleMover opened on July 1, 1975, almost six months after Space Mountain. The construction of Space Mountain did take place after the Park had opened, beginning on December 15, 1972.

Q **What attraction at Walt Disney World was replaced by The Legend of the Lion King? Robert, Marietta, GA**

A —The original attraction in that location was the Mickey Mouse Revue, which featured a large orchestra of Audio-Animatronics Disney characters, led by maestro Mickey Mouse, that played classic Disney songs. It was removed in 1980 so it could be sent to Tokyo Disneyland. The theater saw seasonal use as the Fantasyland Theater, and the 3-D film *Magic Journeys* was shown there for a time. Legend of the Lion King opened in 1994, and it was in turn succeeded by Mickey's PhilharMagic in 2003.

Q **I enjoy going on the Carousel of Progress attraction. Is Walt Disney's voice one of the voices we hear in the main song? Also, who performs the voice of the father? Robert, South Plainfield, NJ**

A —While Walt Disney was caught singing "There's a Great Big Beautiful Tomorrow" with the Sherman Brothers (the song's composers) in a promotional film prepared for General Electric during the building of the original Carousel of Progress, his singing was not used in the attraction. A piece of that film is featured today in the preshow area for the Carousel at the Magic Kingdom at Walt Disney World. Rex Allen provides the voice of the father. Other voices in the current version of the show include Jean Shepherd as Grandfather, Janet Waldo as Grandma, and Noel Blanc, the son of renowned cartoon voice actor Mel Blanc, as various other characters.

Q In the Food Rocks show at the Land pavilion at Epcot, were any of the songs performed by the original artists whose material was being parodied, or are they all the work of impressionists? Jerry, Ormond Beach, FL

A —All the original performers cooperated in the production of Food Rocks, and five recorded the parodies of their music: Tone Loc as Füd Wrapper, Chubby Checker as Chubby Cheddar, Neil Sedaka as Neil Moussaka, Little Richard as Richard, and the Pointer Sisters as the Get-the-Point Sisters.

Q When I visited Walt Disney World in 1994, I rode the train around the Magic Kingdom. I noticed that the locomotive used was a 4-4-0 American type that had to have been built in the 1850s or 1860s. Can you tell me how a 4-4-0 wound up at Walt Disney World? The train at Disneyland appears to be different. William, San Diego, CA

A —First off, some of our readers may wonder what is meant by 4-4-0. This is a standard method of designating the wheel arrangements on locomotives—the number of wheels on the lead truck, followed by the number of drive wheels (the big ones), followed by the number of trailing wheels. The *Roy O. Disney* is the only 4-4-0 locomotive at Walt Disney World among the first five there. It was built in 1916 by Baldwin Locomotive Works and found by Disney in Yucatan, Mexico. This is the oldest locomotive at Walt Disney World. The first two locomotives at Disneyland were built by Disney designers in 1955, but the third, the *Fred Gurley*, dates from 1895 and was found at a Louisiana sugar plantation. It is a 2-4-4, converted from a 0-4-4. For more information, you might be interested in Michael Broggie's book *Walt Disney's Railroad Story* (Pentrex, 1997).

Q **In the movie *Xanadu*, starring Olivia Newton-John, the entrance of the abandoned club that later becomes Xanadu looks similar to the front gate of Disney's Hollywood Studios. Was this planned by the Imagineers, or merely a coincidence? Patrick, Reston, VA**

A —The front gate of Disney's Hollywood Studios was patterned after the entrance to the magnificent old Pan Pacific Auditorium in Los Angeles, which was destroyed by fire in 1987. *Xanadu*, released by Universal in 1980, used that auditorium as a set.

Q **Please tell me I'm not crazy! When Space Mountain first opened at Walt Disney World, there was a "home of the future" at the exit of the ride. In one of the rooms there was a large-screen television, and on it was Kurt Russell singing The Archies' hit "Sugar, Sugar." Am I correct? L., Brooklin, Ontario, Canada**

A —In the early years of Space Mountain, Guests exiting the attraction rode a speed ramp upward past the RCA Home of Future Living, which depicted a new world of home communications and technology for the years to come. There were dozens of television monitors, and on one of them Kurt Russell was indeed singing "Sugar, Sugar." It was taken from a 1970 television show titled *Disneyland Showtime*.

Q I think there used to be more skeleton pirates in the beginning of Pirates of the Caribbean. My father also says there was more than one flume drop. Are we both crazy? Scott, Edison, NJ

A —There are two flume drops in Pirates of the Caribbean at Disneyland and one at Walt Disney World, so your father may have ridden both. The number of skeletal pirates varies in both attractions, too.

Q I've seen signs and benches in Disney's Animal Kingdom that are decorated with animals walking in a line. There is a dragon among them. What does it have to do with the Park? Emily, Luling, LA

A —Original concepts for Disney's Animal Kingdom included an area "to be known as Beastly Kingdom, which would be devoted to mythical creatures." That area has never been built.

Q Which Walt Disney World hotel was the first to be built? How many rooms are there? And is Walt Disney World considered the biggest resort in the world? Katielu, Knoxville, TN

A —The Contemporary Resort and the Polynesian Resort opened first, in 1971. Today, there are almost 25,000 rooms in Walt Disney World hotels, making it by far the largest resort in the world.

Q Are the "hidden Mickeys" in the Parks officially placed there, or do the employees hide those on their own? Sheila, Palm Beach, FL

A —"Hidden Mickeys" are usually unobtrusive elements put into an attraction unofficially by a designer.

Q **Is the huge baobab tree in Walt Disney World's Animal Kingdom real? Susan, Long Beach, CA**

A —No, the tree is a creation of Disney Imagineers.

Q **Is there any truth to the rumors that there are still animals living on the old Discovery Island in Bay Lake at Walt Disney World? Was all the wildlife transferred to Disney's Animal Kingdom when Discovery Island closed? Jennifer, Bristol, CT**

A —While Disney no longer has any animals on the island that are cared for by its Animal Programs staff, there are now quite a few wild animals, including many buzzards, that call the island home. Some of the original animals were transferred to Disney's Animal Kingdom, while others were sent to zoos.

Q **There is a pin I've seen featuring Professor Ratigan on a Trade Parade float. Was there ever a real parade called the Trade Parade in a Disney Park? If so, did Ratigan appear in it? Linda, Yatesville, PA**

A —This pin, from a set of ten, was created for a pin-trading event at the Contemporary Resort at Walt Disney World on September 22, 2001. It was not a real parade.

Q **Before the Nemo ride in The Living Seas at Epcot, I remember another ride but cannot remember its name. It started with a movie. Do you know the name? Carrie, Poland, NY**

A —When The Living Seas first opened, Guests would see a film, *The Seas*, then "descend" into the depths of the sea in Hydrolators. They would board two-passenger Seacabs for a three-minute ride through a four-hundred-foot-long tunnel, offering views through large windows of the coral reefs teeming with fish and other sea creatures, before arriving at Sea Base Alpha. The short ride in the Seacabs did not have a name; it was closed around 2001.

Q How did Walt choose Orlando as the site of Walt Disney World? M.G., Tampa, FL

A —Walt wanted an East Coast site in an area with a climate allowing year-round operation. He also needed an abundance of land at a reasonable price. Central Florida fit those criteria.

Q Why is the Epcot of today so different from the original plans given by Walt in the *Disneyland* show? Also, what happened to those original plans that hung on the wall in the background? Joe, Springfield, MO

A —Walt Disney's 1966 film giving his ideas for EPCOT was shown on local television stations in Florida but not on his regular television show. Since Walt did not have time to refine his ideas before his untimely passing, plans had to be changed in ensuing years to make the project viable. The original plans for EPCOT are filed at Walt Disney Imagineering.

Q How were the countries selected to create World Showcase? Larry, Marion, IN

A —Disney originally sought sponsorship from governments of different countries (they had in mind a group of key countries which they felt had to be in World Showcase, such as Canada, Mexico, England, China, France, Germany, Italy, and Japan) but found such a pursuit to be difficult. Disney then sought sponsorship from companies that operated within the countries, and here they had more success. Canada and Mexico were placed closest to Future World, as they are the countries that border the U.S. (originally, The American Adventure was to be placed between them). As sponsors were found, the countries of Norway and Morocco were added, though some pavilions, including Costa Rica, Spain, and Equatorial Africa, never came to fruition.

Q **Years ago my wife and I attended a Christmas dinner and show at Walt Disney World. I believe it was called the** *Holly Jolly Christmas Show.* **We were picked up by a bus in front of the Contemporary Resort and were taken to a large building that looked like a warehouse. We went several years in a row and then it was gone. What was the real name of the show, and during what years was it presented? Dave, Fleming Island, FL**

A —You may be recalling the *Jolly Holiday Dinner Show Spectacular,* which was held at the Contemporary Resort Convention Center's Fantasia Ballroom starting during the holiday season in 1992. It featured an all-you-can-eat Christmas dinner and a show featuring one hundred performers; it continued until 1998.

Q **I remember seeing the Electrical Water Pageant at the Contemporary Resort at Walt Disney World in the 1970s, and I've heard that its development eventually led to the development of the Main Street Electrical Parade. Was the original music used for the show a version of "Baroque Hoedown," the song later (and still) used for the Main Street Electrical Parade? Alan, Chicago, IL**

A —"Baroque Hoedown" was indeed originally used by the Electrical Water Pageant in 1971, but in 1972 it was transferred to the Main Street Electrical Parade at Disneyland. Over the four decades that the pageant has been operating, the music it uses has changed many times.

Q The Osborne Family Spectacle of Dancing Lights at Disney's Hollywood Studios is fantastic. This year I noticed that of the five soldiers, the middle soldier (with Mickey ears) had a name tag. Can you tell me what the name on the tag was (it was too far away to read), and why did that soldier have a name tag? Greg, Snohomish, WA

A —According to John Phelan, show director for the light show, "The name tag reads 'Dan.' It is in honor of Dan Summers, who was an entertainment technician who passed away in January 2009 from cancer. Dan worked for many years on the display, and he was very passionate and dedicated to it. He was one of the key individuals who figured out how to make the lights 'dance.' But most of all, Dan loved to be on the street with the Guests, answering questions about the display. The crew came up with the idea of honoring Dan with the name tag."

Q In December 1976 my family went to Walt Disney World, and there was a place called the Donald Duck Juice Factory with the name on a water tower. In 2008 I returned and noticed a water tower at Downtown Disney that looked just like the tower I remember. Is that where the juice factory used to be? Robert, Baldwin, WI

A —Would you be thinking of Citrus World, Inc., headquartered in Lake Wales, Florida, not far from Walt Disney World? That is where Donald Duck orange juice is packaged. I do not remember a water tower, but I do remember a large billboard picturing Donald Duck on the roof of their building back in the 1970s.

Q I was just wondering what ever happened to Alien Encounter at Walt Disney World. I visited Disney World just once and loved that attraction because it really got my adrenaline pumping. I had hoped it would eventually come to Disneyland, but now I guess that won't happen. How long was it open, anyway? Pamela, Garden Grove, CA

A —The ExtraTERRORestrial Alien Encounter at the Magic Kingdom was open from 1995 to 2003. It had taken the place of the Mission to Mars attraction, and was then followed in turn by the current Stitch's Great Escape, which opened in 2004. Disney Imagineers are always looking for ways to enhance the Guests' experiences at the Parks, so sometimes they feel that a change in an attraction is advisable.

Q Is there an exclusive club restaurant hidden in Walt Disney World similar to Club 33 in Disneyland? Steve, Huntsville, AL

A —When Walt Disney World was built, Imagineers felt that no exclusive restaurant was needed in the Park because the Resort included hotels with elegant restaurants that could serve the same purpose as Club 33 did at Disneyland—that of entertaining important Guests.

Q My question is about Fantasmic! I was in Walt Disney World in 1988. At that time only Magic Kingdom and Epcot were open. I seem to remember that Fantasmic! was at Epcot. Am I correct, or has it only been at Hollywood Studios? Michael, Manassas Park, VA

A —Fantasmic! premiered in Disneyland in 1992, and although it would open in Disney's Hollywood Studios in 1998, it was never featured in Epcot. However, the Splashtacular show on the Epcot fountain stage greatly resembled it, as this 1993–94 spectacular was host to Disney characters, dozens of performers, and a dinosaur-like alien villain. Epcot also had Laserphonic Fantasy, the predecessor to IllumiNations in the lagoon, from 1984 to 1988.

Q How often do they have to shut down rides like Pirates of the Caribbean or the Haunted Mansion to do maintenance? Also, what is done to the Audio-Animatronics characters? Todd, Buford, GA

A —The ride and show engineering departments at our Parks have various refurbishment schedules for each of our attractions. Some attractions, like Splash Mountain at Walt Disney World, tend to close every year for a period for routine maintenance, while others receive extensive refurbishments, as did The Haunted Mansion at Walt Disney World in 2007. Audio-Animatronics characters are sometimes removed from attractions to be repaired. It isn't uncommon to find several animals from Pirates of the Caribbean or dolls from It's a Small World missing from time to time if they need work.

Q How many ceramic tiles were used to create the beautiful pictures in the walkway of the castle in Walt Disney World? Are any of the gold ones gold-plated ? Jeanne, Florida, NY

A —The beautiful Cinderella mosaics were designed by Disney artist Dorothea Redmond and crafted by famed mosaicist Hanns-Joachim Scharff. No one has counted the pieces of Italian glass—a press release says "hundreds of thousands." Some were fused with silver and 14-karat gold. The smallest pieces were the size of the head of a tack.

Q Each time we ride the bus from the Port Orleans hotel to the Magic Kingdom, we see what appears to be an airport just east of the Magic Kingdom parking lot. What's the story? Brad, Plano, TX

A —That airstrip was called the STOLport, for Short Takeoff and Landing, and it was built in 1971 for use by smaller planes. For a time Shawnee Airlines actually ran daily shuttle flights from McCoy (later Orlando International) Airport, but for various reasons, including safety concerns, the STOLport was closed, and the runway is today primarily used as a staging area for buses.

Q **If Orlando hadn't been chosen, were there other locations being considered for Walt Disney World? Mike, Runnemede, NJ**

A —Walt Disney had at one time considered doing something in Palm Beach, but soon decided that central Florida was the ideal location. After several surveys of the area, the decision was narrowed down to three choices: between DeLand and Daytona Beach, in Osceola County, and in Orange County near Orlando. We ended up combining the last two choices.

Q **Are you still able to visit Discovery Island? I remember taking a boat ride to a little island between the Polynesian Resort and the Magic Kingdom—it was like a minizoo of exotic birds and animals. When I look at a map it appears to still be there, but I can't find any mention of it in promotional materials or visitor information. I've tried several times to show my kids the island. I must have been in seventh or eighth grade when I went there. Sara, Algonquin, IL**

A —You are thinking of the 11.5-acre Discovery Island, which is actually in Bay Lake, near the Contemporary Resort and Fort Wilderness. It was set up as a nature preserve that Guests could visit and included one of the largest walk-through aviaries in the world. It closed in 1999, no longer needed after Disney's Animal Kingdom opened.

Q **Is there an underground tour open to Guests that allows you to view the actual operations and controls of the Walt Disney World grounds? Robin, Lafayette, LA**

A —Walt Disney World offers a special seven-hour tour called Backstage Magic, which includes Epcot, Disney's Hollywood Studios, and the Magic Kingdom. Disney's Animal Kingdom has a separate tour called Backstage Safari. You can find more information about these tours on the Walt Disney World Web site.

Q I love *Impressions de France* at Epcot, and I never tire of seeing it. No one seems to know who the narrator is. Can you help with this? I think it may be an old-time movie star whose name escapes me. Carla, Orlando, FL

A —The narrator is Claude Gobet.

Q How do the performers in parades and shows at the Disney Parks get their jobs? Richard, Topeka, KS

A —The Entertainment Divisions at the Disneyland and Walt Disney World Resorts regularly hold auditions for the parades and shows, looking for young people who are agile and are talented both in singing and dancing.

Q Did Walt originally plan for there to be so many Parks at Walt Disney World? What was his vision for the property? Charmaine, Mobile, AL

A —Walt's initial plan was only for Magic Kingdom and Epcot, but because of his foresight in acquiring so much land, the company was able to add other Parks that he had not considered.

Q What was the first parade at Walt Disney World? Lydia, Dayton, OH

A —The very first parade at the Magic Kingdom was a Character Parade, presented daily from October 1, 1971, until December

20 of that same year, when it was superseded by a Holiday Toy Parade. Meredith Willson led a 1,076-piece band featuring seventy-six trombones, playing his song from *The Music Man*, for a special Grand Opening Parade on October 25.

Q **Have any baby animals been born at Disney's Animal Kingdom? Shelley, Richmond, VA**

A —Yes indeed. There have been well over one hundred species that have reproduced at Disney's Animal Kingdom, including rhinos, gorillas, giraffes, and elephants. The first birth there, before the Park opened to Guests in 1998, was a kudu, a large African antelope.

Q **Our family has been visiting Walt Disney World since it opened. We can't remember what attractions used to stand in the places where Epcot's Mission: SPACE and Test Track are now located. Can you refresh our memory? Russ, Naples, FL**

A —Mission: SPACE took the place of Horizons (1983–1999), and Test Track took the place of World of Motion (1982–1996).

Q **In the 1970s, was Snow White's Scary Adventures a different type of ride? Shanan, Crown Point, IN**

A —The Snow White attraction at Walt Disney World actually went through a major revision in 1994. Prior to that time, while it was not a roller coaster, it was very dark and scary, using the Witch to emphasize the ominous aspects of the film. The new concept was to have Guests experience the show from Snow White's point of view—the heroine hadn't even appeared in the original version.

Q **What brought about the idea of having bands from different schools march through the Park during the day at Walt**

Disney World? And which band was the first one to do it? Hope, Wiggins, MS

A —It seems as if guest high school bands started performing at Walt Disney World in conjunction with its first holiday festival. The earliest one I found listed in a press release or entertainment schedule is the St. Petersburg High School Green Devil Band, on December 18, 1971. Eventually, the Magic Music Days program began attracting hundreds of high school and college bands every year.

Q **A Cast Member told me that the *Empress Lilly* was originally managed and run by Lillian Disney and that she used to throw big parties there for all her friends. What is the history of this restaurant, and what was Lillian's involvement? Marisa, Bloomington, MN**

A —Lillian Disney's only connection to the *Empress Lilly* was that it was named after her. The riverboat opened in 1977 and originally contained three restaurants—the Fisherman's Deck, the Steerman's Quarters, and the Empress Room.

Q **I am a former Cast Member, and many people have asked me about the ability to "take down the castles overnight" during extreme inclement weather. I'm pretty sure this wasn't a part of "traditions" training. Can you shed some light on this persistent rumor? Brent, Orangeville, FL**

A —This is indeed an urban legend—Cinderella Castle at Walt Disney World was built to withstand hurricanes and could not be so easily dismantled.

Q **I recently went to the Magic Kingdom after being there over thirty years ago. Two rides were no longer there. One was**

20,000 Leagues Under the Sea and the other was a cable car ride. My friend says the Magic Kingdom in Florida never had them, only Disneyland in California, but I'm sure they were there. Who is right? Philip, Valhalla, NY

A —You are right. 20,000 Leagues Under the Sea closed in 1994 and the Skyway in 1999.

Q Does the Rock 'n' Roller Coaster play a different song for every ride? John, Bridgeport, CT

A —At the Disney's Hollywood Studios attraction, there are actually five specially recorded Aerosmith sound tracks—each Limotrain features a different Aerosmith song. Lead singer Steven Tyler and guitarist Joe Perry recorded custom lyrics and riffs for each tune.

Q In October of 1971, Disney World had a 1,076-piece marching band led by Meredith "Music Man" Willson. What can you tell me about the Music Man? Richard, El Paso, TX

A —Author and composer Meredith Willson (1902–1984) was best known for composing the Tony Award–winning musical *The Music Man*, which debuted on Broadway in 1957 and was made into a popular movie starring Robert Preston and Shirley Jones in 1962. Willson's showstopper song in the musical was "Seventy-Six Trombones." Disney did a TV version of the musical for *The Wonderful World of Disney*, starring Matthew Broderick, in 2003.

Q One of my favorite things at Animal Kingdom is the Flights of Wonder show. The birds are magnificent. Has this show been part of Animal Kingdom from the beginning? What can you tell me about the birds and the trainers? Sandy, Pittsburgh, PA

A —Flights of Wonder was indeed an Opening Day show at Disney's Animal Kingdom in 1998, and it has been performed ever since for appreciative audiences. The show was developed by Walt Disney World Entertainment in collaboration with Steve Martin of Natural Encounters, Inc., a company renowned for producing educational animal shows. Which birds show off on any given day is part of the surprise; there are at least twenty species in the cast.

Q EPCOT stands for Experimental Prototype Community of Tomorrow, but Walt called it Experimental Prototype City of Tomorrow. Who changed this, and why? Trish, Yardley, PA

A —Walt Disney meant for the name to be Community, but once in a film he made a slip and referred to it as "City." Over the years the EPCOT name evolved until now it is written as Epcot, having become a word in its own right.

Q When I was recently in Walt Disney World, there was a character at the Monsters, Inc. Laugh Floor who said that he was Mike's nephew. He is orange with a purple eye. He was so cute, and I would love to know what his name is. Clemmons, NC

A —Mike's nephew in the show is Marty; the character was not in the film but was created especially for the Laugh Floor.

Q I have seen either a picture or a commercial of Mickey standing on top of the famous Epcot globe. How did he get up there? Is there a trapdoor on top? Tammy, Atlanta, GA

A —There is indeed a trapdoor in Spaceship Earth that allows access to the top. The Matterhorn at Disneyland also has access to the peak.

Q In the 1970s I remember seeing an attraction at Walt Disney World where they showed a movie all about Walt's dream and how Disneyland was born. In the queue area before entering the theater, there was a mural along the length of the wall featuring most if not all of the Disney cartoon characters. I'd like to know what happened to that mural. Was it covered up? Does it still exist somewhere? Davanna, Tampa, FL

A —The mural, painted by Bill Justice, with additions by Russell Schroeder, was located at the entrance to The Walt Disney Story attraction. It has been removed and is in storage.

Q Is there a particular rhyme or reason to the lineup of presidents in the Hall of Presidents? Also, I noticed that Andrew Jackson appeared to be talking with a fellow president. Who is he next to, and did they know each other? Is there any significance to the outfits that they are wearing? Sue, Westerville, OH

A —The presidents are grouped by era, more or less by clothing styles; Imagineers wanted them to be introduced in a more interesting fashion than straight left-to-right chronological order. Andrew Jackson appears to say something to John Tyler, who is standing on his right. Jackson and Tyler were contemporaries but did not always agree politically. For the Hall of Presidents, two retired Hollywood film tailors did extensive research before creating suits that were authentic to what each president would have worn.

Q My wife and I went to The American Adventure during a recent trip to Epcot. The movie we saw there has a segment on the Civil War that tells the story of two brothers—one fighting for the North, the other for the South. Is the family factual, or fictitious? If they are real, can you tell us more about them? Ama, Safety Harbor, FL

A —The song, "Two Brothers," is a traditional-sounding Civil War ballad written by Irving Gordon in 1951 and sung by Ali Olmo. I am not aware if Gordon based his song on any particular family, but I have read of many instances where families were divided by the Civil War. The family shown in the vintage-looking photos in the film is composed of actors.

Q **The narrator on Spaceship Earth sounds like Dame Judi Dench—with the accent and the huskiness. Is it? Barb, CA**

A —Dame Judi Dench does narrate Spaceship Earth. Her narration was added when the attraction reopened in December 2007 after extensive renovations.

Q **I've been to Walt Disney World many times as a child and as a father. My daughter thinks the highest point in the Magic Kingdom is Cinderella Castle, but I say it's Expedition Everest in Animal Kingdom. Please help! Tim, Louisville, KY**

A —Expedition Everest is the Walt Disney World Resort's highest point, followed by The Twilight Zone Tower of Terror at Disney's Hollywood Studios. Cinderella Castle is the highest point in the Magic Kingdom.

Q **Around the late nineties in Walt Disney World, I noticed a short film playing in the Main Street Cinema that featured Mel Brooks as an old-time Hollywood director, directing Mickey Mouse before he met Walt Disney. Can you tell me more about this short? Michael, Clarksburg, NJ**

A —That film was called *Mickey's Big Break*. In it Roy E. Disney portrayed his uncle Walt. Besides Mel Brooks, there were also cameo roles by Dom DeLuise and Ed Begley, Jr. The film was originally known as *Mickey's Audition* and was used during the summer of 1991 at Disney-MGM Studios as a temporary attraction on a soundstage. It appeared at the Main Street Cinema first in 1994 and four years later in the Town Square Exhibition Hall.

Q **My husband and I have been going to Walt Disney World every year for the past twelve years. We wonder every time we're at Epcot what in the world the Odyssey Center is (or was)? It drives us both crazy because I have looked for the answer in countless books and on the Internet, and I've asked Disney employees. No one seems to know. Can you help us? Heather, Cape May, NJ**

A —Odyssey, located between Future World and World Showcase at Epcot, actually opened as a quick-service food facility in 1982 and remained open until 1994. Since then it has been used for special events and banquets only.

Q **I was just on It's a Small World in Walt Disney World, and I noticed that as you get off your boat at the end, there are a bunch of numbers on the wall in random order. Do they mean anything? Mary, Shamong, NJ**

A —During the 2005 redesign of It's a Small World, elements were added, including graphics from the clock tower at the entrance to the Disneyland attraction, as designed by the attraction's original artist, Mary Blair. There is no significance to the placement of the numbers—they simply refer to "time."

Q **When I was a child, our family stayed at the Contemporary Resort several times. Above the bed, I remember seeing a large, framed map of the resort that featured the Magic Kingdom, the monorail line, the Contemporary, the Polynesian, and some hotels that were never built. I believe there are**

now office buildings where these nonexistent hotels were shown. Do you know the story behind those pictures and what happened to them? I'd love to own one! Julia, Rising Sun, MD

A —When those prints—an early depiction of what Walt Disney World was going to consist of—were removed from the Contemporary Resort, many were sold to Cast Members at warehouse sales of surplus property. They occasionally turn up on eBay.

Q I have an early map of Walt Disney World that shows the Magic Kingdom, Bay Lake, and Seven Seas Lagoon. Included on the map are things we know today . . . the Polynesian, the Contemporary, the Campground, and old Treasure Island (Discovery Island). There were three other hotels pictured on the map: one where the Grand Floridian is now (but the theme looks different), another one just north of the Transportation and Ticket Center, and a third, which appears to be Persian, north of the Contemporary on Bay Lake. Can you tell us about these planned hotels? Richard, Davenport, FL

A —The early plans for the Walt Disney World property included several hotels around the Seven Seas Lagoon. Clockwise from the Magic Kingdom were the Contemporary Resort, Venetian Resort, Polynesian Resort, and Asian Resort. There was also a Persian Resort proposed, but it was to be on Bay Lake rather than on the Seven Seas Lagoon. The Grand Floridian Resort was eventually built on the site of the proposed Asian Resort, and one can see the site of the Venetian Resort between the Contemporary and the Transportation and Ticket Center, near the water bridge.

Q I've heard that all Disney rides are less than two hundred feet tall, because if they were taller they would require a flashing red light on top to warn airplanes. Is this true? Catherine, Las Vegas, NV

A —That is correct. The Federal Aviation Administration requires flashing lights on structures over two hundred feet in height.

Q The original Disney-MGM Studios tour showed several house facades from TV shows and movies, including the house from *The Golden Girls*. *The Golden Girls* premiered on television in 1985, but the Park did not open until 1989. Where did this facade come from? Was it a replica, or was it the actual one used in the show? How about the other houses? Jeff, Burbank, CA

A —It was a replica, not the one actually used in the show. Little filming took place on that residential street; it was primarily there for the tour trams.

Q I was recently going through some old family vacation photos, and I came across some pictures from a trip to Epcot in 1987. It looks like there are live elephants performing on the fountain stage. I was young at the time; were there live elephants in the Park back then? If so, what was the show about? Jonathan, Clermont, FL

A —From October 1, 1987, to March 19, 1988, Epcot hosted Epcot's Daredevil Circus Spectacular on the Communicore Stage in Future World. It included "The Greatest Show in Space" and Jay Cochrane, Skywalker. The opening act in the show was the four Cristiani Elephants—Carey, Babe, Shirley, and Emma—who had played in circuses all over the world. They were billed as "mutant prehistoric pachyderms from the steaming jungles of a little-known planet in the Archturian Cosmos." Their stunts were performed four times a day.

Q **Could you tell me who put together the wonderful montage of movie clips that is shown at the conclusion of The Great Movie Ride at Disney's Hollywood Studios? T.R., Marlboro, NJ**

A —That fantastic film compilation seen at the conclusion of The Great Movie Ride was originally created by Academy Award-winning filmmaker Chuck Workman. It has since been updated several times.

WALT DISNEY

Q I have found the quotation, "If we can dream it, we can do it," attributed to Walt Disney, on the Internet. Do you know when he said it? Thomas, Lincoln, NE

A —Despite its frequent publication, that is not a Walt Disney quote. We checked with Imagineer Tom Fitzgerald for the definitive answer: "I am very familiar with that line, because I wrote it! It was written specifically for the Horizons attraction at Epcot and used in numerous ways, from dialogue in the ride to graphics. I find it amusing that The Science of Disney Imagineering DVD series attributes it to Walt Disney, but I guess I should be flattered."

Q Did Walt ever win the Nobel Peace Prize? I heard that he did. Gray, Vicksburg, MS

A —No, he did not. But that is not to say it hasn't been suggested. . . .

Q The fall 2010 issue of *Disney twenty-three* magazine says that you catalogued Walt's office in 1970 and one of the books on the shelf was Victor Gruen's *The Heart of Our Cities*. What were the other books? Edward, Fairfield, CT

A —Some of the books alongside Victor Gruen's were the 1965 *International Motion Picture Almanac*, *The Magic Bed-knob* (which became *Bedknobs and Broomsticks*) by Mary Norton, *The Year of the Horse* (which became *The Horse in the Gray Flannel Suit*) by Eric Hatch, *Blackbeard's Ghost* by Ben Stahl, *Jimmie Dale and the Phantom Clue* by Frank Packard, and *Travels with Charley* by John Steinbeck.

Q Could you please tell me if you have any idea what book Walt is referring to in this quote? "Everyone has been remarkably influenced by a book, or books. In my case it was a book on cartoon animation. I discovered it in the Kansas City Library at the time I was preparing to make motion-picture animation my life's work. The book told me all I needed to know as a beginner—all about the arts and the mechanics of making drawings that move on the theater screen. From the basic information I could go on to develop my own way of movie storytelling." Amber, Griffith, IN

A —The book was *Animated Cartoons* by E. G. Lutz, published in 1920 just as Walt Disney was getting into the field. It is still regarded as an important primer.

Q **When was the last time Walt Disney visited Disneyland? Salvador, Redondo Beach, CA**

A —The last date for a visit to Disneyland that I find on Walt Disney's desk calendar is October 14, 1966, when he met with Presidential Medal of Freedom winners. This visit took place just two months before he died.

Q **I recently saw an old Jack Benny television special with Walt Disney as one of the guest stars. Did Walt Disney and Jack Benny do anything else together during their careers? How well did they know each other? Erik, Maple Grove, MN**

A —I put together a Jack Benny bibliography when I worked at UCLA back in the 1960s; Benny's archives are at the university. Walt only made that one appearance on *The Jack Benny Hour*, on November 3, 1965. I am unaware that they were personal friends. That particular show also featured guests Bob Hope, the Beach Boys, and Elke Sommer.

Q **Can you provide me with some information on the Disney family's connection with Canada? I'm quite sure that Walt's**

father, Elias, was from Canada (possibly from Clinton, Ontario), but I've been unable to find details. Michael, St. Catharines, Ontario, Canada

A —Walt's great-grandfather (Elias) and grandfather (Kepple) came over from Ireland in 1835, settling in Holmesville, near Goderich, Ontario, where the elder Disney managed a gristmill. Walt's father, Elias, named after his grandfather, was born in Bluevale, near Wingham, Ontario, in 1859. He was baptized in Clinton and educated both in Bluevale and Goderich. The Disney family emigrated to the United States in 1878.

Q **I recently saw a photograph of Walt Disney's brother Roy holding a small statue of Mickey Mouse. I've heard that Walt gave it to him. What is the history of this statue? Chris, Las Vegas, NV**

A —The Mousecars, Disney's version of an Oscar, are bronze-colored Mickey statuettes presented to those who have done a special service for The Walt Disney Company. Walt gave the first Mousecar to Roy, in 1947. We don't know how many have been given out, because no accurate lists were kept. There is also a Donald Duck version called a Duckster.

Q **When Walt Disney passed away, in December 1966, no mention was made of it in *Disney News*. Was this simply a matter of editorial timing? Roy's death was mentioned in the spring 1972 issue. Tim, Henderson, NV**

A —I think your guess is probably correct. When Walt died, the winter issue (for December, January, and February) had already gone to press. Perhaps because of the extensive coverage of his passing in other media, by the time the spring issue (March, April, and May) was being prepared, the editors felt it was unnecessary to repeat the news. Roy's death did not receive as much news coverage, so a mention in *Disney News* was called for.

Q I am an amateur historian of the 1939–40 Golden Gate International Exposition (held on Treasure Island in San Francisco Bay). I came across a publicity photo of Walt holding a poster dated 1939 and inscribed "Walt Disney . . . on Treasure Island." Do you know when and for what occasion Walt may have visited? Anne, Menlo Park, CA

A —While I don't have any specifics about your picture, I did find out that Walt Disney visited the exposition. Walt, along with fifteen animators and sketch artists, was there February 17–21 in 1939, in part to attend a concert of the San Francisco Symphony Orchestra conducted by Leopold Stokowski. These artists were working on the early stages of what became *Fantasia*. Walt felt it would be beneficial for them to see Stokowski in concert and observe his mannerisms.

Q On the bronze statue of Walt Disney at Disneyland, there is a small symbol that looks rather like an Asian character on his tie. What is this, and what does it mean? Alfonso, Irvine, CA

A —Walt Disney had a vacation home at the Smoke Tree Ranch (STR) in Palm Springs, California, and enjoyed wearing ties with the ranch's stylized STR emblem.

Q Like millions of others, I've always been amazed at the lifelike Audio-Animatronics figures in the Parks. Has there ever been a move to create an attraction featuring an Audio-Animatronics Walt Disney? Also, I've read all the biographies on Walt Disney currently available, and I've noticed in pictures and films of him that he seemed to always wear two rings. I assume

one was his wedding band. What significance did the other have? Jeff, Ramseur, NC

A —Walt wore a normal wedding band on his left hand and a claddagh ring, an Irish ring featuring two hands holding a heart, on his right. He and Mrs. Disney both had these, which they probably got in Ireland.

While there have been suggestions of an Audio-Animatronics Walt Disney from people outside our company, it has never been seriously considered. Walt was extremely modest and would probably have been appalled at the idea. As a more fitting tribute, we created *The Walt Disney Story* film—which played at the Parks for years and was released on video—and the *Partners* statues (Walt with Mickey Mouse) on display in our Parks. We also have the One Man's Dream exhibit at Disney's Hollywood Studios.

Q **I collect autographs and am interested in Walt Disney autographs. Do you have any comments on the range of values between an autograph, a signed photograph, and a signed document? Mike, Appleton, WI**

A —Walt Disney's autograph has become quite valuable in recent years, but unfortunately, that rise in value has led to a number of forgeries coming on the market. In addition, Walt Disney occasionally authorized some of his artists to sign his autograph for him. Generally, a simple signature, which is the most difficult to authenticate, has been selling for about $1,000 to $1,500. A signed photograph, a letter, or a document would have higher values, depending on the content. An inscription on the mat of a cel would also have a higher value.

Q **As Walt Disney had two daughters, will the name continue? Did Roy or Roy Jr. have any sons? Craig, El Cerrito, CA**

A —Yes, the Disney name will continue. While Walt had two daughters, his brother Roy O. Disney had one son, Roy E. Disney. Roy E. had two sons and two daughters.

Q **I read that Walt Disney was an ambulance driver in World War I, as was Ray Kroc (of McDonald's fame). Did they ever meet during the war? Patrick, Los Angeles, CA**

A —They didn't meet during active service (Walt Disney did not arrive in France until a week after the war ended), but both Walt and Ray Kroc trained at the same place, Sound Beach, Connecticut, before shipping out. There are photos showing both of them as teenagers posing at Sound Beach together as part of the entire training group.

Q **Is it true that "Disney" is actually a changed version of Walt's family's original name? If so, what was the original name, and why did he change it? Gregg, Agoura Hills, CA**

A —The Disney ancestors came from a small town in France called Isigny-sur-Mer. In the French language, someone from Isigny would be identified as "d'Isigny." That was later anglicized to Disney.

Q **Which of his many accomplishments was Walt most proud of? Susan, Honolulu, HI**

A —Walt often said that he was most proud of the organization he had created and that the public accepted and appreciated all he had done through the years.

Q **I know the Disney company is very active in volunteer work. Did Walt give money to charities, and did he have a favorite charity? Susan, Long Beach, CA**

A —Walt had many favorite charities, but the most important to him was the California Institute of the Arts, an institution he helped found. He left the school a large portion of his estate. Other groups included the Jules Stein Eye Institute, the Children's Hospital of Orange County, and the Los Angeles Zoo.

Q **Did any of Walt or Roy Disney's children work at the Parks? Ellen, Montebello, CA**

A —No, none of the kids has ever worked at the Parks. Some of the grandkids, however, have worked brief stints at the Disney Studios in Burbank, California. For example, grandson Walter Elias Disney Miller worked one summer in the Walt Disney Archives sorting and mounting photographs of his grandfather.

Q **Was Walt himself an animator, and did he personally animate any of his cartoons? Sara, Iowa City, IA**

A —Walt gave up animating in the mid-1920s when he discovered that he could hire animators who were more talented than he; instead, he turned to story work and directing, where his major talents lay. He did animate some of his early Laugh-O-gram and Alice Comedy cartoons.

Q **I've seen photos of Walt Disney with dogs. Was he a dog lover? How many dogs did he have? Millie, Eugene, OR**

A —Walt Disney was indeed a dog lover—his family traditionally had pet dogs. In the 1930s, the Disneys had a chow named Sunnee. Later they had a huge poodle named Duchess Disney.

Q **Where is Walt Disney buried? Is it open to the public? Ellen, Montebello, CA**

A —Walt Disney's grave is at Forest Lawn Memorial Park in Glendale, California. Disney fans do come to pay their respects.

Q Was Walt or his brother Roy ever in the military? Victoria, Superior, WI

A —Roy O. Disney served in the Navy during World War I. Walt's service was with the American Red Cross; he was too young to get into a military unit.

Q What did Walt do during World War II? How did the Studio help with the war effort? Mark, Darien, CT

A —During the war, about 93 percent of the output of the Studio was devoted to the war effort, with the production of military, training, and propaganda films along with insignia for military units and war-themed cartoons that attempted to raise morale on the home front. Walt himself was a bit too old to be drafted; he turned forty-two days before Pearl Harbor. He was also a father of two daughters and ran a company heavily involved in the war effort.

Q I've always wanted to know why Walt Disney and his brother Roy have not yet been inducted as Disney Legends. Is there a specific reason why? Joe, Livonia, MI

A —Good question, and I'm not sure what the answer is. I guess that Walt and Roy Disney essentially *were* the company during their lives, and it didn't seem necessary to give them the Disney Legend award (which bore their name). They have already been sufficiently honored.

Q I used to live in northern Nevada and would visit Squaw Valley at Lake Tahoe often. A friend showed me a home there and said it was Walt Disney's home during the Olympic Games. It is an

adorable home; it looks like Snow White could walk out the door at any moment. Is this story true? Debby, Windermere, FL

A —Walt Disney did have a vacation home he used at Squaw Valley at the time he produced the pageantry for the 1960 Winter Olympic Games, but I do not have a record of its location.

Q **Is it true that the last thing Walt Disney did before he died was write the words "Kurt Russell"? Victor, Chicago, IL**

A —Not exactly. On his desk was a notepad on which he had scrawled some notes about future films and television shows. One of the names that he wrote was "Kurt Russell." The notes are undated but are certainly among the last things he wrote in his office. When Kurt was at the Studio filming *Now You See Him, Now You Don't*, I took him up to Walt's office to show him the notes.

Q **Walt Disney was the mystery guest on the November 11, 1956, episode of *What's My Line?* At the end of the show, he told viewers that next week, *The Saturday Evening Post* would feature an article written by his daughter about Walt Disney. I would love to read this article and know more about it. Marcio, Rio de Janeiro, Brazil**

A —Walt referred to the serialized version of Diane Disney Miller's biography of her father, "My Dad, Walt Disney." It appeared in *The Saturday Evening Post* for seven weeks, beginning on November 24, 1956. The book version was entitled *The Story of Walt Disney.*

Q **My cousins told me about a great documentary that was made about Walt Disney. They also told me it was directed by his grandson. Do you know where I can find it? Gavin, Auburn, IN**

A —You are referring to *Walt: The Man Behind the Myth*. It was released on VHS in 2001 and DVD in 2002 and may still be available. You can also find copies on eBay. It was shown on cable TV in 2011. The executive producer was Walter Elias Disney Miller, Walt's grandson, for the Walt Disney Family Foundation.

Q I know Walt Disney received the esteemed Silver Buffalo Award from the Boy Scouts of America. Was it in response to any specific activities, or because of his work and life in general? Denise, Tallahassee, FL

A —Walt was presented with the Silver Buffalo Award by the Boy Scouts in 1946, and it was essentially for his life's work. The commendation explains it was for "contributing to the joy of youth in every land . . . and the elevation of their standards of good taste."

Q Did Walt Disney ever name a favorite among his movies? Ken, Bangor, MN

A —Walt's current project was usually his favorite; when he finished it, it was forgotten and he went on to the next. But some artists have reported that he told them he had a special fondness for *Bambi* in the early days and later, of course, for *Mary Poppins*, which was the pinnacle of his career.

Q Walt took a lot of chances. Was there ever a movie that Walt said afterward he wished he hadn't made? Shari, Chesterfield, MO

A —Movie producers often have second thoughts about films that are released to disappointing box-office results. Walt certainly worried about *Fantasia* when it took so long to make a profit. Audiences complained about the heavy Scottish accents in

Greyfriars Bobby. And he had second thoughts about *Alice in Wonderland*—he wondered if he had been right in trying to adapt such a classic story, with so many avid fans, in the Disney style.

Q **Did Walt Disney ever appear in one of his films? Gina, Minneapolis, MN**

A —Walt only appeared in one of his theatrical films—*The Reluctant Dragon* (1941). Humorist Robert Benchley brings a story to Walt, along the way learning about the process of animation, only to discover on meeting Walt in a screening room that the Studio has already made a film of the book. Walt also had a cameo in television's *Moochie of Pop Warner Football.*

Q **I've heard that Walt Disney loved to play polo. When and where did he play? George, Raleigh, NC**

A —In the 1930s Walt played polo to get his mind off his work, and he enlisted several of the Disney staffers, including his brother Roy, to join him. He played at a club started by actor Victor McLaglen and later at the Riviera Polo Club. He finally gave up the sport after suffering a serious neck injury.

Q **I've heard that Walt and his family didn't mingle very much with the "Hollywood" crowd. Is that true? Louis, Queens, NY**

A —That is true. Walt was quite different from the other studio heads in Hollywood, being the only one raised on a farm in mid-America, and he had small-town-boy sensibilities. He was more at ease socializing with his staff, neighbors, and close friends.

Q **Was there an award that Walt received that he was particularly proud of? Harold, Kalamazoo, MI**

A —Walt kept a few of his favorite awards behind the desk in his office. These included his first Oscar for the creation of Mickey Mouse; an ornate cut-glass pitcher from Russia for *Snow White and the Seven Dwarfs*; and the prestigious Irving Thalberg Award, presented by the Academy of Motion Picture Arts and Sciences for Best Producer.

Q **I understand that the last time Walt voiced Mickey Mouse it was for the cartoon short "Mickey and the Beanstalk" (a segment of *Fun and Fancy Free*). Why did Walt decide to stop voicing Mickey when he did? Beverly, San Francisco, CA**

A —It was during the production of *Fun and Fancy Free* that Walt decided he had just gotten too busy, so he asked his sound-effects man, Jim Macdonald, to take over the chore for him. Macdonald continued for three decades, when he was succeeded by Wayne Allwine. Bret Iwan now provides Mickey's voice.

Q **When Walt Disney's house was sold, the miniature railroad and all its associated buildings and tracks were removed. What became of them, and who has the train? Richard, Baltimore, MD**

A —The tracks were taken out many years ago and donated to the Live Steamers group at Griffith Park in Los Angeles. After Lillian Disney's death in 1997, the barn in which Walt operated the train was also moved to Griffith Park, where it is maintained with exhibits and open to the public on the third Sunday of every month.

Q **What high school did Walt Disney graduate from, and when did he graduate? Becky, Lancaster, CA**

A —Walt attended only one year of high school, at McKinley High in Chicago. He left to become an ambulance driver at the end of

World War I and never returned to school. However, many have told me that if you met Walt, you would think he was one of the most educated people you had ever met. He was very inquisitive and seemed to remember everything he was told.

Q **I heard a rumor that Disney did not accept major credit cards until about the nineties because Walt Disney could not get loans from the major banks back in the day. Is this true? Bob, Bristol, CT**

A —Until the mid-1980s at Walt Disney World, only American Express, which was the official credit card of Walt Disney World, was accepted for admission, though other cards were accepted for accommodations, shops, and sit-down restaurants. Disneyland did not accept any credit cards for admissions before the mid-1980s. There was no relationship to Walt Disney's earlier bank loans.

Q **I heard somewhere that Walt was once an Eagle Scout, but it's not mentioned in the latest authorized biography on Walt Disney. Was he? Popski, Philadelphia, PA**

A —Walt Disney was never a Boy Scout, though he had great admiration for the organization.

Q **My father visited Disneyland almost fifty years ago. He is convinced that when he went to the restroom, Walt himself handed him a towel when he was done. Would it be possible that Walt was in the Park? (If not, I won't tell my father, because he loves that memory!) Jenny, Westminster, CA**

A —Walt Disney frequently visited the Park, so this might have been a possibility. I ran into Walt in the Park myself around 1956, when I was a teenager.

Q After watching *The Wizard of Oz* for the fifteenth time with my three-year-old, I was wondering what Walt thought about the picture. After all, it was made directly as a result of the fervor around *Snow White*, which was released a year earlier. Dan, Penfield, NY

A —Walt was intrigued with the Oz stories, first inquiring about their copyright status in 1937, even before MGM had begun production on its film. I have never seen any comments by Walt on the MGM film, but in 1954, Disney bought the film rights to eleven of the original Oz books by L. Frank Baum and soon announced plans for a film to be called *The Rainbow Road to Oz*. Other than a couple of production numbers performed by the Mouseketeers on an episode of the Disney TV show, the film was never made. It wasn't until 1985 that Disney finally took advantage of the rights and made *Return to Oz*.

Q Being a Disney fanatic, I pick up on the little "Disney details" (scenery, names, etc.) in many of the Disney films. I was wondering if the animated star WALL•E was named for Disney founder, creator, innovator, and genius Walter Elias Disney? Anita, Waukee, IA

A —Interesting thought! Not knowing the answer, I checked with Pixar, and their answer was "Nope. Sorr-E." WALL•E actually stands for Waste Allocation Load Lifter, Earth-Class.

Q Can you tell me what Walt Disney's favorite food was? C.K., Bellevue, WA

A —Walt had a passion for chili and beans. According to his biographer, Bob Thomas, Walt "was a connoisseur, preferring to combine a can of Gebhardt's, which had more meat and few beans, with a can of Dennison's, which had less meat and more beans."

Q **When was Walt Disney's final visit to Walt Disney World? Susan, Lowell, MA**

A —Walt Disney's last trip to view the Florida property was in May 1966. He died in December of that year, so he never saw the finished Park, which opened in 1971.

Q **Where did Walt Disney get the idea for the name Mouseketeers? S.C., Trenton, NJ**

A —Way back in 1936, Walt Disney made a Silly Symphony cartoon called *Three Blind Mouseketeers*. The title was a takeoff on both *The Three Musketeers* and "Three Blind Mice." No doubt he remembered that title when he was planning the *Mickey Mouse Club*. We have in the Archives a memo from Walt dated April 15, 1955, in which he says, "The talented kids on the Mickey Mouse Club Show will be called Mouseketeers." The TV program began six months later.

Q **I was told that Walt Disney's collection of miniatures was the forerunner of Disneyland. Is this true? G.T., Helena, MT**

A —Yes, Walt was a miniatures collector—furniture and household items, which he displayed in little room settings. Out of this collection came an idea for a miniature Americana display with dioramas that would travel the country by truck and teach people about how life in the United States developed to the present. His first completed model was Granny's Cabin, which he exhibited at a Festival of California Living at the Pan Pacific Auditorium in Los Angeles in 1952. But because of the obvious problem of not being able to show dioramas to large numbers of people, Walt had to put aside his idea of a miniature display and expand his sights to what eventually became Disneyland.

Q **How did Walt Disney get his interest in trains, which eventually led to the live-steam setup he had in his backyard? J.L., Huntington Beach, CA**

A —When Walt was a boy in Marceline, Missouri, his Uncle Mike was a train engineer. Walt would run down to the tracks to wave when he knew Uncle Mike would be steaming through. Later on, as a teenager living in Kansas City, Walt got a summer job as a news butcher, selling newspapers, candy, and soft drinks on the trains that ran from Kansas City through half a dozen states. What an ideal job for a kid who loved trains! Years later in California, after having fun building an electric train layout for a nephew for Christmas, Walt decided to build an even larger railroad at his home, and this was followed eventually by the trains at Disneyland.

Q **When I was in Chicago I looked for Walt Disney's birthplace at 1249 Tripp Ave., but I couldn't find it. Is the house gone? J.K., Springfield, IL**

A —The house is still there. The reason you didn't find it is that all of the houses along the street have been renumbered. The house is now 2156 Tripp Ave.

Q **Was Walt Disney ever filmed while recording the voice of Mickey Mouse? T.W., Sykesville, MD**

A —Since Walt often energetically acted out the role while recording Mickey's voice, the animators felt it would be useful for them to have film of him doing just that. Walt resisted, but finally gave in during a recording session for *The Pointer*, which had more Mickey dialogue than usual. He only agreed if the camera would be hidden in the control booth. The animators were delighted with the result; unfortunately, that unique film no longer exists.

But more recently a short film clip of Walt doing Mickey's voice from *Mr. Mouse Takes a Trip* surfaced in the film library.

Q **Did Walt Disney personally design any of the attractions at Disneyland? A.L, Antioch, CA**

A —Until his death in 1966, Walt Disney was highly involved in creating all of the attractions that were built at Disneyland. He spent more time on some attractions than on others. For example, when Walt was planning the Mine Train Through Nature's Wonderland, he wasn't satisfied with his designers' creations. So Walt took drawing materials home and sketched out the entire ride himself. Today, this drawing of Walt's is part of the Archives. (The Mine Train ride has since been replaced by Big Thunder Mountain Railroad.)

Q **Did the United States issue a postage stamp to honor Walt Disney? G.D., St. Paul, MN**

A —The 6-cent commemorative stamp to honor Walt Disney was issued on September 11, 1968. The Archives acquired the original 1967 letter from then–California Governor Ronald Reagan, written to the postmaster general, suggesting that a stamp be issued for Walt Disney. Reagan wrote, "I hesitate to even mention California's pride in his vast accomplishments for fear of detracting from his true image as a world-renowned and world-beloved figure. There is no necessity for me to itemize his contributions to humanity; they can be summed up by simply saying that because of him the world is a richer, better place."

Q **What were Walt Disney's first and last films? B.T., Anaheim, CA**

A —Walt's first films were called Newman Laugh-O-grams. They were short advertising films made for a movie theater in Kansas

City in 1920. The last film released before his death in 1966 was *Follow Me, Boys!*, but he had also worked on several that were released the following year, such as *The Happiest Millionaire* and *The Jungle Book*.

Q

Did Walt Disney travel to all of the areas where the True-Life Adventures were filmed? C.F., Natick, MA

A

—Walt Disney relied on individual nature photographers to provide him with the film footage he needed for the True-Life Adventures. While Walt did not travel to the sites himself, he was very interested in personally screening all of the film footage that the photographers sent back.

Q

Is it true that Walt Disney was once an actor? L.M., Renton, WA

A

—I probably wouldn't dignify it by calling it "acting," but when Walt Disney was a boy in Kansas City, he and a friend named Walt Pfeiffer would occasionally put on skits at the local vaudeville theater. The boys called themselves "The Two Walts," and one time they were delighted to win a prize of 25 cents. The stage always fascinated Walt Disney, and if he hadn't gotten into animation, he just might have tried to make acting a career. He enjoyed doing the lead-ins for his television shows. If you want to see how good an actor Walt Disney was, catch him in *I Captured the King of the Leprechauns*.

Q

What happened to Walt Disney's backyard train, which we saw on *Where Do the Stories Come From*? L.H., Seattle, WA

A

—The small-scale Carolwood-Pacific Railroad, which Walt built at his home in Holmby Hills in 1950, remained in place for only a few years. After Walt had a much larger train on which to ride at Disneyland (1955), he removed his setup at home, and the train went into storage. Several of the cars were exhibited as part of the Walt Disney Story at Walt Disney World from 1973 to 1981 and after various exhibitions are now on display at The Walt Disney Family Museum in San Francisco.

Q **What was Walt Disney's birth date? T.J., Tyler, TX**

A —Walt was born on December 5, 1901. December was a notable month for the Disneys. All of Elias and Flora Disney's children except Roy were born in December, and Walt, Roy O., Roy E., and Lillian died during that month.

Q **Was Walt Disney the first one to combine animated cartoon characters with live actors and actresses? J.M., Martinez, CA**

A —No, the combination of live action with animation began before Walt Disney got into the business, but he improved on the process. His first series was called the Alice Comedies, in which a live actress cavorted with cartoon characters. Walt tried different processes later on with such films as *The Reluctant Dragon*, *The Three Caballeros*, *Song of the South*, and *So Dear to My Heart*. The technique was perfected in the 1960s and 1970s with *Mary Poppins*, *Bedknobs and Broomsticks*, and *Pete's Dragon*.

Q **How did Walt Disney get the idea for his great series of nature films? E.B., Wilmington, DE**

A —Walt had a husband-and-wife team, the Milottes, in Alaska shooting film for him. As he screened the footage that was sent back to the studio, he fell in love with scenes of seals on the Pribilof Islands. So he telephoned the Milottes for more coverage, which resulted in the Academy Award–winning *Seal Island*. That 1948 True-Life Adventure film was followed by twelve more in the series. Eight of them won Academy Awards for Best Documentary.

Q **I enjoyed seeing Walt Disney in *The Reluctant Dragon*. What was the last TV show he hosted? P.F.G., Mokena, IL**

A —Walt Disney died on December 15, 1966. He had, however, already filmed his TV show introduction for the entire season, so the remainder of the shows were aired with Walt as host. The last original show (before the summer reruns) was *A Salute to Alaska*, which aired on April 2, 1967. Our series at that time was called *Walt Disney's Wonderful World of Color*.

Q **For what did Walt Disney win his first Academy Award? J.T., Concord, MA**

A —Walt Disney actually received two awards at the Academy Awards banquet on November 18, 1932, held at the Ambassador Hotel in Los Angeles. One award was for *Flowers and Trees* as Best Cartoon, with 1932 being the first year there was such a category; the second was a special Oscar given for the creation of Mickey Mouse. The award came exactly four years to the day after Mickey's debut in *Steamboat Willie* at the Colony Theater in New York.